Scotts

Lawns

Your Guide to a Beautiful Yard

Meredith Books
Des Moines, Iowa

CONTENTS

YOUR DREAM LAWN 4

Consider how lawns enrich our environment, our communities, and our lives.

CHOOSE A PROGRAM 16

Have a beautiful lawn no matter how much time, effort, and resources you can devote to it.

MOWING 34

Such a simple task has a big impact on the health of your lawn. Learn the best way to mow.

FERTILIZING 52

Make sure your lawn has adequate nutrients to keep it healthy, dense, and weed free.

WATERING 66

Grasses are remarkably drought tolerant. Save money, labor, and natural resources by watering correctly.

TROUBLESHOOTING 80

Get to know the major lawn pests and learn how to deal with them without tearing out your hair.

BRAND NEW LAWN 156

Although most people get a lawn when they buy a house, sometimes you may want to have more control.

REVIVING YOUR LAWN 144

Whip your lawn back into shape after heat, drought, or other problems have ravaged it.

HOME SPORTS LAWNS 200

The ultimate status symbol: Set up your backyard to host all sorts of backyard games or practice your swing.

othing's quite as nice as the sight of a beautiful green lawn welcoming you when you pull into the driveway of your home or quite as satisfying as watching children tumble and play on the soft grass on a sunny summer day. A healthy, well-tended lawn certainly enhances your enjoyment of your home. At the same time, it improves the value of your property and the aesthetics of your neighborhood and community.

Lawn care doesn't have to be difficult or expensive. With a little time, good basic equipment, and the know-how you'll find on the following pages, a terrific lawn is easily within your reach.

This book makes it easy to create a lawn care program perfectly suited to your lifestyle. Each chapter walks you through a component of basic lawn care and provides the fundamentals on how to make it happen. Use the Digest pages at the beginning of each chapter for quick overviews of what you need to know about tasks from mowing, fertilizing, and watering, to solving problems, making repairs, and starting a brand-new lawn.

BENEFITS OF A LAWN

A single blade of grass may not seem very impressive. But together with the millions of other blades in a lawn, they form an incredibly diverse and active ecosystem that benefits homeowners and everyone else on the planet. Some of the benefits are easily measured; others may be less readily apparent.

Above: Attractive homes with well-kept lawns sell faster and bring top-dollar prices.

Right: Lawns make the world cooler and quieter and form the perfect backdrop for a backyard retreat.

Opposite right: Lawns produce oxygen, trap dust, and absorb pollutants from smoggy air, making the outdoors a much more comfortable place to be.

Ask any real estate agent. An agent knows how much easier it is to sell a home with the curb appeal of a well-kept lawn than one with a lawn full of weeds. An attractive lawn sends a signal to buyers that the rest of the home is likely well kept and is worth a premium price. In fact, it can add 5 to 15 percent to the home's value.

Less easy to evaluate are the ways in which lawns can contribute to your sense of well-being. Most people say that the best place to relax is in their own backyard. But the benefits of green space go much deeper than just relaxation or recreation. For example, when cities install landscaping in blighted urban areas, people begin to take greater pride in their surroundings, and vandalism and graffiti decrease. It has even been shown that a hospital patient who can see a landscape from bed heals faster after an operation than one who can't.

Quality-of-Life Benefits

Healthy, well–maintained lawns provide truly marvelous environmental benefits, which can be seen in the ways a green, growing lawn contributes to the world around it. Consider just a few of the roles that healthy grass plays in our well–being.

Heat and noise reducer When the heat is on, grass helps keep you cool. Street or sidewalk temperatures may reach 100°F or higher, but the grass remains at a pleasant 75°F. The front lawns on a block of eight houses could perform the same cooling work as 70 tons of air–conditioning— enough to cool 23 homes.

Grass also makes your life a bit quieter. It effectively absorbs and deflects sound. When combined with trees and other landscaping, a lawn can significantly reduce harsh, unwanted noise.

Oxygen producer A healthy lawn is an amazingly efficient production system. Grass plants remove carbon dioxide from the air and produce oxygen in return. Just 625 square feet of grass supplies all the oxygen a person needs for one day. A 5,000–square–foot home lawn produces enough oxygen for eight people each day. In comparison, it takes two 100–foot trees to provide the same amount of oxygen for eight people.

Soil saver Grass controls erosion by knitting the soil together, trapping runoff water, and eliminating many of the problems caused by dust and mud. And it's one of the more efficient water savers you'll find in nature. A healthy lawn absorbs rainfall six times more effectively than does a garden area of the same size.

Dust trap If you've ever walked through a dry, unplanted area, such as a construction site, on a windy day, you have some idea of what life might be like without healthy lawns. Clouds of windblown dust make for difficult breathing, irritated eyes, and reduced visibility. Grass is an effective air cleanser. It slows the air moving across its surface, so dust particles settle onto the blades and are eventually washed back to the ground. Every year grass traps millions of tons of dust that would otherwise blow unhindered.

Pollution fighter In one year's time the blades and roots in an acre of healthy grass absorb hundreds of pounds of pollutants from the air and rainwater. Among them are sulfur dioxide, nitrogen oxide, hydrogen fluoride, nitrates, and other gases blamed for acid rain and the greenhouse effect.

Safe surface Perhaps the most important benefit is the recreational value lawns provide for young and old. Dense turf is a safer playground and playing field than nearly any other surface. It reduces the potential severity of many injuries and helps to cushion falls.

Above: Grass prevents soil erosion even on the steepest slopes.

Left: A well-kept lawn is one of the safest surfaces on which children can play. It cushions falls and prevents skinned knees.

Top right: Lawns are integral to good landscape design. They allow you to step back and actually see the garden.

So Long, Artificial Turf

A healthy lawn beats artificial turf, no contest. It didn't always seem that way.

In the early 1970s athletic-field managers cheered the introduction of artificial turf for its consistent, year-round playing surface that could be adapted for different sports or activities in days instead of weeks. Annual maintenance costs were less, and maintenance personnel required less technical skill.

Yet today many stadiums have gone back to natural grass. Why? With artificial turf, there are 10 to 32 percent more injuries to athletes than on natural grass, and temperatures get way above comfort level. While fans may be enjoying a mild 78°F fall day, football players on the field struggle in 125°F heat. In summer, temperatures as high as 160°F have been recorded on artificial playing surfaces.

WHAT'S GOOD FOR THE LAWN IS GOOD FOR THE ENVIRONMENT

When used correctly—meaning you follow all label directions—lawn fertilizers have no negative effects so you can feel confident in letting your children and pets play on the lawn.

Although issues related to the environment are often subjects of heated debate, it's clear that today, more than ever, everyone needs to be a partner in the stewardship of the planet. To be sure, the actions you take today result in the legacy you leave for the generations that follow.

The great debates over the environment and how to best care for it are frequently driven by emotion rather than logic and clear thinking, which can make it hard to determine the best path on matters of public policy. Each individual, however, can make a personal effort to be as informed as possible about the effect his or her choices and actions may have on the environment. The lawn is a perfect example of a subject of environmental consideration that people encounter right at home.

Lawns have become a point of contention among those who wonder about their impact on the environment. Are lawns harmful? Should you feel guilty about spending valuable natural resources such as water on your lawn? Do the fertilizers and pesticides you apply cause damage to the environment?

The truth is, a well-tended lawn looks good and is beneficial to the environment. A healthy lawn absorbs water so efficiently that it prevents damaging runoff from heavy rainfall. It also prevents soil erosion, moderates temperatures, reduces glare and noise, serves as a firebreak in wildfire-prone regions, and provides an ecoculture for insects and microorganisms that are important to the overall health of the soil and the air.

The thicker and healthier the lawn, the better it's able to do its job. If you follow the advice in this book, which favors using fertilizer, water, and pesticides judiciously, your lawn will be healthy and contribute to the critical balance of our living environment.

Fertilizers and Pesticides

So what about fertilizers and pesticides (controls for weeds, diseases, and insects)? Dozens of research studies have shown that these materials have little chance of harming the environment when applied to lawns correctly. Unlike cropland, where pesticides and fertilizers fall on bare earth, lawns trap the materials within their dense canopy and prolific root systems. Ninety-nine percent of a pesticide applied to a lawn stays in the lawn. And lawns retain 190 times more nitrogen and 235 times more phosphorus than does farmland.

In addition, most pesticides sold for lawn use today have undergone intense scrutiny, and their effect on the environment has been rigorously tested. They are less water soluble than older pesticides, so they don't get into groundwater, and they are easier on soil microorganisms and earthworms and other beneficial species in the soil. In addition, these newer pesticides are effective in smaller quantities than were needed when using older pesticides, and they provide protection over an extended period of time.

Federal and state regulations and tough federal and state testing and evaluation requirements ensure that lawn care products present no unreasonable health risks to users, their families, or their neighbors. As long as pesticides and fertilizers are used correctly, they won't harm the environment or you.

Bottom Line

Does all this mean you can use fertilizers and pesticides on your lawn with impunity? No. Misuse is harmful and unsafe. Instead, follow these simple rules, and you'll be assured that you're taking care of the environment while you care for your lawn.

Read and follow all label directions. Use no more or no less of the product than the label recommends and heed all safety precautions.

Fertilize only when the grass is actively growing. If the lawn is dormant or suffering from heat stress or the ground is frozen, the fertilizer is more likely to be wasted and might run off rather than be used by the lawn.

Use pesticides only where you have or anticipate a problem and use only as much pesticide as it takes to treat the problem.

Apply fertilizers and pesticides accurately. If any of the material lands on a hard surface such as the driveway, sidewalk, or street, sweep it back onto the lawn to keep it from being washed into the storm sewer.

HOW GRASS GROWS

The way grass grows is what allows it to form a lawn. It's how it is able to withstand abuse. It's also the reason a lawn can deteriorate even when you believe you're giving it the best of care. By taking the time to understand how grass grows you'll discover the secrets to a beautiful lawn.

Lawn Grasses

Mowing is the one activity that truly distinguishes a lawn. Most plants can't stand up to mowing because they grow from the ends of stems at the top of the plant. After a few weeks of mowing, nearly any plant would die. The growing points of grasses, on the other hand, are at the bases of their leaves, close to the ground, usually below the reach of the mower's blades.

Many grasses tolerate mowing, but not all of them look beautiful afterward. Of the 10,000 grass species, only about 50 make a good lawn. These are the smallest, most compact grasses that mowing actually helps turn into a dense, uniform stand.

The Crown

The foundation of the dense stand of grass plants is the crown. Located at the base

---

Parts of a Grass Plant

Remember making grass whistles when you were a kid? If you stopped to take a close look at the blades as you tore them apart, you may have noticed that they have some unique features, such as tiny fingerlike ears that curl around the front of the leaf at the base of the blade or a hairy fringe between the leaf and the stem. These and other features on this page are clues to the identity of the grass growing in your yard. (See the grass profiles starting on page 182, for grass descriptions.)

Ligule: A structure that grows from the collar on the inner side of the leaf. If the grass has a ligule, it may be membranous, hairy, or a combination of the two.

Collar: The point where the blade and sheath meet. If the collar is distinct, its size is the main distinguishing feature.

Auricles: An extension of the collar to the front of the sheath. Size, shape, and presence differentiate grasses that have them.

Vernation: A cross section of the leaf blade as it emerges from the sheath. Most grasses are either round, rolled, or flat (folded).

Blade: The upper, broad portion of the leaf. Its size, width, and orientation help distinguish one grass from another.

Leaf tip: Size and shape—including whether it is blunt, boat-shaped, pointed, or sharply pointed—differ among grasses.

Daughter plant

Sheath: The lower portion of the leaf, which wraps around the stem. Some sheaths are distinct.

Tiller

Crown

Stolon

Roots

Rhizome

of the plant, it is the growth point where new leaves and roots originate, and it is the plant's center of activity. A grass plant can lose its roots, as happens when it is harvested for sod. It can lose most of its leaf surface as when you mow it. But as long as the crown is intact, the plant will survive because the crown can generate new leaves and roots.

The crowns of all grasses form buds from which new, independent plants arise. In lawn grasses, mowing encourages more of these buds to develop. During the life of a grass plant, buds constantly form and grow into new plants—called daughter plants—with their own crowns. How these daughter plants originate determines their growth habit, which in turn determines how quickly a particular grass species forms a lawn and how readily a lawn can thicken or fill in damaged areas.

Daughter plants that develop directly next to the crown are called tillers. All grasses form tillers, but a few, such as perennial ryegrass, form them exclusively. These are called bunchgrasses because they grow in clumps. Every year a tight cluster of daughter tillers forms around each crown, and the clump gradually expands outward. Bunchgrasses grow into a tough, dense turf, but their slow expansion means they are slow to heal any damage to the lawn. They also don't grow into a good sod because they don't knit together.

In some grasses, the buds also develop into stems that grow laterally above or below the ground. Aboveground stems are called stolons; below ground they are known as rhizomes. Both travel far from the mother plant and form new plants wherever they go. Grasses with rhizomes or stolons quickly recover from damage and can be harvested as sod.

Bermudagrass and zoysiagrass have both rhizomes and stolons. They are aggressive, spreading species that form a durable turf well suited for use in lawns and high-stress situations such as sports fields. They'll also keep you busy trying to keep them from spreading into adjoining garden areas

Most stoloniferous grasses—those with stolons only—tolerate very low mowing. (It's no surprise that creeping bentgrass, the grass on golf greens, is stoloniferous.) The exception is St. Augustinegrass, which does better mowed at 3 inches tall. Rhizomatous grasses—those with rhizomes only—include Kentucky bluegrass. These tolerate moderately low mowing and recover quickly from damage.

Cool- and Warm-Season Grasses

Grasses come in two categories: cool season and warm season, which are determined

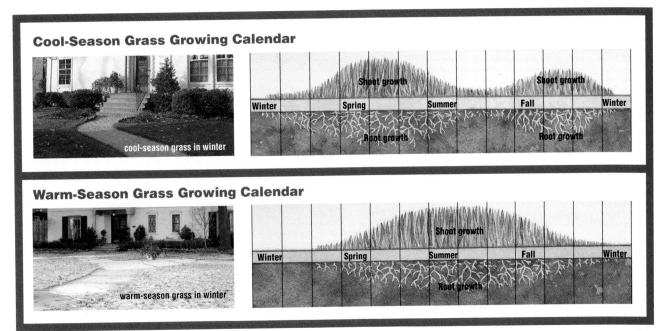

Cool-Season Grass Growing Calendar

cool-season grass in winter

Shoot growth | Shoot growth
Winter | Spring | Summer | Fall | Winter
Root growth | Root growth

Warm-Season Grass Growing Calendar

warm-season grass in winter

Shoot growth
Winter | Spring | Summer | Fall | Winter
Root growth

by when and where the grasses grow best. (See the illustrations on page 13 to compare their growing times.) Which type you can grow depends on your climate. With a few exceptions, cool-season grasses do best in northern regions; warm-season grasses are adapted to southern areas.

More important, the categories influence when you perform certain lawn tasks. Fertilizing, starting a lawn, renovating, removing thatch, and many other lawn activities are most effective and easiest on the grass if done during the grass's peak growth period—when temperatures are 65°F to 75°F for cool-season grasses and 80°F to 95°F for warm-season grasses. The chart below shows the different timings for common lawn tasks for each type of grass.

Food Sources

Like all plants, grasses get their green color from chlorophyll, a key component in photosynthesis, a process in which plants take carbon dioxide from the air and turn it into carbohydrates. These carbohydrates are the plants' food, which fuels growth of grass shoots and roots.

Any excess carbohydrates are stored within the plant. When stressful periods arise, such as a spell of hot, dry weather during summer, the grass has these reserves to call on. The plant also uses stored carbohydrates to begin growth after its dormant period and to form into a dense turf when growth resumes.

Mowing removes the leaf tissue the grass uses for photosynthesis. Lawn grasses compensate for the loss by becoming denser or growing a larger number of leaves. That adaptation is not without cost. The plants must use carbohydrates to constantly replace the leaves rather than for root growth or storage. They end up with a less extensive root system and fewer reserves. The shorter you mow the grass, the greater the stress on the system to rejuvenate itself.

Fertilizing helps compensate for mowing, although there are limits to how much it can help when you routinely mow too short. By fertilizing, you ensure that the grass leaves are loaded with chlorophyll so they can continue photosynthesizing at a normal rate. Fertilizing encourages new growth and may reduce the amount of roots lost from mowing.

The Simple Secret to Success

It's easy to have a fantastic, picture-perfect lawn. Grow a grass adapted to your climate, then treat it well. Feed it at least three times a year—and preferably four or five times, or every two months—during the appropriate seasons. Mow often and mow high. Give the lawn regular drinks of water. It really is as simple as that.

Cool-Season Grasses

Early Spring	Midspring	Summer	Late Summer	Late Fall
■ Clean up leaves and other debris ■ Begin mowing ■ Prevent crabgrass ■ Fertilize	■ Fertilize ■ Control broadleaf weeds ■ Mow	■ Give a light feeding if needed ■ Control insect pests ■ Prevent grubs ■ Mow ■ Water	■ Fertilize ■ Sow grass seed ■ Dethatch or aerate if needed ■ Mow ■ Water as needed	■ Fertilize ■ Control broadleaf weeds ■ Mow as long as grass grows ■ Rake leaves ■ Water as needed

Wake up to a beautiful lawn. It's easy. Choose a cool- or warm-season grass depending on where you live and care for it following the calendars below.

Warm-Season Grasses

Early Spring	Midspring	Summer	Late Summer	Late Fall
■ Clean up leaves and other debris ■ Prevent weeds ■ Fertilize (if grass is dormant, wait until growth begins) ■ Dethatch or aerate if needed ■ Mow	■ Little or no maintenance required ■ Fertilize if you have not done so earlier ■ Control weeds	■ Fertilize ■ Control insect pests ■ Mow ■ Install or repair lawn with seed, sod, sprigs, or plugs ■ Water	■ Water ■ Fertilize ■ Mow ■ Control weeds ■ Control insect pests if needed ■ Overseed	■ Little or no maintenance required

CHOOSE A PROGRAM

he simple truth about your lawn is that whatever you put into it, you get out of it. How much or how little you invest in your lawn is up to you, of course, so it's good to know that whatever time and other resources you have to spend on your lawn, your efforts will have a visible, tangible, and valuable result.

Spending even the least bit of time or money will yield an improvement. And if you want to lavish time and resources on your lawn, your efforts will really bring results.

On the following pages, you will see four lawn care programs for folks with different goals for their lawns. From that information, you can craft a seasonal lawn care routine that reflects your personal standard of quality.

CHOOSE A PROGRAM DIGEST

Save Mowing Time

If your distaste for mowing keeps you from giving your lawn better care, here are some ways to ease the task:

Make sure the mower blade is always sharp. Dull blades don't cut grass very well. With a dull blade, you'll end up using 20 to 30 percent more gas, exert more effort to push the mower, and spend more time mowing.

Match the size of your mower to your yard. With a mower that's too small you'll travel back and forth more often to cut the lawn than you would with a right-size mower. With one that's too big, you'll spend all your time backing up, turning around, and trimming areas the mower wouldn't fit.

Trim before mowing. Then when you mow, the trimmings are chopped up, plus you won't be tempted to try to get in closer with your mower than is efficient.

Use a good, well-balanced fertilizer to avoid surge growth, which forces the grass to grow too tall too fast.

TO DO

- Determine how much time you have to devote to your lawn's short- and long-term care.
- Fertilize appropriate to your region, type of grass, and resources.
- Mow regularly, never cutting off more than one-third of the leaf.
- Water as directed after fertilizing, and throughout the season appropriate to your location and time and water resources.
- Address weeds, pests, and diseases as necessary.
- Groom and tend to the details of your lawn according to your personal resources.

Plan for *Your* Ideal Lawn

An annual lawn care program takes into consideration the amount of fertilizer a lawn will need and anticipates problems, such as weeds or grubs, that the lawn is likely to face. It also accounts for the amount of time and resources you can (or want to) devote to your lawn. The result is a calendar for applying pest controls and fertilizer, in addition to regular mowing and watering.

Whether you're a barebones minimalist or an all-out lawn fanatic, setting up an annual program ensures you put down the right product at the right time to eliminate problems, as well as build the thickness, density, and health of your lawn with proper nutrition.

Almost a Fanatic

What if you have a very large lawn and want a better lawn but not the commitment to the work? One alternative is to put a small part of your lawn on a full-season program while keeping the remaining grass on a less stringent schedule. Decide which part of the lawn you care most about looking good. Follow the full-season program on this part. For the rest of the lawn, feed once or twice a year on this schedule:

COOL-SEASON GRASSES

1. **August–September:** Fertilize for fall root growth.
2. **October:** Winterize with a fertilizer-plus-weed control to prepare the lawn for winter, promote early spring greenup, and kill broadleaf weeds.

WARM-SEASON GRASSES

1. **March–May:** Fertilize and apply controls for broadleaf weeds.
2. **June–August:** Fertilize and protect against insects, which thin the lawn and turn it brown.

Which type of product to use when?

You can save time and energy by choosing the right product at the right time.

Fertilizer only	■ Your lawn needs a feeding.
	■ Your lawn is, and you expect it to remain, problem free.
Fertilizer plus control	■ Your lawn needs a feeding.
	■ You need to treat a problem that is in, or may be in, your whole lawn.
	■ You want to precisely apply a product to every square inch of your lawn.
Control only	■ Your lawn does not need a feeding.
	■ You are spot treating a few weeds with ready-to-use spray. (Note: With insect controls, it is best to protect the whole lawn with a granular product because you cannot easily predict where problems will occur.)

Start Any Time

You don't have to wait until spring to start an annual lawn care program. Annual programs are cyclical, which means you can start anywhere in the cycle and keep going from there.

Get Back What You Put In

0 feedings	1 feeding	2 feedings	3 feedings	4 to 5 feedings
Never-fertilized lawns are weedy, have short, thin root systems, and few resources to get through stressful periods.	Add one feeding per year and the lawn grows a little denser, not quite as weedy, and a bit healthier.	Two feedings per year really help to thicken the lawn. The roots grow thicker and denser too. The lawn begins crowding out weeds.	Three feedings are almost ideal. After three feedings, the lawn will be thick, dense, and healthy. And it will outcompete weeds and ward off pests.	Four to five feedings are ideal. Although they won't make your lawn much denser than three feedings, they provide more resources allowing the lawn to survive stresses of all kinds.

A MINIMALIST LAWN CARE PROGRAM

Weekend Warrior

Even a minimalist can find time to give the VIP treatment to his lawn for one or two weekends a year, setting the stage for a whole season of effective low-key lawn maintenance. Pick a Saturday in spring (early spring for a cool-season grass), a little later for a warm-season grass, and try to knock out these basic tasks:

- Remove any leaves and winter debris from the lawn.

- Give your mower a tune-up and balance and sharpen the blades.

- Make sure your hose and sprinkler are in working order.

- Clean out your spreader, fill it with fertilizer (follow the instructions for your type of spreader, grass, and the size of your lawn), and apply the fertilizer.

- Water, if necessary, at the appropriate time after fertilizing.

Just because you can't—or just plain don't want to—spend a lot of time or money cultivating the "perfect" lawn, doesn't mean you have to settle for a yard full of weeds. With a minimal investment of time and resources, you can have a perfectly acceptable modestly groomed green lawn.

Fertilizing

Do you even need to fertilize? Each year you don't fertilize, the nutrients your lawn needs to thrive are further depleted. The grass is less able to handle extremes of weather or stand up to insect pests or diseases. Eventually the soil becomes so infertile and your grass so weak that the weeds begin to dominate. Where now your lawn consists of an amiable mix of grass and weeds, someday you'll be the lord of a lawn that's more weeds and bare spots than grass. For many a minimalist, though, green and growing is good enough.

Fertilizing once or twice a year is a better idea. You won't have the lushest lawn in the neighborhood, but one application can thicken your lawn enough to choke out some weeds and give the roots a stronger base to absorb water and nutrients. A second feeding thickens the lawn and improves its health even more.

If fertilizing just once a year, do it when the grass is actively growing: For cool-season grasses, that's in early fall; for warm-season grasses, it's in midspring. Use timed-release or all-in-one fertilizer. These are a bit more expensive than other fertilizers, but if you're fertilizing just once, you ought to make it worth your while. If you will fertilize twice, make the second application in late fall for cool-season grasses, early summer for warm-season ones.

Watering

Some people never water their lawn. They take what nature gives them and leave it at that. If this sounds like you, it's unlikely you will ever be inclined to install an elaborate sprinkler system or even get out there with a hose and sprinkler from time to time.

Just know that not watering during a season with ordinary rainfall is one thing. Not watering during an extremely dry, hot summer will have an effect on the long-term health of your lawn. At the least, your lawn will be quite stressed by the drought and weakened in its natural defenses against weeds, insect pests, and diseases. At worst—and especially depending on the type of grass that prevails in your lawn—your lawn might not survive extreme weather. If your lawn really gets away from you due to drought, it may turn brown and stay brown—as in dead brown.

The only time you really must consider watering is if you decide to fertilize. For the best and fastest results, give the lawn a good soaking soon after an application of fertilizer. Either water after you fertilize, or fertilize just before a rain and let nature do the work for you.

Mowing

The most important part of a minimalist lawn care program is mowing. Sure, if you aren't fertilizing and the grass isn't vigorously growing, the lawn won't need to be mowed as often as the lawn of a more motivated lawnkeeper. But you still have to mow. The key is to mow the grass high enough that it is able to naturally muscle out some of the weeds. Set the mower at its highest setting, which will usually leave the grass about 2½ to 3 inches tall. Mow when the grass needs it, but don't take more than one-third off the top of the grass blades in any given mowing. For instance, if you let the grass grow to 6 inches tall and then lop off 3 inches when you mow, you've cut too much. Your grass will become stressed and weak, perhaps creating bigger problems for you than just an overgrown lawn.

Under a minimalist program, your lawn will be healthier than if you never fertilized, but it will still have weeds and be lighter green.

Problems

Weeds, insect pests, and diseases drive most lawn owners crazy. The lawn care minimalist isn't so concerned about weeds because they're probably green and blending agreeably with the grass plants in the lawn. They cut just as easily as the grass, so everything looks fairly uniform after you mow.

As for insects, most lawns can take a host of critters living in the grass. Unless you suddenly notice severe insect damage, you probably don't have to deal with making advances in the insect war. Diseases can creep up, but if you mow correctly and keep your mower blade sharp, you'll avoid shredding the tips of the grass, which is the same as an invitation to all sorts of lawn diseases. The key to avoiding lawn problems is to make sure that whatever you do for your lawn, you do it right.

Extra Points

Even a minimalist can see the wisdom in spending a little more on a mulching mower. A mulching mower cuts grass clippings into tiny pieces, which are left right on the lawn (no raking—every minimalist likes that) to break down quickly and deliver nutrients back to the grass. That's doing something good for the lawn that takes no more time than the mowing that had to be done anyway.

Minimalist: What It Takes

- **Spring** Basic winter cleanup (for example, rake, remove yard debris), fertilize, especially if you did not fertilize in the fall; water after fertilizing (if it doesn't rain); mow regularly as necessary.

- **Summer** Mow regularly as necessary.

- **Fall** Fertilize; mow as necessary through the end of the active growing season.

- **Tools and materials** Basic or mulching mower, spreader, fertilizer (get a weed-and-feed fertilizer if weeds are a problem), and hose and sprinkler (if necessary).

AVERAGE LAWN CARE PROGRAM

The extra feeding under the average care program greens up the lawn and helps crowd out weeds.

Like most homeowners, you care about tending your lawn to the best of your ability. You don't want to pay someone to do it for you, nor do you want to spend much time working on your lawn yourself. But you do have standards for the quality of your lawn and are willing to spend some time and resources on its care.

Fertilizing

Applying fertilizer three times a year during the peak growing seasons will go a long way toward making your lawn healthier and protecting it from stress.

Three yearly feedings won't necessarily result in an award-winning lawn, but it will give the lawn some protection from weather, weeds, insects, and diseases. Buy the best fertilizer you can afford. If your lawn has weeds or insects, use a two-in-one fertilizer, which both feeds your grass and controls the problem.

Use this product during the first period of active growth in the year. You'll control the weeds before they take hold in the lawn, and you'll give your grass nutrients so it can become strong enough to prevent other weeds from moving in.

The second and third fertilizations should be done during the next periods of active growth of the year. This schedule will strengthen the roots to help the grass withstand winter. Fertilize cool-season grasses in early to midspring and in early and late fall, and warm-season turf in midspring, midsummer, and early fall. Giving your grass a shot of nutrients at these points throughout the season will create a good base to build on year after year.

Watering

A good dose of water after fertilizing will move the fertilizer off the top of the grass (where it does no good) and into the soil. Thoroughly water all fertilized areas, or you could end up with a patchy-looking lawn. You can rely on rain to water in the fertilizer or run your sprinkler.

As for regular watering, a lawn needs about 1 inch of water a week—including any rainwater. If your lawn is looking a bit dry, pray for rain or pull out the sprinklers and hoses. Understand that if you don't water during dry spells, your lawn might suffer and could ultimately die. Lawns often go dormant during summer heat as a natural survival mechanism. If your lawn does go dormant, you may wish to water deeply once a month during the dry season to give it a better shot at survival. If at the end of the extreme weather your lawn doesn't revive from being dormant, it likely never will, and you'll have to deal with that if it occurs.

When you water, do it in the morning; it's less likely to be windy (which can disturb your watering pattern), and the grass will have plenty of time to dry before nightfall. Soggy grass that sits overnight is a perfect breeding ground for many lawn diseases.

Mowing

Mowing correctly is the biggest weapon you have in your lawn care arsenal. You can avoid a ton of stress on the lawn simply by paying attention and mowing when the grass needs it. Taller grass is better able to recover from the stress of weather conditions, so keep the mower deck at a high setting. No matter how long the grass, never take off more than a third of that length when you mow. If you cut the grass shorter, it has to work harder to recover from the mowing. This stresses the lawn, especially during a dry spell.

Low-Maintenance Grasses

If you want to spend less time and money on your lawn, consider one of these low-maintenance grasses. (See the profiles beginning on page 182 to learn more about them.)

- **Buffalograss** warm-season, drought tolerant, slow growing

- **Centipedegrass** warm-season, low growing, requires little fertilizer

- **Tall fescue** cool-season, drought resistant

Average: What It Takes

- **Spring** Do basic winter cleanup (for example, rake, remove yard debris); tune up your lawn mower and sharpen the blades; fertilize cool-season grasses in early spring and warm-season grasses in midspring (water afterward if necessary); mow regularly as necessary when the growing season begins.

- **Summer** Mow regularly as necessary.

- **Fall** Fertilize in early and in late fall for cool-season grasses and early and mid-fall for warm-season grasses (water afterward if necessary); mow as necessary through the end of the active growing season; clean equipment for winter storage.

- **Tools and materials** Rake, trimmer, mulching mower, spreader, fertilizer, weed-plus fertilizer as necessary, hose and sprinkler.

Set your mower to its highest setting. Mowing high strengthens a lawn so it stands up to heat and drought stress.

Keep mower blades sharp. Shredded grass blades create stress and offer millions of invitations for disease to settle in your lawn. A clean cut will give you some insurance against lawn diseases and makes for an all-around nicer looking lawn. Tuning up your mower and sharpening the blades once a year are worthwhile so that your mower starts up the first time every time and the grass isn't shredded by dull blades. If you're not into doing the tune-up yourself, take your machine to a lawn mower repair shop and have a professional do it. This is one task you shouldn't skip.

Problems

Weed-and-feed fertilizer may not take care of all stubborn weeds. Keep a long-handled weed digger and a sprayer on hand to help you spot-control the weeds that really bug you. Dig up individual weeds or spray them with an appropriate herbicide and let the grass grow to fill in the vacant areas. You may feel like you're doing some hard time, but you're saving yourself the expense of applying a product to the whole lawn when the whole lawn may not need it. And if you're not the type to be bothered by

Extra Points

A good trimmer can last for years and give your lawn a neat, finished look without much extra effort. Invest in a trimmer with a vertical edger. It's worth the extra money you'll spend on it because it does two jobs—trimming and edging. Used horizontally, it trims the lawn in hard-to-mow spots. Vertically, it creates neat edges along driveways, walkways, and patios.

some weeds, just dig out the biggest and most obvious ones and let it go at that. Or just concentrate on the front yard and let the backyard be. (For more on controlling weeds, see the chapter starting on page 80.)

Insect pests and diseases can create havoc in a lawn. The healthier the grass is, the less likely the lawn will succumb to problems. If you fertilize three times a season and mow the lawn regularly and well, you'll have some protection. But if you suspect insect or disease damage, you need to find out exactly what you're dealing with. Use the Lawn Detective section of this book (see pages 88 to 91) to help you figure out what your problem may be; use your county extension service as an additional resource. Once you've determined what you're up against, be sure to use the right product for the problem. There is no bigger waste of your time and money than using the wrong product or technique to solve a problem. Take the time first to identify what's going on, and then apply the proper treatment.

Bare spots in a lawn can drive some homeowners crazy. Even if you're not one of these people and you don't mind a little patchiness, understand that bare spots are perfect areas for weeds to creep in and establish themselves. As with any insect or disease problem, if you can identify why the grass won't grow in that spot, you're on your way to filling it in once and only once. For example, gasoline or driveway salt may have damaged an area of your lawn while diseases and insects have nothing to do

It's All In the Seed

If you're going to the effort to fix patchy areas of your lawn, now is not the time to skimp on quality, especially when it comes to seed. You won't need much of it for patch-seeding, so buy the best seed available. Look for seed with the highest germination rates (the rates are noted on the package) and with little or no weed seed. This gives you the best chance of success for the trouble you take to solve your little patch problem.

with the bare area. In this case, dig up the damaged spot, add some good topsoil, and seed the area to head weeds off at the pass. If mole crickets or spring dead spot are the culprit, this technique won't work. You will need to apply an appropriate pest control.

Smaller bare patches scattered throughout the lawn can result in your lawn mower cutting unevenly so you unwittingly scalp the surrounding area of grass. Overseed these bare areas of your lawn to take care of that problem. And if you have patchy areas you just can't lick—such as a perpetually shady spot or a path the kids have worn in the lawn—decide whether you can live with them or just how much effort you're willing to spend to fix them.

FULL-SEASON LAWN CARE PROGRAM

It's obvious you care for your property: You have high standards and good habits and are willing to spend the time and money necessary for one of the nicer lawns in the neighborhood. You understand that keeping a nice lawn demands your attention throughout the season—and from year to year as well.

Fertilizing

The full-season fertilizer schedule calls for you to fertilize four times a year. This not only will help your lawn to green up in spring but also will shore it up against the stress of weather, weeds, insects, and diseases throughout the year.

The first fertilization will get the grass growing early in the season and help develop a healthy root system. The last application will continue to feed and protect the grass over the long dormant span. You would do well to use a fertilizer and weed preventer for the first application and a weed-and-feed for the last one. That way, you'll take care of whatever weeds might have sneaked in throughout the year.

Make the first application to both warm- and cool-season lawns in spring as they green up. Follow up with applications every two months after the first. Make the final feeding in fall for an extra boost that helps both cool- and warm-season grasses prepare for the long winter. This last feeding should occur no later than midfall for warm-season grasses.

It is important to note that you don't have to wait for the beginning of the growing season to start fertilizing. If you missed the first two applications of the year, don't hold off until the next year to start. You can begin the cycle of fertilizing toward the end of the year, get a couple of applications in, and then start up again the next season. There is no reason to wait—dive right in when you can, and your lawn will be better for it.

Sprinklers with automatic timers save labor and ensure your lawn receives the right amount of water.

Watering

You know your lawn well enough to notice when it starts to show signs of drying out. When you can see your footsteps in the grass—that is, when the grass takes too long to spring back after you walk on it—you're at the ready with the sprinkler. You pay attention to the weather and know to get the sprinklers and hoses lined up and to water thoroughly if you haven't had rain in a week and a good soaking isn't on the horizon. And while you know you don't have to water after fertilizing, you've found that the lawn responds faster when you do.

Invest in effective sprinklers and you will be rewarded with greener, healthier grass. Set up a few sprinklers around the lawn for full coverage and to decrease the amount of time you have to spend rearranging them around the yard. You might also consider sprinklers with automatic timers—either ones you can set to apply a certain amount of water, or ones you can set for a certain amount of time. This saves you from losing track of time and ending up with a soggy lawn. Overwatered lawns can create the opportunity for disease, so irrigate thoroughly but just for the prescribed amount of time and water. And water in the morning, before the wind picks up so that your carefully placed sprinklers water the areas you intend them to.

Mowing

Anyone who admires the look of his or her own lawn knows that the secret is in the mowing. Get your lawn mower tuned up and the blades sharpened once a year. The blades may even need to be replaced every few years, so pay attention to the grass and make sure the cut's nice and clean every time. If your grass is thick (thanks to your good habits), you can lower the mowing height to about 2 to 2½ inches. Thick turf naturally crowds out weeds, so you won't need to let the grass grow as

Under a full-season program, your lawn will be dense and weed free, providing the perfect frame for a home.

Full Season: What It Takes

- **Spring** Basic winter cleanup (for example, rake, remove yard debris); tune up your lawn mower and sharpen the blades; do a soil test; aerate (if necessary); add amendments (as recommended); fertilize with preemergence weed control in early spring for cool-season lawns and mid-spring for warm-season grass; fertilize again in late spring; water if necessary after fertilizing; mow regularly as necessary when the growing season begins.

- **Summer** Mow and water regularly as necessary; fertilize; watch for insect pests (use a fertilizer plus insect control if necessary); treat to prevent grubs if they have been a problem in the past.

- **Fall** Remove leaves and debris; fertilize twice (early fall and late fall for cool-season grasses, early fall and mid-fall for warm-season grasses); water as necessary after fertilizing; mow as necessary through the end of the active growing season; clean equipment for winter storage.

- **Tools and materials** Rake, trimmer, mulching mower, spreader, leaf blower (if desired), fertilizer (if weeds are a problem, use a regular weed-and-feed or one with a preemergence weed control), hose and sprinkler, long-handled weed digger, aerator (available for rent).

Consider aerating once a year to avoid thatch and soil compaction. Leave the soil plugs on top of the lawn to disintegrate on their own.

are finely chopped to help them break down faster into the soil. To make sure all grass trimmings are mulched, string-trim the edges of your lawn before you mow. Those clippings will be mulched as you mow over them.

Problems

For the most part, a healthy lawn chokes out weeds on its own. And with applications of fertilizer plus weed control, you should have little trouble with weeds. If some do develop, the extra fertilizer treatment with preemergence weed control at the beginning of the year should help stamp them out. If

Check that your spreader is operating properly before spreading fertilizer and other materials on your lawn. Practice your pace and be sure to set the spreader to the rate specified on the package label.

high to choke out the weeds. Because you regularly fertilize and have been watering as necessary, the grass will need to be cut more often during the active growing season. Never take off more than one-third of the grass blade when you mow. If you're going to be away for a week or so, arrange to have someone else mow (using your mower since it's already set to the correct height for your lawn) while you're gone.

Don't be tempted to rake up and bag your clippings. Those clippings are from well-fed grass, and as they decompose into the soil they'll feed your lawn. Your mower should be a mulching model or have a mulching attachment so that the clippings

you have some weeds here and there, use a long-handled weed digger to get them out of the ground, and let the surrounding turf take over. Or spot-treat them with an appropriate herbicide.

Insects and diseases are unlikely to bother a healthy lawn, but every once in a while you may notice something is amiss in that sea of green. Insects live in your lawn anyway, but an overabundance of them can cause problems. Stay alert for signs of infestation. Identify the culprit, and treat the lawn with an insect control labeled specifically for dealing with that bug. If parts of the lawn have been ravaged, dig up the topsoil involved, replace it with fresh

Moderate-Maintenance Grasses

These grasses take a little attention but pay you back in green good looks:

- **St. Augustinegrass** warm-season, shade tolerant

- **Zoysiagrass** warm-season, heat and drought tolerant

- **Bahiagrass** warm-season, thick

- **Kentucky bluegrass** cool-season, needs regular watering and fertilizing

- **Perennial ryegrass** cool-season, good shade tolerance, not very drought tolerant

- **Tall fescue** cool-season, drought tolerant

topsoil, seed those areas with good–quality grass seed, and keep the surrounding grass healthy to help fill in the gaps quickly. If grubs have been a problem in the past, consider applying a grub control as a preventive treatment.

Diseases may crop up in the lawn, so once again you need to identify the problem and treat it with the proper formula for that particular disease. Your county extension service can help you identify the culprit and recommend the correct treatment.

Keep an eye on the thatch in your lawn. If you notice it is growing thicker, it's time to either aerate or dethatch the lawn so that moisture and nutrients can get into the soil to help break it down. Consider aerating every year or every other year as part of your routine maintenance. Because you keep your grass healthy, it can handle this treatment. (To learn more about thatch and aerating your lawn, see pages 136 to 139.)

Soil Amendments

Have your soil tested at least once a year. The results of the test will give you valuable information about what your soil needs to make it perfect for your lawn to thrive. The results of the soil test will include recommendations for the amendments you need to add. Check with your extension service for the best time of year to add these amendments.

Cruise Control

You've got a great spreader, you take care of it, and you calibrate it carefully every time you use it. But a spreader is only as good as the person operating it. When you're applying fertilizer with a spreader, it's important to keep moving at a steady pace so that the product is applied evenly. Practice your pace. Fill your spreader with a bit of sand, then take a walk down the driveway and back again. If the sand is evenly dispersed, you've got your pace down. If some areas are either heavier or lighter in coverage, you know you have to pay attention to your pace to help ensure an even application throughout the lawn.

What is an extension service?

The Cooperative Extension Service is a joint program between states, counties, and the federal government. The mission is to provide the public with information and education on a variety of topics including lawn care.

Mow and Blow

Blowing grass clippings with a leaf blower is the last leg of the regular mowing ritual for many people. It gives a clean-swept look to driveways, walkways, and patios.

An electric blower will do the job nicely if you have a smaller lawn and easy access to an AC power outlet. A gas-powered blower is necessary for a big area, but it is noisy and downright unpopular in some neighborhoods, so work as quickly as you can.

Determine an efficient route around the areas that need to be cleared, blowing the clippings back onto the lawn, where they'll break down and feed it.

Soil test results ensure your lawn's roots grow in the best possible environment.

No effort is too ambitious and no expense too great when it comes to the meticulous care and grooming of your baby—your lawn. It's a year-round challenge that you relish because you are a lawn fanatic.

Fertilizing

It is likely that you will feed your lawn as many as five times a year using the best fertilizer at exactly the right times:

Cool-season grasses Fertilize first in early spring (use a fertilizer plus crabgrass control to prevent annual grassy weeds if you have had problems with them in the past). Fertilize again in late spring, using a fertilizer plus broadleaf weed control as necessary. In midsummer, fertilize and protect against insects as necessary. In early fall, fertilize for root growth. Make the final application—a winterizer—in late fall.

Warm-season grasses Fertilize and prevent crabgrass as needed in early spring. Fertilize and control broadleaf weeds if any are present in late spring. In early summer, fertilize and protect against insects. Fertilize for fall root growth in late summer; and winterize in early fall.

If you're going to fertilize that often, be sure to apply the correct amount of fertilizer each time. The idea is to see that your lawn gets a constant, appropriate level of feeding throughout the year, not bursts that will overly stimulate it.

Precise fertilizer application requires precise equipment. Calibrate your spreader so you know exactly how much fertilizer is being spread onto your lawn. Precise application also involves making sure all areas of the lawn are covered. Be particular about lining up each pass with the spreader to avoid unsightly lines of unfertilized grass in the lawn—or super-green lines of double-fertilized grass.

Watering

Use a rain gauge to ensure your lawn is getting the right amount of water. Adjust your watering schedule so that your lawn receives a total of 1 inch of water a week, including any rainfall.

Whether you have a top-of-the-line automatic sprinkler system or a good sprinkler-and-hose setup, test it to find out exactly how much water is coming out. Use the tin-can test (see page 70) to see how long it takes your sprinkler to provide ¼ inch of water, then use that time measurement to calculate how long the sprinklers need to run for the lawn to get the water it needs. If your sprinkler system can be set to apply a certain amount of water instead of running for a certain length of time, test that system too, so you know if the output is really what the sprinkler is set for. Water deeply after fertilizing so that the fertilizer sitting on the top of the grass blades won't burn the lawn.

Mowing

Ultrameticulous mowing is a sure sign you're a lawn fanatic. Every line is straight, and the grass looks like a battalion of soldiers standing at attention when you're done. To achieve this clean look, sharpen your mower blades at least once a year to ensure a clean cut every time. Buy a mulching mower so the grass clippings can be cut so finely that they'll decompose right into the soil, feeding the grass their nutrients every time you mow.

String-trim around the edges of the lawn before you mow to capture all those clippings into the mulcher as you mow. Mow the grass to a height of 2 to 2½ inches for an extra lush look, since shorter grass looks fuller than taller grass. Edge around driveways and walkways to give your lawn that look of military precision your neighbors will envy.

Problems

Your lovely lawn looks like a tempting feast to pests, so protect against these snackers with a light summer feeding with insect

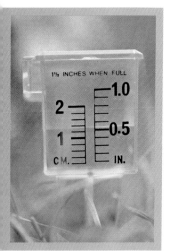

A rain gauge helps ensure your lawn receives at least 1 inch of water each week.

A lawn grown under a manicured program is as inviting as the softest carpet. Uniform texture, healthy color, and lack of weeds is the hallmark.

Manicured: What It Takes

- **Spring** Basic winter cleanup (for example, rake, remove yard debris); tune up your lawn mower and sharpen the blades; do a soil test; aerate (if necessary); add amendments (as recommended); fertilize (with preemergent weed control) in early spring; fertilize again in late spring; water if necessary after fertilizing; mow regularly as necessary when the growing season begins.

- **Summer** Mow and water regularly as necessary; make a light application of fertilizer with insect control (cool-season grasses) in early summer; treat to prevent grubs if they have been a problem in the past.

- **Fall** Remove leaves and debris; fertilize twice (early fall and late fall for cool-season grasses, early fall and midfall for warm-season grasses); water if necessary after fertilizing; mow as necessary through the end of the active growing season; clean equipment for winter storage.

- **Tools and materials** Rake, trimmer, mulching mower, leaf blower, edger, spreader, fertilizer (combination products as necessary, such as weed-and-feed, crabgrass preventer plus fertilizer, and fertilizer plus insect control), hose and sprinkler, long-handled weed digger, aerator (available to rent), rain gauge.

control. If insect pests do invade your lawn (they can travel from a neighbor's yard), identify them and apply a control for that specific pest. Keep watch to make sure the pests are gone, and seed any areas that show stress from an infestation.

Diseases aren't likely to appear in your lawn, but they can happen, perhaps as a result of environmental influences beyond your careful control. Pinpoint the disease you're dealing with, and apply a product to help rid the lawn of it. Seed over any sparse areas with high-quality seed, and let the surrounding grass blend in with the new plants to fill in those spots.

Above and Beyond

To maximize your lawn's ability to absorb nutrients and to stop thatch and soil compaction, aerate the lawn once a year. Rake the soil plugs or just mow over them to break them up so the soil can easily blend back into the lawn. Dethatch only when necessary—when the thatch is over $\frac{1}{2}$ inch thick—because dethatching is hard on the lawn.

While picking up grass clippings isn't necessary when you mow properly, leaves are another matter. If you let them stay on the lawn all winter, they'll smother the grass. Either run a mulching mower over them to chop the leaves into small pieces that break down quickly, or collect them with a bagger attachment, which makes quick work of the job.

The Perfect System

If making sure your lawn is never thirsty is high on your priority list and dragging sprinkler hoses around your yard is getting tiresome, it may be time to invest in an automated sprinkler system. The cost of installing such a system can be daunting—anywhere from $1,500 on up—but if your property is large and hose sprinklers are impractical, it may be your only choice if you really want a lush green lawn. These systems can be timed to go off in the morning (the best time to water) and stop when a specific amount of water has been dispersed. The sprinkler heads pop up when in use, then withdraw back into the ground when not in use so the lawn can be used and maintained.

Do a soil test every year to determine what amendments your lawn needs. Apply the correct amount of amendments according to the soil test results, and continue to fertilize throughout the season to keep a balance of nutrients in the soil. Use good topsoil if you need to seed a specific area to ensure that the new soil is as good as the surrounding soil.

Trees can present a challenge to your lawn–maintenance skills. Shady areas around the bases of trees require special consideration—they should be seeded with grasses that are shade tolerant. Shade tolerant means the grass will still need at least four hours of dappled sunlight. You may need to thin the canopies of your trees to be sure the lawn gets enough sun. If you don't want to touch the trees, consider planting shade–loving groundcovers to maintain the uniformly green color of the whole lawn.

Rake up any fallen tree leaves because they can deprive your lawn of light and moisture. And don't just rake in the fall, but all through the season.

The Cutting Edge

An edger will give your lawn that perfect finish—military straight lines that showcase your beautiful grass. Manual edgers give you more control, which is precisely what you're looking for in your lawn maintenance program. Edge around your driveway, walkways, and plantings every few weeks to keep the lawn looking polished. If your lawn is just too large for a manual edger, invest in a power edger and practice around some inconspicuous area in the yard to be sure you have the hang of it before heading out into the more noticeable areas of the lawn.

MOWING

The hum of a lawn mower is part of the soundtrack of summer. For some, mowing may be the least favorite item on the to-do list. But for others, it's a means of artistic expression. Either way, if you own a home with a yard, you know you will be mowing. Whether you are a casual clipper or consider yourself a contender in the suburban Olympics, consider that without the mower, there would be no lawn in the first place.

The next time you head out to mow your overgrown lawn, remind yourself that you're contributing to the beauty of your property and your neighborhood, and that you're doing your part to promote a healthy environment by cultivating a healthy lawn. Think of mowing as a form of therapy: Put your worries on the back burner and enjoy the fresh air, the exercise, and the opportunity to enjoy the simple pleasures of a labor of love.

MOWING DIGEST

When to Mow

Mow when the lawn is dry and no more than a third taller than the recommended height for your grass. Avoid letting the grass outgrow your mower. If the highest your mower can go is 2 inches, mow before the lawn reaches 3 inches tall.

TO DO

- Mow high, mow often.
- Confirm ideal mowing height and make sure that's the height you're mowing at.
- Mow according to growth rate, not calendar.
- Keep mower blades sharp.
- Leave clippings on the lawn (if they're small enough to not smother the grass).

Mowing Heights

Mowing height is based on the growth habit of the grass. Some grasses grow tall and straight, others low and wide. Check the box on page 40 to find the recommended mowing height for your grass.

If you're not sure how high your mower cuts, insert a ruler or your finger into the grass after mowing. (Hint: Your index finger measures about 3 inches long.)

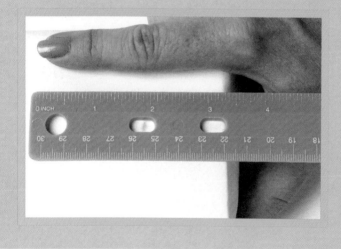

Match the Mower to the Size of Your Lawn

- Less than 2,000 square feet: manual reel mower or rotary push mower

- 1,000 to 5,000 square feet: 20-inch-wide gasoline-powered or rechargeable electric rotary mower

- 5,000 to 20,000 square feet: 22-inch-wide, self-propelled gasoline-engine rotary mower

- More than 20,000 square feet: riding mower or tractor

- Putting green: self-propelled reel mower

Highs and Lows

Mowing high results in	Mowing low results in
- More grass leaves	- A thicker lawn
- More upright growth	- Shallow roots
- More shade tolerance	- Less vigor
- Deeper roots	- More rapid regrowth after mowing
- Drought tolerance	- More weeds, pests
- Slower regrowth after mowing	- Higher maintenance
- Fewer weeds	- Scalped patterns in the grass on uneven ground
- Fewer pests	

Did You Know?

- Walking at an average pace, it will take 2½ hours to mow a half acre of unobstructed lawn with an 18-inch mower. A 36-inch riding mower cuts the same lawn in about 30 minutes.

- The higher you mow, the deeper the roots. Roots of tall fescue clipped at 3½ inches grow to 4 feet deep. The same plants clipped at 2 inches result in roots typically only 18 inches deep.

- Before 1830, lawns were trimmed unevenly at best—with the same tool used to harvest grains.

- Bermudagrass and creeping bentgrass are most tolerant of low mowing, and St. Augustinegrass and tall fescue of high mowing.

- Fine golf course putting greens are routinely mowed ⅛ to ¼ inch tall.

- With an estimated 1.1 million-plus acres of lawns, Texas is the most turfed—and mowed—state in the nation. First runner-up is Georgia and next is Michigan, both with more than three-quarters of a million acres.

If you're not into tuning your mower and sharpening the blades once a year yourself, take your machine to a lawn repair shop and have a professional do it. This is one task you shouldn't skip.

Care for Your Mower

Spring tune-up	Season's end
■ Remove engine shroud and clean around air-cooling fins	■ Fill fuel tank, and add fuel stabilizer (unless it voids your warranty)
■ Change oil	
■ Check, clean, or replace air filter	■ Remove spark plug and drop a teaspoon of oil into cylinder; replace spark plug
■ Clean deck top and bottom	
■ Change spark plug	■ Brush or wash away dirt and debris
■ Lubricate controls and linkages	
■ Sharpen blades	■ Store in a dry, ventilated area

This Blade's for You

Lawns mowed high have more leaf blades, so they capture more sunlight. More sunlight means more energy for the grass, and more energy makes for a stronger, tougher lawn with deeper roots.

Myths, Facts, and Good Advice

Myth: Always mow to the recommended height.

Fact: Not if the lawn is growing fast and doing so would remove more than a third of its height.

Advice: During peak growth periods, you might have to mow several times a week. If the lawn gets away from you, raise the cutting height and mow. Wait three or four days, then mow at the normal height.

Myth: The sharpness of a mower blade makes little difference.

Fact: A sharp blade cuts grass more cleanly, making for a better-looking, less disease-prone lawn. It reduces the effort required to cut the grass, so a sharp blade means faster, easier mowing.

Advice: The more you mow, the more your mower blade needs sharpening. Average users should check the blade at least twice a year.

Tip: Keep a sharp spare mower blade on hand.

MAKING THE CUT

As long as you mow your lawn at the right height and at proper intervals, clippings quickly break down.

There are really only two rules to mowing: Remove no more than one-third of the grass blade at a time, and mow at the upper range of the recommended cutting height for your grass.

Growing heights vary for each grass species, but the taller you mow the lawn, the stronger it is and the better able to survive periods of stress. This is especially important during summer, when the taller height also keeps weed seeds from germinating and insulates the soil during periods of drought.

A Change in Tradition

Turf specialists used to recommend cutting the grass shorter than normal the first time you mow in spring. This low cutting was believed to allow the sun to reach into the crowns of the grass plants and stimulate new growth for early greenup. Experts now say this early scalping may do more harm than good. In fact, scalping at any time of year can severely damage your lawn—especially during times of stress, such as hot, dry periods for cool-season grasses.

That's because scalping—cutting off more than a third of the leaf—forces the plant to put its energy into regrowing blades instead of roots. It also exposes the lower, shaded parts of the plant to sunlight, usually turning them into an unsightly grayish brown stubble. So even though taller grass may not look as trim and tidy as you might think is ideal, it is healthier grass.

Mowing Tips

■ Be sure your mower blade is sharp. A sharp blade cuts the grass cleanly and helps mulch clippings into small pieces, which break down quickly. Conversely, a dull blade shreds the grass, leaving a ragged cut at the top of the leaf, which gives the lawn a gray, tired look. Some grasses, such as perennial ryegrass, take on a particularly ragged look if mowed with a dull blade.

■ Change the direction and pattern each time you mow. Doing so reduces turf wear from mower wheels—that damage is even more pronounced in thin or shady areas. If you mow repeatedly in the same direction, the mower tends to push the grass over rather than cut it cleanly. Eventually the grass begins to lean in the direction mowed, producing light and dark patterns or stripes.

■ Don't let newly seeded grass grow excessively long before the first mowing. If the grass gets too tall before mowing and you mow it to, say, half its height, you'll shock the plants, stressing them and slowing or impairing the process of forming a healthy lawn.

Ragged leaf tips from dull mower blade

To avoid scalping, mow often enough that you never remove more than a third of the grass blade. The recommended height for Kentucky bluegrass is about 2 inches, which means you should mow as soon as it is 3 inches tall. Similarly, tall fescue thrives at 3 inches; mow it when it is 4½ inches tall.

How do you know how high your mower cuts at each setting? Mower decks generally have a cutting range of ⅝ inch to 3½ inches. To check the actual height that your mower is cutting, place the mower on a hard surface, disconnect the spark plug, and measure the distance between the blades and the hard surface with a tape measure (or use a stiff piece of paper and a pencil).

Keeping in mind the basic concept of mowing high and often, here are specific recommendations for mowing cool- and warm-season grasses.

Cool-Season Grasses

With most cool-season grasses (bluegrass, ryegrass, and fescue), you can set the mower as high as it will go and never touch the setting again. If you want athletic-field or golf-course-quality turf, though, start the season mowing at the lower end of the ideal height range, then raise the height to the tallest recommendation for the rest of the season. Hot weather stresses grass; the taller grass shades the soil, lowers its temperature, and slows water loss. Long grass blades also have more surface area, allowing the plants to manufacture more carbohydrates to feed the roots.

Tip
Unless your lawn is bermudagrass, creeping bentgrass, or zoysiagrass, you can set your mower as high as it will go, up to 3 inches, and never adjust the height again.

Bag or Mulch

Contrary to common opinion, grass clippings neither add to thatch nor increase diseases. As long as you mow at the right height and proper interval, clippings break down without a trace because they're mostly water. As they break down, they contribute nitrogen and other nutrients to the soil and supply it with organic matter.

The clippings from a 1,000-square-foot lawn contribute ½ to 2 pounds of nitrogen, depending on how much you fertilize. The more you fertilize, the more nitrogen the clippings return to the soil.

Even so, you may have reasons to collect clippings. If you pick up clippings, the best place to use them is in the garden as mulch (where kids won't track them into the house) or in your compost pile. Throw out clippings from the first three mowings after applying weed control or weed-and-feed rather than putting them in the compost pile.

Comparing Mowing Heights

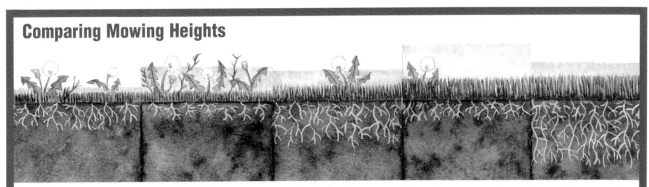

Some people mow low, thinking it will keep the grass from growing back so fast. What they get instead are weeds and shallow-rooted grass.

Letting the grass grow tall and then scalping it is even worse. Roots shrink even further, and the lawn is much less resilient.

Mowing at the low end of the recommended height range is better for the lawn but not optimum.

Even if you mow at the high end of the range, removing more than one-third of the blade at once causes the grass shoots to grow at the expense of the roots.

Grass is healthiest, most resilient, and weed free when you mow at the high end of the height range and never cut off more than a third of the blade.

Mow frequently; too-tall grass becomes coarse, stemmy, and matted.

Cool-season grasses grow vigorously during the spring and require more frequent cutting then. Continue mowing until the grass stops growing in fall, when the weather turns cooler and the trees start to change color.

Warm-Season Grasses

Warm-season grasses (bahiagrass, bermudagrass, buffalograss, centipedegrass, seashore paspalum, St. Augustinegrass, and zoysiagrass) are naturally better adapted to warm weather than cool-season grasses. They thrive in heat, and they experience more vigorous growth during the summer. So you don't need to raise the mower height to protect them from heat stress. Instead, keep the cutting height the same all summer for these grasses.

Some warm-season grass species can survive mowing heights as low as $\frac{1}{8}$ inch, but others won't do well if cut shorter than $1\frac{1}{2}$ inches. Bermudagrass and zoysiagrass lawns will build up excessive thatch if mowed taller than $1\frac{1}{2}$ and $2\frac{1}{2}$ inches, respectively. Warm-season grasses can thrive at low heights because

Recommended Mowing Heights in Inches

Bahiagrass	2–4
Bermudagrass	$\frac{1}{2}$–2
Buffalograss	2–3 or unmowed
Centipedegrass	1–3
Creeping bentgrass	$\frac{1}{2}$–$\frac{3}{4}$
Fine fescues	$2\frac{1}{2}$–4
Kentucky bluegrass	$2\frac{1}{2}$–4
Perennial ryegrass	$2\frac{1}{2}$–4
Seashore paspalum	1–2
St. Augustinegrass	2–4
Tall fescue	$2\frac{1}{2}$–4
Zoysiagrass	$\frac{3}{4}$–2

Hints for Smooth Mowing

1 **Mow header strips at the ends of the lawn and around flowerbeds and shrub beds.**

2 **Mow back and forth between the header strips. The headers give you room to turn and work around any curves.**

3 **Overlap each cut by 1 or 2 inches; this helps you avoid leaving ridges of uncut grass.**

they have stolons; they spread by sending out lateral stems along the ground, making it possible for them to grow under conditions that kill more upright grasses.

Figure the Frequency

How often should you cut the grass? The simple answer is, as often as it takes to maintain its recommended height. That depends on the grass species, the season, the growing conditions, and the amount and type of fertilizer you use. Generally, every five to seven days is plenty, keeping the basic one-third rule in mind. It's important to cut the grass regularly throughout the growing season. The more moisture the grass receives, the more often you'll need to mow. You may find yourself mowing twice a week during extended rainy periods. During wet spells some specialists suggest a practice known as double cutting. This involves moving the mower height up a setting and then, after the clippings dry, lowering the mower to the normal height and mowing again in a different direction.

It's a Jungle

When you return from vacation and find the grass so tall you could lose your dog in it, your first inclination might be to cut everything back to its original height. Resist the temptation; instead, spend the next few weeks gradually lowering the grass to its proper height. The key is to mow every few days, never removing more than one-third of the grass blade at a time.

Sharpening the Blade

- For a clean cut, the mower blade must be sharp. A dull blade tears grass, which then takes on a grayish brown cast. Sharpen the blade whenever it shows signs of wear. Follow the installation instructions in the owner's manual, especially because it's possible to install a blade backward on some mowers. Keep a spare sharp blade on hand so you won't ever have to use a dull one.

- Remove the spark plug wire. Clamp a 2×4 block to the deck to keep the blade from turning as you remove it. Squirt some penetrating oil on the bolt that holds the blade, and give it about 15 minutes to work its way into the threads. Turn the nut counterclockwise with a socket wrench and remove it. Mark the bottom of the blade with a grease pencil.

- Carefully examine the blade. If you see cracks or large nicks, replace the blade with a new one. If the blade is just dull, sharpen the cutting edges with a grinder. A hand file works, but a grinder is faster. Closely follow the factory angle of the cutting edge; apply minimal pressure as you move the blade across the wheel. Dunk the blade in a bucket of water after each pass to cool it, then wipe it with a rag. Finish with a 10-inch mill file, keeping the angle consistent. File away from you with long, broad strokes.

- Next rebalance the blade. Balancing kits are available at most hardware stores. Set the center of the blade on the plastic balancing device provided with the kit so the blade swings free like a teeter-totter. Let it settle, and mark the light end. Grind the heavier side, then recheck the balance. Both sides must be even.

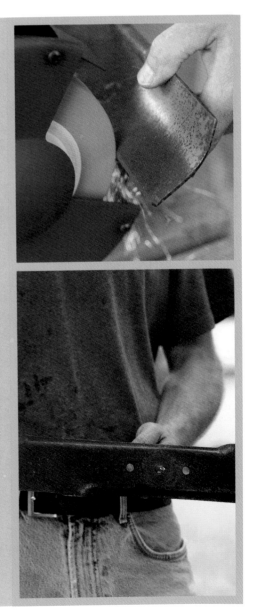

LAWN MOWERS

Reel mowers provide a precise, even cut. Manual models are best for small lawns. Their cutting height is shorter than other mowers. Dense or tall grass limits their effectiveness.

The two most common types of lawn mowers are rotary and reel. Reel mowers have blades that are mounted cylindrically; they rotate across a stationary bed knife and shear the grass like scissors. Because of the blade arrangement, reel mowers operate as effectively when the blades are spinning slowly as when they spin fast.

Most mowers on the market, however, are gas-powered rotary models with 2- or 4-cycle engines. Rotaries employ a single blade that is mounted horizontally and spins at speeds up to 200 miles per hour.

Choosing the style of cut is only the beginning when buying a mower. You can select from an array of features and models. If you want to avoid exertion and your pockets are deep enough, there are even high-tech robotic models.

Reel Mowers

If your lawn is less than 2,000 square feet, consider a push reel mower. These vintage-looking models are powered by inexpensive and abundantly available muscle power. A reel mower will give you not only a handsome yard but also a valuable aerobic workout. If you remember reel mowers as the heavy, bulky clunkers your grandparents used, you haven't seen the newest models, which are lightweight (as low as 16 pounds) and durable. Many have ball-bearing wheel assemblies that glide over a lawn. The better models let you adjust the mowing height from $\frac{1}{2}$ to $2\frac{1}{2}$ inches, and they come in 14-, 16-, 18-, 20-, and 24-inch widths (the wider the reel, the faster the job). Affordable power models are also available in many areas, but not in every market.

Reel mowers slice through the grass with an efficient scissorslike cut, which is actually better for your grass than the cut of rotary units. They cut cleanly with little injury to the grass, which helps keep moisture in the grass blade and disease out. Other than wiping down the blades after use and sharpening the reel every two years, which you can do yourself, these mowers need almost no maintenance. They're also easy to store; just hang them on a shed or garage wall.

Reel mowers produce a high-quality cut on short turf. One disadvantage is that they can't handle grass much taller than 2 inches. Also, if your lawn is riddled with dandelions or other tall, tough weeds, a reel mower won't cut as well. Wiry weeds tend to fold under the blades, so your freshly mowed lawn will be dotted with weed stems. Mowing with a manual reel mower is slower than with a power model. A lawn that requires 45 minutes to mow with a gas-powered mower might take 60 to 70 minutes with a manual reel mower.

Rotary Mowers

Rotary mowers are by far the most common type used in the United States and Canada. You'll find electric, gas-, and battery-powered models. Power rotary mowers are less expensive than their powered reel cousins and cost less to maintain. The blade is easy to remove, and anyone with a grinding stone or file can sharpen one with practice. Or you can take the blade to a shop for sharpening.

Rotary mowers are much safer than they were even a few years ago. Two types of safety systems are available. The most common is what is known as a zone restart, a lever or switch that stops both the blade and the engine. More expensive models feature a blade-break clutch (or deadman's switch), a safety bar on the handle that only stops the blade from spinning, not the engine, as soon as it's released. Use these safety devices, whatever type of rotary mower you have. The spinning blade can sever fingers, toes, hands, and feet.

One safety issue remains: The blade spins at a high rate of speed and can throw debris with enough force to injure anyone within range. Make sure your lawn is free of debris (large sticks and stones) before mowing. Read the owner's manual and follow all safety precautions.

Rotary mowers—which come in side-discharge, rear-discharge, bagging, and mulching models—are best suited to tall mowing heights and are apt to scalp bumpy or uneven lawns at levels lower than 1 inch. Don't skimp on power. Engines on lower-priced models tend to have power ratings between $2\frac{1}{2}$ and 3 horsepower. Tall, dense grass can bend their crankshafts. A mower with $3\frac{1}{2}$ horsepower or higher is better for such lawns.

Mulching mowers will do a better job of dicing clippings into small pieces so they'll disappear quickly. The key to getting clippings to break down rapidly, though, is to mow often enough that the clippings are never so thick they smother the grass beneath them.

Selecting a Power Source

Gas-powered mowers If your yard is up to a half acre in size, you'll probably want a gas-powered, walk-behind model, although the engine makes for a heavy mower (up to 100 pounds) that's not as easy to handle as an electric model. Even so, gas mowers have been the most popular sellers for many years. They have more power and work better for large lawns. Self-propelled versions take the work out of mowing slopes and thick turf.

Electric mowers Electric push mowers don't pollute the air and are quiet, easy to maintain, and relatively

Walk-behind mowers offer an unlimited range of options, from width of cut to horsepower, matching any situation.

Safety Comes First

- Understand how the equipment works. Read the owner's manual before using equipment for the first time. Know where all the controls are and how to use them
- Dress to mow. Wear sturdy shoes and close-fitting clothes, including long pants.
- Clear the area. Pick up rocks, twigs, cans, golf balls, and anything else the mower could throw or that could damage your machine.
- Handle gasoline carefully. Fill the tank before starting, while the engine is cool. Avoid spills. Store gasoline in an approved container in a cool, well-ventilated area, and never smoke around it. When you're ready to start the mower, do so outdoors.
- Fill the gas tank only when the

mower is on pavement. Gas spills kill grass and sterilize the soil.
- Keep children and pets away from the mower. Never allow kids to play with a mower or operate it without supervision. Don't carry a child with you on a riding mower. A child could fall off and be cut by the blades before the engine stops.
- Mow when the grass is dry to avoid slipping and falling. Wet clippings also clog the mower deck or chute.
- Mow during daylight. Keep a sharp eye out for debris by looking 3 to 4 feet ahead of the mower.
- Watch your footing on hilly terrain, and never mow on a steep incline. Mow slopes on the diagonal. Better yet, consider planting a groundcover that doesn't need mowing on slopes.

- Keep hands and feet away from moving parts at all times, even if safety devices are engaged. Never work on equipment when the motor is running. And never remove or tamper with warning labels or safety devices; they're provided to protect you and your family.
- Never pull a mower toward you. If you should slip, you could catch a foot under the mower blade.
- Operate equipment carefully, and always follow the manufacturer's recommended operating procedures. Turn off the engine and disconnect the spark plug before attempting to unclog or work on any power equipment. Also remember to remove the key of riding mowers when you leave a machine unattended.

Battery- and electric-powered mowers are especially trendy in cities with tough anti-pollution standards. They produce no emissions and run quietly.

inexpensive. They may be powered by an electric cord or a battery. Corded machines are good for small lawns where maneuverability isn't a problem.

The main disadvantage of corded mowers is that you have to drag around an extension cord. Look for models with a handlebar that flips over or that allows the cord to slide across to reduce the chance of slicing through it when turning. Also, you don't want to stray much farther than 100 to 150 feet from an electrical outlet, because the longer the cord, the greater the drop in voltage.

These machines are a snap to start, and they are generally lightweight (30 to 60 pounds). Just don't use them on moist lawns because they lack the power to cut through wet grass. More important, a frayed cord can pose a serious danger. Store the mower where it will stay dry, because moisture can cause electrical faults.

Battery-powered mowers are much easier to maneuver around a yard—and a bit more expensive—than their tethered cousins. You'll find them to be heavier (55 to 80 pounds), so you might wish to buy a self-propelled model, especially if your lawn slopes. Note, too, that the battery makes the machine a bit top-heavy, so test-drive one before buying.

Battery-powered mowers are available with 12-, 24-, or 36-volt batteries; they can cut up to 5,000 square feet on a single charge—about 45 minutes of mowing time.

If you decide on a battery model, plan to store it where you can keep it constantly plugged in (recharging the battery takes about 20 hours). Consider buying an extra battery to ensure you can finish a mowing job in one try. Batteries generally last five to seven years.

Riding mowers The next step up is a riding mower—more expensive and more powerful than any of the walk-behind varieties. A riding mower makes the most sense for homeowners with large lawns or physical conditions that limit their activity. The typical 30- to 42-inch mowing path is a major plus for big jobs.

Riding mowers vary from no-frills models designed for mowing large, flat areas to models fitted with a variety of features and attachments that allow you to take on numerous jobs. A hydrostatic, or automatic, clutch is one option that makes the work easier, so you might decide to pay a little more for this extra.

Consider buying a garden tractor if you have several acres or more to maintain. These machines not only cut the grass, but also till soil, scoop snow, and pull loads. Take care when using any type of riding mower on steep slopes.

Sizing Up the Lawn

A lawn's size, features, and rate of growth will influence your choice of mowers. Begin by measuring the area of your lawn, then consider peculiarities of the terrain. A smaller plot (less than 5,000 square feet) suggests a smaller, basic, inexpensive mower. Such a mower also might be appropriate for trim-mowing a larger lawn with a complex shape or with many trees and other landscape features.

For sloping lawns or those up to 20,000 square feet, opt for a self-propelled mower. A more spacious lawn (greater than 20,000 square feet) may justify a riding model.

Powering Up

One of the most important considerations in buying a power mower is the engine. Match the horsepower to the grass as well as to the size and the terrain of your lawn. A thick, dense turf, such as a zoysiagrass lawn, requires more horsepower. Although there's no sense paying for more power than you need, you'll kick yourself if you end up with an undersize mower that requires extra time and energy to use.

Gas mowers (3½ to 4 horsepower or more) are the most powerful. For a small, relatively flat lawn, consider buying a manual reel, corded electric, or battery-powered mower.

If you prefer a gas version, you'll need to choose between a two- or four-cycle engine. Two-cycle engines are not as widely available and may soon no longer be on the market. They run on a mix of gasoline and oil, which lubricates the engine without an oil pump and produces a great amount of exhaust (the reason they're being phased out). Four-cycle engines run on gas only; oil is added separately.

Both gas engines perform satisfactorily. Two-cycle mowers are a good choice on slopes, where engine lubrication is difficult. They also tend to be lighter in weight.

Self-propelled gas mowers have more powerful engines, 4 to 6½ horsepower, so they are ideal for hilly properties. Riding mowers have larger engines—8 to 20 horsepower or more.

Storage

If you have limited storage, think about a mower with a collapsible or folding handle. You can hang some reel and electric mowers on the wall. Riding lawn mowers are space hogs; before buying one, consider how much space you have available for storing it.

Comparison Shopping

Because it's not always possible to test-drive a lawn mower, you'll find it helpful to talk to friends and neighbors about their mowers. Consumer groups and manufacturers' websites are also good sources of information. Watch for media stories and reports; check for recall notices. Look for recognized brand names. Established manufacturers with a strong reputation are more likely to stand behind their products and to supply parts for them. They also offer more substantial warranties.

Baggers vs. mulchers

Rotary mowers come in side- and rear-discharge models (for bagging), and mulching models. Side-discharge versions throw the clippings to the right side of the cutting path. (You can fit most mowers with a bag attachment to catch clippings that are discharged either to the side or the rear. One has no advantage over the other; it's a matter of preference.) Riding mowers typically have rear attachments for bagging clippings; the bags are easy to remove and save strain on your back from raking.

If you prefer to leave the clippings on your lawn, mulching mowers chop the clippings into small pieces that quickly disappear. The key to getting clippings to break down quickly, even with mulching mowers, is to mow often enough that clippings don't build up on the surface.

Easy start Nothing is more frustrating than being ready to mow and then spending a half hour trying to start the motor. Fortunately, newer models start up much easier than older ones, thanks to innovations in engine design. Today's pull-start mowers should fire up after a couple of strong pulls.

Older adults or those with limited mobility may still want to consider buying an electric-start model. Most of these start with the push of a button or the turn of a key. Avoid buying one that doesn't give you the option of starting it with a rope, just in case you have problems with the electric-start or your power source isn't working.

Decks The deck is the housing that covers the rotating blade; it is made of aluminum, steel, or tough plastic (the same plastic in football helmets). Aluminum decks are lighter weight and more rust resistant than steel, but they cost more.

Garden tractors are versatile, multipurpose machines well suited to large properties. Optional accessories allow you to use these tractors for snow removal, garden tilling, and many other jobs.

Zero-turn mowers, which have rear wheels that operate independently, were developed for professional use but are now popular among homeowners. They're fun to drive and make quick work of your lawn but take a little getting used to. Consider buying one if you have an extra-large lawn to mow.

Heavy-duty mowers usually have a steel deck, as do most push mowers. Steel decks can rust, but this is entirely avoidable with proper care.

Deck widths vary. Average commercial walk-behind models come with 36- to 42-inch decks, whereas riding mowers may have 6-foot decks. The wider the mowing swath, the faster you can mow your lawn. But with a wider deck, the mower is heavier, less maneuverable, and more expensive. Wider decks are also more likely to scalp uneven spots in the lawn. But no matter the size of your mower deck, scalping can be a problem if the lawn has high spots or bumps. Larger mower decks often have a floating or oscillating feature that allows the mower to move with the ground's contours and prevents scalping.

Before deciding on a wide deck, measure your yard to make sure the mower will fit through all of the small openings and around any special landscaping features.

Cutting-height adjustment Changing the mowing height can be a snap or a chore, depending on the mower. Some models have easy-to-use levers that raise or lower the cutting height by raising or lowering the deck; a lever is usually located on each wheel of the mower. Some newer models let you change the height with the flick of one lever. Riding mowers often have a handle mounted on the side that moves the deck up or down. With inexpensive push mowers, you often have to take the wheels off to adjust the cutting height. If you own such a mower, set the height as high as it will go (or to the tallest cutting height for the grass) and leave it there.

Turning on a dime Though you won't be competing in a slalom race, you do want to be able to maneuver around flowerbeds and through narrow spaces with ease, especially if you're thinking about getting a riding mower. Today's models offer a variety of steering capabilities. Some riders—zero-turn mowers—are designed to turn by pivoting around their rear wheels. Four-wheel-drive and all-wheel-drive riding mowers really will turn on a dime. This ability allows you to cut closer to objects, turn tighter corners, and reduce the amount of trimming you need to do.

One word of caution: Driving these mowers can be tricky because their wheels move independently. Until you become proficient with the mower, your flowerbeds may be in peril. Reasonably priced residential models are available.

Front vs. rear drive Riding mowers may have front- or rear-wheel drive. Most people report little difference between the two, although some believe the front-wheel-drive option makes their mowers more maneuverable and gives them greater control. With front-wheel drive you need to push down on the front wheels to compensate for the weight of the bag as it fills with clippings. Take both types out for a spin to find out which feels best.

Maintaining Your Investment

You've spent a lot of money on your lawn mower, and you want the machine to last. The best way to ensure that is to set up—and follow—a comprehensive maintenance schedule. Your owner's manual is a good place to start your to-do list. If you bought a used lawn mower or don't have the owner's manual, follow the schedule on the opposite page.

Spring prep Most manuals tell you exactly what you need to know. Pay close attention to the viscosity and quality of oil recommended for the engine. The wrong oil can cause overheating and excessive wear on the internal parts, which in turn shortens the engine's life.

Keeping the air filter clean A dirty filter causes the engine to work harder and waste energy. It also permits particles to enter the internal workings of the mower, wearing them down and causing damage. Eventually, the mower will begin burning oil, like a worn-out car engine.

Inspect or change the spark plug at either the beginning or end of each mowing season. Use a spark plug gauge to check the gap; most manuals list the most favorable gap thickness. Take care not to damage the porcelain insulator. If the porcelain is cracked, replace the plug.

Winter storage At the end of the mowing season, put the machine away for the winter. Allow the engine to cool completely. Drain most of the gas from the fuel tank, then run the mower until the entire fuel system is completely dry. Or add a fuel stabilizer to the tank. (First consult the owner's manual because using an additive may void your warranty.)

Drain and properly dispose of the old crankcase oil and replace it with fresh oil per the manufacturer's recommendations.

Remove the spark plug using a spark plug wrench. Lubricate the cylinder by pouring a teaspoon of oil through the spark plug hole (again, check the instructions in your owner's manual). Slowly rotate the engine several times by turning the crankshaft or pulling the starter rope to distribute the oil. Replace the spark plug with a new one, but don't reconnect the spark plug wire to it.

Thoroughly clean all dirt and debris from the machine. If you have a self-propelled mower, grease the rear height-adjuster brackets. Check the blade and engine-mounting bolts to make sure all are tight. This is also a good time to inspect and sharpen the blade.

Store the mower in a clean, dry place, well away from appliances with pilot lights or other potential ignition sources.

Maintenance Steps

Beginning of season
- Add fresh gas
- Replace spark plug
- Sharpen blade
- Clean or replace air filter
- Check oil level
- Inflate riding mower tires
- Reconnect spark plug wire

Before each use
- Check fuel and oil levels
- Check tire inflation
- Check for loose or worn parts

After each use
- Clean clippings from underside of mower and from top of deck

Throughout the season
- Check blade sharpness and general condition
- Balance the blade after sharpening
- Check all visible moving parts for wear and looseness
- Use correct fuel and oil

Periodically
- Clean or change air filter after every 25 hours—more often if working in dusty conditions
- Lubricate wheels and moving joints after 25 hours
- Check belts and chain drives of riding mowers

End of season
- Change oil
- Drain gas or add gas stabilizer, if the warranty allows
- Lubricate cylinder
- Thoroughly clean mower
- Grease where necessary
- Disconnect spark plug wire
- Store safely

FINISHING TOUCHES

Straight-shaft trimmers are powerful and comfortable to use. Try out a trimmer before buying to make sure that its length and weight fit your body.

Power edgers easily and quickly slice through the buildup of soil and grass along sidewalks, driveways, and other paved areas.

The edges of a lawn, where grass meets planting beds or paved areas, can have a big impact. Letting them grow shaggy gives the whole lawn a messy, unkempt appearance. It takes little effort to keep edges looking orderly, and string trimmers and power edgers can help you attain that well-manicured appearance you desire and make the job easier.

String Trimmers

String trimmers may be powered either by a gasoline engine or an electric motor. Gas models are the most powerful and versatile.

Electric models are effective and not nearly as noisy as gas versions. They are also less expensive. With electric trimmers, the greater the amperage, the better the cut. Corded types can be used anywhere that can be reached by an extension cord. Battery-powered models are a good alternative, giving you more flexibility. Look for electric models with the motor on the top of the shaft rather than the bottom; those with bottom-mounted motors are not as well balanced.

You can choose between straight- and curved-shaft models. Those with straight shafts are more powerful and comfortable and offer a greater reach. Curved-shaft models are easier to handle, lighter in weight, and less expensive. Trimmers with antivibration engine mountings cut down on fatigue. A head that rotates allows you to use the trimmer as an edger.

Angle the trimmer to send the trimmings away from you. Trim before mowing. That way, the mower will chop up the trimmings, reducing the need for raking and bagging later.

Always wear eye protection when using a string trimmer. The spinning string can throw small objects at a high rate of speed and damage eyes. Long pants also take the sting out of the job. If using a gas-powered model, be sure to wear ear plugs; the high pitch of the engine can damage hearing.

Mowing Strips

The term mowing strip refers to a hard surface—usually concrete or brick—that borders a landscape feature such as a flowerbed, tree, or wall.

Mowing strips eliminate the need to trim grass that mowers can't reach. They serve as a barrier to roots and rhizomes.

The surface of the strip can be anywhere from a few inches to a foot wide. It should be flush with or slightly above ground level. When you're mowing, the wheel of the lawn mower rides along the strip. Because the mowing strip provides a tidy edge, the result is a neatly manicured lawn that doesn't require use of trimmers or edgers.

Edgers

As a lawn grows, it builds up organic matter and collects windblown soil at its edges. The resulting buildup lets grass grow a few inches over sidewalks, driveways, and street curbs. You can easily remove it with an edger—a tool designed to cut a neat line between pavement and lawn. Manual or power edgers are available.

Manual edgers come in two types: stick and roller. Stick edgers consist of a half-moon blade at the end of a handle. Roller

A gas leaf blower takes you to all parts of your yard without fighting with a cord.

Leaf Blowers

These portable tools are either handheld or mounted as backpacks. You sweep a hand-operated wand back and forth, blowing debris ahead of you as you walk. Leaf blowers clear clippings and leaves from lawns, sidewalks, and driveways. Some models give you the option of vacuuming debris into a bag.

Gas and electric blowers are available. Electric blowers either attach to an extension cord, which limits mobility, or are powered by a rechargeable battery. Gas leaf blowers allow more freedom of movement and are more powerful than their electric counterparts. However, they are noisier than electric leaf blowers.

The true test of a leaf blower is not the horsepower of its motor, but the amount of air expelled over a given period of time. Leaf blowers are ranked by the cubic feet per minute of air they put out. The more air, the better and the more expensive the blower is.

Use Caution

Be careful when operating power equipment. Follow the safety procedures in the owner's manual. Always turn off equipment that isn't being used, and disable machines while servicing them. Wear eye protection, long pants, and ear plugs.

edgers have a star-shape cutting wheel attached to a wheel guide. With either type, you push the cutting edge into the ground along the pavement to slice away unwanted grass. A roller edger requires considerable arm muscle, depending on the thickness of the buildup. Stick edgers put your leg muscles to work. Step edgers, a type of half-moon edger, use your body weight as the driving force.

Power edgers get their muscle from either gasoline or electricity. Electric ones have star-shape cutting wheels, like roller edgers. Gas-powered edgers have a narrow, rapidly spinning cutting blade. Both are effective. Consider a power edger if your turf is a tough, aggressive species, such as bermuda.

Power and roller edgers are easiest to use on long, straight edges. Half-moon edgers and string trimmers are good for cleaning up around curved or irregular shrub beds and flowerbeds.

Edging gives the lawn a neat, well-kept appearance. You can edge at any time of year, but doing it in the spring helps the lawn look its best as it emerges from dormancy. Some homeowners edge the lawn every few weeks or whenever it starts to look ragged.

Whichever tool you use, work when the soil is moist—but not wet—because moist soil takes less effort to cut than dry soil. When using hand tools, you'll find it easier if you work from the area you've already cut toward the uncut edge, rather than the other direction. Sweep up debris as you go so it doesn't get in the way.

Protecting Tree Trunks

- Never use a string trimmer to trim grass near a tree trunk or bang your mower against the bark. That little bit of damage can kill the tree, especially if you repeat it every time you mow. Eventually it will destroy the tree's water- and food-conducting tissue and provide an entrance for insects and diseases.

- A good way to protect the tree is to install a ring of mulch around the trunk. Start the ring at least 3 inches away from the trunk and extend it as wide as the drip line of the tree (the outside edge of the

canopy). This not only protects the trunk but also makes the tree healthier, because grass inhibits tree root growth.

- Another option is to plant groundcover around the tree.

PATTERN PERFECT

Your lawn will join the big leagues when you mow patterns into the grass. Make it fancy or plain, and change the pattern every week if you like.

Use a regular roller to press patterns into your lawn. Avoid rolling the lawn when soil is wet and easily compacted.

Mowing may be a necessity, but take it one step further and you can call it art. Inspired by the snappy designs mowed in the grass at major league baseball parks and other professional sports venues, homeowners are beginning to have fun adding similar embellishments to their own lawns. Stripes, checkerboards, and diamonds are common field patterns, and easy to do at home if you have the right tools and technique. Try a mowing pattern in your own lawn and give the neighbors something to talk about.

The designs are the result of light reflecting off the grass. Mowing naturally bends grass a bit, so when light is reflected off grass that's mowed and bent one way, it looks a different color from the row of grass that was mowed and bent the other way. Add to that the weight of a heavy roller reinforcing the impression on the grass, and you have a pattern that seems to pop right off the lawn.

So how do the professional groundskeepers get the patterns to look so sharp? They use good equipment. They use souped-up field mowers outfitted with weighted rollers to press down the grass and highlight the pattern. You can use your own mower and a ground roller and get the same dazzling effect.

Even though you only need a mower and a roller to make a pattern, understand that your pattern will only be as good as your mower. For beginners, mowing a straight line is the first challenge. So before you cut a single row, sketch out the pattern as you would like to see it on your lawn, with a mind to the vantage point from which it will be best appreciated (for example, from the road, your living room window, or your back deck). Next identify a straight line in your yard that will be the baseline against which you will begin to mow and create your pattern. This line can be a first pass at the edge of a straight driveway or curb, or you can mark it with string and chalk and begin mowing there. Mow from one end of your baseline to the other, make a turn at the end, and mow back in the opposite direction, slightly overlapping the tire marks from your first row.

To ensure that your lines stay straight as you mow back and forth, it's better to look ahead than to look down at the mower. If you focus your gaze at a point about 10 feet in front of you, you can keep in line with the previous pass and anticipate any adjustments you need to make. Looking down at the mower while you work will gradually set you off course.

If trees, shrubs, or other obstacles block the path of your mow lines, lift the deck of your mower (like popping a wheelie on a bike) as you go around them, so you don't disturb any adjacent lines you have made. Resume mowing against the edge of the previous pass when you've moved beyond the obstacle.

Once you've cut your pattern in the lawn with the mower, it's time for the roller to close the deal. Rollers are sold at most home improvement stores or garden centers—they're the same piece of equipment you use to prepare the soil to plant a brand new lawn or to level the ground to lay a patio or walkway. Your roller should be the same width as your mower deck, so that you're reinforcing exactly the same pattern you created with the mower.

Fill the roller with water or sand to give it weight (water's best because you can use it in your garden when you're done, and you won't have to lug a full roller to the garage). Run the roller over your lines in the same direction as you mowed, sticking as close to your original lines as possible to keep the edges of the pattern sharp. (Avoid using a roller when the soil is wet to avoid compacting clay soil.)

Start With Stripes

Stripes are the simplest pattern to mow. Mow back and forth in straight lines, as described above, and follow up with rolling in the same direction as you mowed. Think about laying your stripes on a diagonal (if the contour of your lawn permits).

Check It Out

A checkerboard is a simple variation on the basic stripes pattern. Once you've mowed the entire yard in stripes, mow it all again at a 90–degree angle to your first set of stripes, mowing in alternate directions just as before. Although you mow twice, you roll only once. Go back to your first set of stripes and roll every other stripe in the direction that you first mowed to reveal your checkerboard pattern.

Stripes
Mow straight lines back and forth across your lawn as normal, traveling in the opposite direction with each pass.

Checkerboard
Mow a second time at a 90-degree angle to the first mowing. Again mow in straight lines and travel in opposite directions with each pass.

Highlight the pattern
Go back to the stripes you created with the first mowing. Roll every other one traveling in the same direction as you traveled with the mower. Finally, mow around the edges of your lawn to clean up any stray unmowed blades of grass.

Making Turns

At the end of a pass make your turns carefully, to protect both the grass and the design. Approach the end of a row slowly, and mow to the end. Lift the mower deck up off the grass while turning to prevent scalping the grass in the turn area. Once the turn is completed, line up the mower at the beginning of the next pass carefully to make sure you're exactly in line with the previous pass. This will help keep the lines straight and protect the integrity of the mowing design.

Cleaning Up

Giving the pattern a nice clean look actually starts before you mow a single row. Trim the grass around trees, shrub beds, driveways, or buildings before you start to mow. This way when the pattern is mowed, those grass clippings get mowed right in with the rest of the grass, and you won't have to leave unsightly footprints all over your pattern by cleaning up after the fact. Finish off the pattern by making a final pass around the outside edges of the lawn to get rid of any marks you may have made turning and to give the design a polished look.

FERTILIZING

The simple secret to a healthy, gorgeous green lawn is good food. It's true. The single most important thing you can do for your lawn is to provide it with proper nutrition by fertilizing regularly. This is the easiest, most effective, and least expensive way to make a real impact on your lawn.

Many homeowners feed their lawns once or twice a year and wonder why the lawn isn't thriving. That's because lawns suffer on this feast-or-famine approach. During the famine—the long stretch between feedings—the grass is deficient in nutrients and doesn't have the resources to stand up to normal, everyday stresses. When feasting, the diet is too rich and the grass becomes so "flabby" that diseases and insect pests readily move in. Providing your lawn with regular meals is the best way to ensure it develops into as healthy and hardy a lawn as it can be.

This chapter explains all you need to know about fertilizing. It shows you how to figure out what your lawn needs and how to select the best product for your yard. It offers tips and techniques for evenly applying the right amount of fertilizer to avoid leaving yellow stripes in the grass.

The good news is that fertilizing is easy to do and the results of regular feeding are remarkable. You'll pat yourself on the back every time you look at your lush, healthy lawn.

FERTILIZING DIGEST

A = L×W
Calculate the Size of Your Lawn

To apply the right amount of fertilizer, you need to know the area of your lawn. It's easy: For any rectangular space, simply multiply the length by the width (so a lawn 60 feet wide and 40 feet deep contains 2,400 square feet). For a lawn with an irregular shape, divide the lawn into rectangular sections and add up their areas. A quick solution for a yard that is mostly lawn: Calculate the total lot area and subtract the area covered by the footprint of the house and driveway.

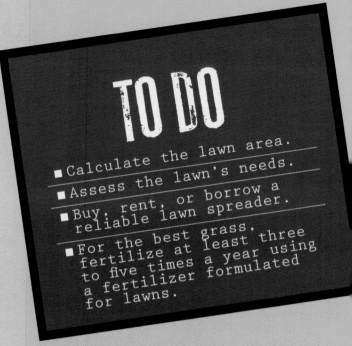

TO DO

- Calculate the lawn area.
- Assess the lawn's needs.
- Buy, rent, or borrow a reliable lawn spreader.
- For the best grass, fertilize at least three to five times a year using a fertilizer formulated for lawns.

Q&A

Q The hardest thing about spreading fertilizer actually makes the job easier. What is it?

A Getting up early. Morning is the best time for the job, while the breeze is light and the dew is heavy. Why? The spreader leaves tracks in the dewy grass, so it's easy to see exactly where you've been. Also, gentle morning breezes mean the fertilizer doesn't blow around. Finally, it's just a beautiful time of day to be outside. (Follow watering directions on the bag, even though the grass is dewy.)

Spreading Joy

The spreader you use makes a difference in your perception of fertilizing. Give yourself and your lawn a break: Rather than trying to coax another season out of some rusty relic that won't roll straight or spread evenly, get a new one that works better and lasts longer.

Drop or broadcast? As the names imply, some spreaders drop fertilizer; others broadcast it. Drop spreaders are precise. They're the best choice if you have adjacent beds you don't want to treat. Broadcast spreaders are quicker and easier to use and some models prevent fertilizer from getting into adjacent areas.

Take care to overlap each pass so you don't leave gaps. Otherwise you may see telltale yellow and green stripes.

Three Key Nutrients

The first key to fertilizer lies in those three big numbers on the label. They represent the three most important nutrients in the bag.

Nitrogen
Boosts growth and green color

Phosphorus*
Feeds seedlings and aids root growth

Potassium**
Strengthens resistance to drought and disease

29-1-4

It's the ratio of the numbers that matters—a 10-10-10 fertilizer is in a 1-1-1 ratio. In other words, nitrogen, phosphorus, and potassium fill the bag in equal proportions. Lawn fertilizers are high in nitrogen, often in a ratio of 10-1-1. You'll learn in this chapter how to get the ideal mix of nutrients for your lawn.

$* P_2O_5$ $** K_2O$

Perfect Timing

For nutrition, people think in terms of three square meals a day. Most cool-season lawns prefer four a year: a spring awakening, an early summer boost, a late summer revival, and a late summer or autumn reinforcement to carry the lawn through winter.

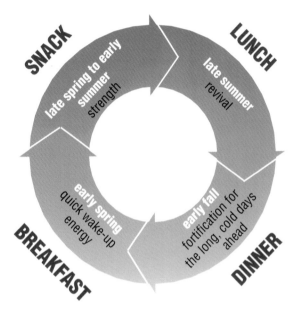

SNACK — late spring to early summer strength

LUNCH — late summer revival

DINNER — early fall fortification for the long, cold days ahead

BREAKFAST — early spring quick wake-up energy

Lawn Lore

Fertilizers in History

The first fertilizer? Let's just say it was distributed free by livestock, which also provided the first system of mowing. A pretty efficient process all in all but hard to manage on today's lawns.

The most celebrated fertilizer? Fish. Squanto of the Pawtuxet tribe taught the pilgrims to plant a fish beside their corn seeds. Squanto is said to have picked up this trick in his travels, which stretched from present-day Massachusetts to Newfoundland. Without it, the colonists might not have survived on the crops they coaxed from their fields near Plymouth Rock.

Inventor of a more scientific fertilizer? Justus von Liebig, a German chemistry professor in the early 1800s.

The first fertilizer made specifically for lawns? Scotts Turf Builder, which was introduced in 1928.

Myths, Facts & Good Advice

Myth: Fertilizing means more mowing.

Fact: It doesn't have to. But if you use a fertilizer composed mainly of quick-release nitrogen, the grass will grow fast. Such fertilizers are a feast-or-famine diet for grass. A high-quality fertilizer, on the other hand, feeds lawns steadily, which means the grass grows steadily too.

Advice: Read the label before buying to ensure you're getting high-quality fertilizer. Look for these terms: extended feeding or slow-release nitrogen, which may also be called slowly available, controlled-release, or water-insoluble nitrogen (WIN).

FERTILIZING FUNDAMENTALS

The ideal fertilizer program is one that provides uniform growth throughout the season. In other words, rather than surging rapidly for a few weeks after being fed, the grass grows at a steady pace for the entire growing season. With a balanced program, the plants build carbohydrate reserves and develop sturdy root systems while the fertilizer meets the needs of the growing grass. The following will help you understand the basics of fertilizing.

Quality

Lawns will survive without fertilizer. However, in the absence of fertilizer, a lawn is prone to deteriorate as a result of seasonal stressors and is less likely to fulfill its promised environmental benefits.

As a lawn runs short of nutrients, the first thing to go is color. The luscious green fades. Over time, the lawn thins and loses resiliency, and eventually thin spots provide space for weeds to move in. Deficient grass is not vigorous, and if diseases and insects attack, it may not survive the damage.

Although it's true that the more fertilizer a lawn receives the better it looks, overfeeding can cause problems. Overfertilizing stimulates leaf growth at the expense of the roots. With a thin, shallow root system, the lawn can't stand up to heat or drought. The succulent shoots are easy prey for diseases and insects. In addition, overfertilizing promotes thatch.

About Fertilizer

You've probably noticed that nearly all lawn fertilizers contain lots of nitrogen and less phosphorus, potassium, or other elements. That's because nitrogen is the element missing from most soils, and it's also the element that grass uses the most.

Nitrogen may be the main nutrient, but it's not the only one required. In fact, 17 elements are essential to lawn survival. All 17 are equally important and must be available for plants to function. They

Nitrogen for color, phosphorus for root growth, and potassium for strength: These are only three of the nutrients grass needs to remain beautiful and healthy.

A healthy lawn is thick and luxurious and has vibrant color. The blades are strong, the roots dense and far spreading. And because the lawn is full of thriving, healthy grass plants, there's no room for weeds to make a home. A great lawn frames everything around it to dramatic effect. The key to such beauty? Good nutrition on a regular schedule, tailored to local conditions.

Grass grows constantly, which means it requires a steady diet of nitrogen, phosphorus, potassium, and other nutrients. Even though many nutrients occur naturally in soil, the soil is usually unable to supply them as fast as or in the quantities the plants need. Good nutrition for a lawn is the result of a balanced fertilizer program that supplies the right nutrients in the correct amounts at the best time for the lawn.

vary only in how much plants use of each. Macronutrients—carbon, hydrogen, oxygen, nitrogen, phosphorus, potassium, sulfur, magnesium, and calcium—are picked up by plants in the largest quantities. Micronutrients—boron, chlorine, copper, iron, manganese, molybdenum, nickel, and zinc—are used in small amounts. Most are soil borne, but carbon, hydrogen, and oxygen come from the atmosphere.

You can't always tell which element is involved when a lawn is deficient. The most obvious and most frequent symptom—yellowing or poor color—is common to many deficiencies. Just the same, knowing about the elements will help you recognize a lawn in trouble and give you insight about what is going on inside the plant. The following elements are those most likely to be deficient in lawns.

The Big Three

Nitrogen As an integral component of many chemicals within a plant, nitrogen has a part in nearly every plant function. It is crucial to chlorophyll, the chemical that gives plants their green color and allows them to manufacture their own food. When nitrogen is low, lawns turn pale to yellow and grow slowly.

Phosphorus Most soils contain plenty of phosphorus, which is a mineral. However, it may not be readily available to plants. The main role of phosphorus is to aid shoot and root growth.

Deficiencies are rare. If grasses do need phosphorus, they first turn unusually dark green, then purple, and they may be more susceptible to disease. (Grasses sometimes turn purple in fall as the weather cools. If the discoloration is due to a deficiency, applying phosphorus will overcome it. If it is due to cold weather, it won't.)

The most likely time you might encounter a phosphorous-related problem is when starting a lawn. Phosphorus is immobile in soil, and a small, developing root system may be unable to tap the supply. Once the roots grow, they are better able to obtain phosphorus.

The Nutrients Plants Need

Nitrogen — N
Good for
- Growth
- Color
- Density
- Chlorophyll formation

Deficiency symptoms
- Pale color, yellowing
- Stunted growth

Phosphorus — P
Good for
- Growth of new roots and shoots
- Seedling root growth
- Seedling plant vigor

Deficiency symptoms
- Rarely seen
- Yellowing or purple cast to leaves

Potassium — K
Good for
- Overall plant health
- Stress resistance
- Cold hardiness
- Disease resistance

Deficiency symptoms
- Rarely visible
- Pale color or no symptoms

Iron — Fe
Good for
- Chlorophyll formation

Deficiency symptom
- Yellowing

Potassium In a nutshell, potassium is involved in the plant's overall health. It helps with resistance to stresses such as excessively high and low temperatures and disease, wear tolerance, and cold hardiness, which is why winter-type fertilizers are often high in potassium. Potassium levels are often low in sandy soils. No easily recognized color changes occur with a deficiency, so it's hard to identify.

Late summer and fall are the best times to fertilize cool-season grasses. Spring is the second best time.

Other Important Nutrients

Iron Iron is the most likely micronutrient to be deficient, particularly in high-pH soils. It is involved in chlorophyll production, so a deficiency turns the grass yellow. Many high-quality lawn fertilizers contain iron. Professional groundskeepers often use iron-rich fertilizer to encourage dark green color without causing a flush of growth.

Calcium Because of its involvement in cell wall development, cell division, and growth of young shoots and roots, calcium is important to plant vigor. Deficiencies are rare and generally show up only in acid soil. The main symptom is slow growth; in extreme deficiencies, leaves develop a reddish hue. Lime, used to raise soil pH, supplies calcium.

Magnesium Because magnesium is a constituent of chlorophyll, the primary symptom of its deficiency is yellowing. Deficiencies are rare, usually occurring in sandy, acid soils.

Getting the Yellow Out

When a lawn loses its healthy green color, most people get out the spreader and fertilize. Sometimes they're surprised when that doesn't help. In such cases, the lawn may be deficient in iron, magnesium, or another element.

The quickest way to determine whether yellowing is due to iron deficiency is to apply iron sulfate or iron chelate to a test area. If lack of iron is the culprit, the area will turn green in 24 to 48 hours. Try magnesium next if it fails to green up. Mix 1 teaspoon of Epsom salts, which contain magnesium, in 2 cups of water in a spray bottle. Lightly mist the same test area. Again, you should see a noticeable change in 24 to 48 hours if a magnesium deficiency is the problem.

Other nutrient deficiencies that could cause yellowing include manganese and sulfur. Using high-quality turf fertilizers containing these nutrients keeps these deficiencies from developing.

A Matter of Balance

As a general rule, a well-fed cool-season lawn requires three to five feedings a year, depending on the type of grass and the desired quality. Most warm-season lawns require three to six, depending on how many months they actively grow. Fertilizer recommendations are based on the amount of nitrogen to provide, usually about 1 pound per application, because nitrogen is the element that is most often lacking in soil. A soil test helps fine-tune the amounts of other nutrients to apply. It measures pH, which influences nutrient availability, and elements such as phosphorus, potassium, and iron.

The number of feedings listed here provides for a lawn of the highest quality. Such a lawn is not only better looking, it is thicker and safer to play on. Several conditions can alter these general recommendations. For example, some grasses, such as centipedegrass and buffalograss, do best with less fertilizer. In Florida and other areas with sandy soil, a lawn may need more frequent feedings. Or if you host the neighborhood kids' summerlong kickball tournament, extra feedings help the lawn survive the activity. In dry periods, lawns need less fertilizer; in rainy periods, they may call for more.

When to Fertilize

It's best to split the total amount of fertilizer required annually into three to five applications. The timing of the feedings and the amount you apply with each one depends on whether your lawn is a cool- or warm-season species. You've heard the advice that people should eat to correspond with their periods of greatest activity: a large breakfast as you start your day, a medium-size lunch, and a small dinner in the evening. It's a similar case with grasses. Feed the lawn when it is actively growing, a time when fertilizer will enhance root growth and carbohydrate storage.

Cool-season grasses These grasses put on the most growth during spring and fall. Roots break dormancy and begin expanding as the soil warms in early spring, then the blades join in. The plants consume carbohydrates stored the previous year. During the summer, growth slows as the grass hunkers down to wait out the heat. When temperatures cool toward fall, the lawn resumes growth, but now it is storing carbohydrates for the winter ahead.

Thus for cool-season grasses the biggest feedings should be in late summer and fall. Provide two meals: one feeding in late summer to thicken the stand and grow healthy roots, and a second feeding a month or so later to winterize the lawn and build food reserves for the coming winter dormant period.

Spring calls for small snacks in early and late spring. If you didn't fertilize in fall, the lawn will need more fertilizer in spring. However, too much fertilizer in spring encourages excess growth; the grass hungrily consumes its carbohydrate supply, leaving little in reserve for the dog days of summer. To avoid this problem, use correct amounts of slow-release fertilizer in the spring.

Avoid fertilizing cool-season grasses in hot weather (above 90°F). Feeding then does the weeds more good than the lawn. However, a light application of fertilizer in summer—such as a fertilizer plus an insect control—can help the grass recover from insect attack.

Warm-season grasses The growing calendar for warm-season grasses is opposite that for cool-season grasses. Because warm-season grasses sit still during cool months and grow steadily from midspring to early fall, they benefit from several small meals all summer long.

The exact date to fertilize depends on your location. In Houston the first round of fertilizer may go down in March, but in Minneapolis the first chance to fertilize may be late April. As a guide, wherever you are, time the first feeding to coincide with your first mowing. You know the grass is growing then.

Fertilize warm-season grasses in spring and summer. Those are the most active seasons of growth for those grasses.

How the Grasses Rank

Needs the most feeding

- Bermudagrass
- Kentucky bluegrass

- Zoysiagrass
- Perennial ryegrass
- St. Augustinegrass
- Tall fescue

- Fine fescues
- Bahiagrass

- Centipedegrass
- Buffalograss

Needs the least feeding

FERTILIZER

Inorganic fast-release sources are salts that pull water from the air; they provide quick growth.

All-in-one granules combine all nutrients and any pest controls in one particle for more complete and uniform coverage.

Liquid fertilizers contain fast-release nitrogen, which must be reapplied often.

Fertilizer quantity recommendations are based on pounds of nitrogen per 1,000 square feet. That assumes you know the size of your lawn, as well as how to get the right amount of nitrogen on the lawn. Luckily, most fertilizer labels do the nitrogen math for you; all you really need to know is the size of your lawn. Read the label, set the spreader to the specified setting, and you're ready to go.

Understanding Labels

Federal and state laws require that all fertilizer labels supply the same information. Once you know the code, reading a label is a cinch.

The analysis All fertilizer packages display three numbers—the fertilizer's analysis. The analysis refers to three essential nutrients: nitrogen, phosphorus, and potassium. Each number stands for the percentage of the package made up of the available form of each nutrient by weight. The analysis shows the nutrients as a ratio. For example, a 29–1–4 fertilizer has approximately a 10–1–1 ratio.

How do you compare two fertilizers with the same analysis ratio? Look at the pounds of nitrogen delivered per 1,000 square feet and the source of the nitrogen.

To convert the analysis to pounds of nitrogen, multiply the package weight by the percentage of nitrogen. For example, a typical 15½-pound bag of 29–1–4 holds 4½ pounds of nitrogen (15½ × 29%). Divide that number by the number of 1,000–square-foot units the bag covers— 5 for the 5,000 square-foot coverage of a 15½-pound bag—and you learn that 29–1–4 fertilizer supplies 0.9 pound of nitrogen per 1,000 square feet (4½ ÷ by 5).

Determining the actual amounts of the available forms of phosphorus (P_2O_5) and potassium (K_2O) in a fertilizer is less straightforward and rarely necessary.

Nitrogen source Many people avoid fertilizing because they think it will mean

more mowing. It doesn't have to. Surge growth results from applying too much fertilizer at a time or from using a bargain product that contains too little slow-release nitrogen. The source of the nitrogen governs the release rate.

Fertilizers are either fast-release or slow-release, or a combination of the two. The lawn doesn't care which you use; it cares about getting the nitrogen. You will, however, notice differences in how the lawn reacts to each kind.

Fast-release inorganic fertilizers include materials such as ammonium sulfate. They are inexpensive, high-nitrogen fertilizers. Highly soluble in water, they dissolve quickly and don't last long. Plants and microbes use them rapidly, or they may leach out of the root zone. These fertilizers provide a sudden growth flush that lasts a few weeks, followed by a rapid slowdown— in other words, feast then famine.

When applied too heavily or not washed off leaves, these fertilizers can damage plants by burning, or desiccating, the leaves.

Slow-release fertilizers include natural and synthetic organics. Natural organics are derived from materials such as animal manures, sewage sludge, and grain byproducts. They are long lasting and safe on lawns. They are naturally low in nitrogen, so it takes quite a bit of product to supply the recommended amount of nutrients. They may be slow to act because microbes must break down the fertilizer to release the nitrogen.

Synthetic organic fertilizers are manufactured materials that combine the best of natural and inorganic fertilizers. They are high in nutrients, long lasting, and safe for plants. They may be fast or slow acting. They include materials such as fast-acting urea and slow-acting methylene urea, polymer– or plastic-coated urea, and sulfur-coated urea.

A coated fertilizer releases nitrogen slowly through the outer coating. Mixing different-size particles or particles with coatings of different thicknesses governs the release rate.

Methylene urea is a form of urea composed of particles with different-size molecules or "chains." The shortest chains release nitrogen first. By creating particles in chains of various sizes, the manufacturer can control how long the effects of the fertilizer last. The best fertilizers provide eight weeks or more of ongoing feeding.

Some slow-release fertilizers have limitations. For example, coated products release nitrogen only in the presence of moisture. Others work only when microbes are active (when the soil is warm, above 55°F, and moist). It may take two to three weeks for a slow-release fertilizer to go to work. For that reason, many lawn fertilizers are a mix of fast and slow materials. The fast-release nitrogen immediately feeds the lawn. It is used up in a few weeks, but by then, nutrients from the slow-release materials become available. In high-quality fertilizers, fast-release materials make up a small portion of the fertilizer. In that way, you're assured of steady, uniform growth.

Another sign of quality is the particle size itself. Fertilizers that have fast- and slow-release materials combined into one small particle are the easiest to use to achieve uniform coverage. With these, more particles are applied per square inch of lawn than with larger sizes.

Liquid or Dry?

Fertilizer can be applied to a lawn in liquid or dry form. People often ask which is better. The truth is, it doesn't matter. Both types contain the same materials and both provide satisfactory results, although liquids are fast-release fertilizers and must be applied more frequently.

The question is more a matter of convenience and skill. It takes more skill to apply liquid fertilizer uniformly at the right rate. Most homeowners generally find dry materials easier to handle, especially if they have a good spreader that accurately and uniformly distributes the fertilizer.

Testing the Soil

Soil tests are the most accurate gauge of a lawn's pH and need for phosphorus and potassium. Test your soil every three to five years or when your lawn is not up to snuff.

1 Collect several soil samples randomly around your yard, using a probe. Probes slide into the ground and pull out a core of soil without damaging the lawn. If you don't have one, use a trowel. Take samples 3 inches deep or follow the instructions from the soil lab.

2 Thoroughly mix the samples, then measure 1 cup of soil to send to the testing facility.

Lawn Growth

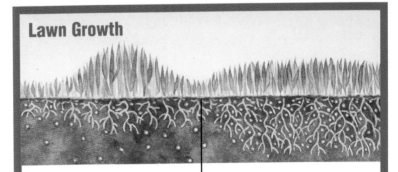

Surge growth
Fast-release fertilizers dissolve and move through the soil quickly. The grass grows rapidly and then slows.

Steady growth
Slow-release fertilizers dissolve slowly. They spoon-feed nutrients, so the grass has steady, controlled growth.

Almost everyone knows firsthand the embarrassment of a yellow-striped lawn. You can't hide it from the neighbors, and it takes weeks to go away. After spending time, effort, and money on fertilizing, you may feel it was all a waste.

Striping means that the fertilizer wasn't applied evenly. Usually it results from

Drop Spreader

- Precise
- Good in small areas
- 18- to 22-inch swath
- Use where you want to avoid fertilizing adjacent areas.

Broadcast Spreader

- Good in large areas or when you want to work quickly
- 5- to 10-foot swath, depending on the fertilizer and your walking speed

Handheld Crank Spreader

- Accuracy depends on how steady you hold your hand and how straight you walk
- 5- to 6-foot swath

overlapping too much or too little between passes. The goal when fertilizing is to put the fertilizer down uniformly at the correct rate over the entire lawn. A high-quality spreader can do both; knowing how to operate the spreader ensures that it does.

Selecting a Spreader

Most stores offer two basic types of lawn spreaders, drop and broadcast, that you can use to apply many materials besides fertilizer. All have a hopper the fertilizer goes into, an opening on the bottom of the spreader to release the fertilizer, a way of adjusting the size of the opening to control the flow from the hopper, and an on-off lever. The two types of spreaders vary in the way they distribute fertilizer, and their distribution pattern is key to which one is appropriate for your yard, as well as to how easy it is to make uniform applications.

Drop spreaders These apply materials in a well-defined, straight path, with the fertilizer dropping straight down from the hopper. On average, they cover a 2-foot-wide strip, but their wheels extend several inches beyond the drop zone. It takes practice to avoid leaving stripes when using drop spreaders because you need to carefully overlap the wheel tracks.

A drop spreader is especially suitable when you need to apply fertilizer precisely, such as around flowerbeds and shrub beds, near water gardens, or along pavement. Because of its narrow width, it takes longer to cover an area than a broadcast spreader.

Broadcast spreaders Also called rotary spreaders, broadcast spreaders have a spinning disk at the base of the hopper that throws fertilizer in a wide fan-shaped swath in front of the spreader. They're fast but not precise. More fertilizer falls near the hopper than at the edge. Different size particles come out of the hopper at different rates, and everything within the swath will be fertilized, whether it needs it or not. (Some models, such as the EdgeGuard, can be adjusted to spread to one side, which keeps materials away from planting beds, sidewalks, and driveways.) It's easier to avoid striping the lawn with a broadcast spreader, but you still must overlap for even coverage.

A broadcast spreader is best for fertilizing large, open lots; a drop spreader is good for small yards with many gardens. If you have a large lot, consider buying one of each type of spreader. Use the drop spreader to make precise applications around flower and shrub beds, then fill in between them with the broadcast spreader. Or use an adjustable–swath broadcast to control the application of fertilizer near the beds.

Handheld crank spreaders A type of broadcast spreader, hand spreaders work best in very small areas you can cover with just one pass. They are inexpensive and useful in small areas but have limitations. They hold only a few pounds of fertilizer and can be even more imprecise than a typical broadcast lawn spreader because many people lack the arm strength to hold a full hopper and steadily turn the crank without wobbling.

Some fertilizer–plus products should not be applied with a handheld crank spreader. Check the label. If it doesn't specify a setting for a handheld spreader, use a drop or broadcast spreader instead.

Accuracy

Most fertilizer labels specify what setting to use to apply the product accurately and at the correct rate. Be aware that several things affect whether the setting is correct in your yard. For example, if your pace is slower than average, you might apply excess fertilizer; walking too quickly can reduce the amount of fertilizer you put down. A spreader you've had for many years could have damaged or worn settings that are inaccurate. It doesn't hurt to test your spreader every spring to ensure its accuracy. The box below explains how; it will also help you find the right setting if your brand of spreader is not listed on a fertilizer label.

Caring for Spreaders

After each use, empty the hopper. Set the opening wide open and thoroughly hose off the spreader—the hopper, the wheels, the spinning rotor, everything. Be sure to get into all nooks and crannies; use a brush on them if you have to, so that no residue is left. Let the spreader dry. Then lightly oil the bottom and inside of the hopper, the spring and rod inside the control housing, and the axle bearing. Finally, store the spreader in a garage or shed with the hopper wide open.

Walking Speed

For both drop and broadcast spreaders, walking speed is a critical factor in checking the spreader's accuracy. Reducing your walking speed by one-half doubles the application rate at any given setting. The person who will do the actual application should be the one to check the spreader. Walk at a speed you can consistently maintain when fertilizing.

Can I Trust My Spreader?

If your spreader runs out of fertilizer before it should or you have leftovers when you finish, you've got a calibration problem. The Scotts Helpline (800/543-8873) can help you readjust your spreader so it is accurate. For other brands, here's how to find a new, correct setting. (Because calibrating a spreader is complicated, it may be easier to buy a new spreader instead.)

1. Weigh the bag of fertilizer, then pour about half of it into the spreader.
2. Measure the spreader's application width, which is the length of the opening on a drop spreader and the width of the fan for a broadcast spreader.

3. Set up a 25- to 100-foot-long test strip. The longer the test strip, the more accurate your results will be.
4. Set the opening on the spreader, then apply fertilizer over the test strip. Open the hopper as you begin walking; close it at the end of the strip.
5. Pour leftover fertilizer back into the bag. Weigh the bag, then subtract the final weight from the original weight.
6. The formula for calculating the application rate is the amount used times 1,000, divided by the area of the test strip (original weight – new weight × 1,000) ÷ (length × width). Examples:
Broadcast: 1 pound of fertilizer used, a 25-foot-long strip, and a 10-foot-wide fan: $(1 \times 1,000) \div (25 \times 10) = 1,000 \div 250$ = 4 pounds of fertilizer applied per 1,000 square feet.
Drop: $5/16$ pound used, a 50-foot-long strip, and a 2-foot-wide hopper opening: $(5/16 \times 1,000) \div (50 \times 2) = 312\frac{1}{2} \div 100 = 3\frac{1}{8}$ pounds applied per 1,000 square feet.
7. Now figure how many pounds of fertilizer the bag should supply to every 1,000 square feet. Say the bag weighs $15\frac{1}{2}$ pounds and is to cover 5,000 square feet; that's $3\frac{1}{10}$ pounds of fertilizer for each 1,000 square feet ($15\frac{1}{2} \div 5$). The drop spreader at $3\frac{1}{8}$ pounds per 1,000 is accurate. The broadcast spreader applies too much fertilizer. Repeat the test using a smaller setting until the application rate comes within 10 percent of the expected rate.

SPREADING HOW-TO

Once you get to the point of actually applying, fertilizing is easy. Fill the hopper and go. A few rules, however, will help you work evenly and effectively.

Push the spreader rather than pull it. Take care to walk a straight line as you push. Set a steady, moderate pace and maintain it. Speeding up or slowing down changes the rate at which the fertilizer comes out of the hopper.

Know where any sharp dips in the lawn are, such as where the soil has settled after removing a tree. Spreader wheels falling into the depression can jar the spreader, letting extra fertilizer spill out there.

Operate the spreader over the long way of the lawn to keep from having to stop and turn as often.

In a square or rectangular yard with few obstacles, first make two header strips as wide as your spreader's application width at each end of the lawn. Then go back and forth between the headers. Headers give you room to turn. Shut the hopper when you reach the header strip, overlapping the strip slightly.

Above: If you have a hard time seeing the wheel tracks, fertilize in the early morning when the lawn is still dewy. That's when it's easiest to see where you've been.

Right: Run adjustable broadcast spreaders 4 to 6 inches from the outside edge of flower and shrub beds.

In an irregularly shaped yard with shrub beds and flowerbeds, make header strips around the various beds, and then fill in between them. Shut off the hopper each time you reach the header.

Leave the hopper closed until you start walking. Close the hopper just before coming to a stop. Also close it when turning, when backing up, and when reaching a section where you've already applied fertilizer. If an obstacle such as a tree gets in the way, shut off the spreader just before you reach the object. Move to the other side and continue spreading.

Keep the fertilizer dry. Dry fertilizer is easier to apply. If you must spread on misty or damp days, use a hopper cover to protect the fertilizer. It fits over the hopper like a shower cap.

Below right: When using a drop spreader around flower and shrub beds, align the hopper with the edge of the bed. You may need to run one wheel in the bed.

Wash the fertilizer off grass blades with $\frac{1}{4}$ to $\frac{1}{2}$ inch of water, especially if the temperature is above 90°F. Sweep sidewalks and driveways to keep fertilizer from ending up in storm drains.

Avoiding Streaks and Stripes

Careful overlapping is the key to avoiding stripes. Even so, it's easy to overlap too much or too little and still have streaks, unless you know the tricks.

Broadcast spreaders are fairly simple. Make sure you know the width of your spreader's throw pattern, then overlap the edge about a foot. For example, say your spreader applies a 6-foot–wide swath. Shut off the spreader at the header strip. Turn, walk 5 feet, then face the lawn again, open the spreader, and apply the next swath.

With a drop spreader, you'll need to pay a little more attention. If you have one of the newer models with an arrow on top of the hopper, simply align the arrow with the previous swath's wheel track.

Without the arrow, you should aim to overlap the previous wheel track by an inch or so. An easy way to do this is to pivot the spreader so that the wheel is just inside the previous track. Take care that you overlap just the wheel tracks and not the hopper; the two hopper tracks should just meet. Applying the fertilizer in the early morning when the grass is still dewy can help you see where you've been. Consider practicing on the driveway so you get used to where the fertilizer drops. Be sure to sweep it up afterwards.

To avoid confusing spreader tracks with mower tracks, apply the fertilizer at right angles to the direction you normally mow.

Apply header strips at the ends of the lawn or, when the lawn is irregularly shaped, around the edges. Then fill in between the headers.

Even Coverage

Before applying fertilizer, give your drop spreader a test spin. This is a simpler test than calibrating the settings. But it is just as important in ensuring accuracy.

Put about ¼ pound of fertilizer into the hopper, then walk it down the driveway a few feet. Check how evenly the fertilizer drops out of the spreader. If you see skips and misses, something is blocking the discharge ports.

A uniform stripe that runs the length of the test strip means a port is clogged. It could be rusted shut or fertilizer pellets could have dissolved and clogged the port, or something else could be caught there.

Fluttery skips mean that foreign material is lodged in the bottom of the spreader. It occasionally bounces out of the way, then falls back to block the ports.

Spills

Fill the spreader on pavement so that any spills are easy to sweep up. However, no matter how careful people are, accidents happen. When they happen on the lawn, take action fast. A spill can kill the grass, and sometimes the effects last for years.

Scoop up as much of the spill from the lawn as you can. Use a wet-dry vacuum to pick up the fine pieces. Then flood the area with water so the soluble fertilizer dissolves and moves below the roots. The grass may still suffer, but it will revive faster.

WATERING

**W**atering a lawn is so easy that it's often taken for granted. Not surprisingly, that's often where problems with your lawn begin.

Lawn watering may be easy but there's still a right way and a wrong way to do it. Here's the secret: Keep the root zone moist, water deeply and infrequently, and don't waste water.

Simple, yes, but given all the different types of soils, grasses, climates, and weather, it can get tricky. The key is to know the growing conditions in your area and water according to those requirements. Do it right and you will have a better-looking, more resilient lawn and likely save water while you're at it.

WATERING DIGEST

Follow the Footsteps: A Sign Your Lawn Wants Water

If you see footprints in your lawn, ignore your watering schedule and the time of day, and turn on the sprinklers. Visible footprints mean the grass is so dry it has lost its resiliency. The color of such weakened turf will be off too—silvery blue instead of green. Wait too long and the color will change again—to brown.

TO DO

- ☐ Calibrate sprinklers.
- ☐ Water deeply and infrequently.
- ☐ Watch for dry spots.
- ☐ Don't waste water.

Rain Gauge

Lawns need at least 1 inch of water a week. To ensure they receive that amount, measure rainfall, then make up the difference with your sprinklers.

Match Sprinklers to Your Region and Lawn

- Any region, a small lawn up to about 600 square feet: portable sprinklers

- Dry western region, any size lawn that must remain green: automated inground sprinkler system

- Wet eastern region, 600 to 5,000 square feet: portable sprinklers

- Wet region, larger than 5,000 square feet: inground sprinklers

- Whatever kind of sprinkler setup you choose, use a timer to automatically shut it off.

Basic Rules of Watering

- Moisten the root zone every time you water, usually with at least ½ inch of water.

- Water deeply and infrequently, once or twice a week, supplying a total of 1 to 2 inches a week.

Lawn Watering During Drought

If the grass is still growing, mow higher to encourage roots to go deeper. Stretch time between irrigations to the maximum; water efficiently, wasting no water to runoff; and water thoroughly. Watering just a little bit encourages weeds. During severe water shortages, let the lawn go brown. A healthy lawn of a perennial grass, though completely brown, can survive without water and recover quickly once rains return.

Did You Know?

- The great grasslands of North America are in semiarid regions; forests cover high rainfall areas.

- Mowed grasses use comparatively less water than most trees.

- Clay soils take as long as five hours to absorb an inch of water; sandy soils need only one hour.

- The earth recycles water; it neither creates nor destroys it. The earth has approximately 300 million cubic miles of water, and it has had that much for eons. Only 2½ percent is fresh water suitable for drinking and growing plants.

- Ten thousand cubic miles of water falls to earth each year as rain.

Q&A

Q When is cycling (on-off-on-off) good for your lawn?

A When your soil is heavy clay or when your lawn is on a slope. Cycling your sprinklers (on-off-on-off) three or more times ensures that the water moves into the soil without runoff. A timer can do much of the work for you.

The Screwdriver Test

Lawn watering theories, rules, or even timing make no difference if water doesn't soak 6 to 8 inches into the soil. You might water long enough to apply several inches of water, but if it doesn't soak in, it's wasted. There is only one way to know for sure. That's by testing. After watering, poke an 8-inch-long screwdriver into your lawn. If it easily goes in at least 6 inches, you've watered enough.

Become a Watering Pro in 20 Minutes

To water accurately, you need to know how much water your sprinklers apply. To find out, all it takes is 20 minutes and some empty cans. Page 70 has all the details. It's simple, and the results will pay off for years.

Hose Smarts: Tips for Selecting a Hose You'll Use

- Look for hoses with four or five layers of reinforcing materials, or plies.

- Rubber hoses last longest but are heavy and expensive.

- Larger-diameter hoses deliver more water faster.

- A 75-foot hose is convenient for large yards but is heavier and more expensive than a shorter hose. A 50-foot, ⅝-inch-diameter hose is suitable for most home lawns.

Myths, Facts & Good Advice

Myth: The best sprinklers are the ones that deliver the water fastest.

Fact: True if your soil can absorb a lot of water at one time, but most soils can't. Sprinklers that water fast may be the most wasteful. If the soil can't absorb the water, it runs off.

Advice: Match your sprinkler's application rate to the soil's absorption rate. Watering slowly, like a gentle rain, is usually best.

Myth: Brief, daily watering is more beneficial to lawns than deep watering several days apart.

Fact: False. Deep watering with a several-day gap in between encourages deep roots for a healthy lawn.

Advice: Watch your lawn and wait for signs that it needs water (footprints remain in the lawn), then run the water until moisture reaches several inches into the soil.

LAWN WATERING BASICS

When you water, the goal is to moisten the lawn's entire root zone—from the soil surface to 6 to 8 inches deep—and to keep it moist. That usually takes 1 to 2 inches of water a week, either from rain or irrigation.

This amount of water is the ideal. It ensures that roots grow deeply and that they always have a ready water supply. Lawns can get by on much less. In fact, healthy turf often survives eight weeks or longer without water. It goes dormant and turns brown but doesn't die.

Use a rain gauge to measure weekly rainfall amounts, then make up the difference with your sprinklers. If you get 1/10 inch of rain the day after watering, it won't have much effect on the lawn. However, if you decide not to water one week because it rained but don't know that only 1/10 inch fell, your lawn will suffer.

Deep and Infrequent

The key to meeting the ideal is to water deeply and infrequently. Irrigate once a week, applying the whole amount at once. Or water twice a week, applying at least 1/2 inch of water at a time.

When you water every day, it may seem as though you are giving your lawn the best of care, but you're not. Frequent watering merely wets the soil surface; the roots proliferate where the soil is moist but grow no deeper. A shallow-rooted lawn lacks the resources to survive stressful periods, and the constant moisture around the blades increases the chances for thatch and disease.

How long to let your sprinklers run to supply 1/2 inch or more of water depends upon two things: how fast the water comes out of the sprinklers and how fast the soil can absorb it.

Measuring how fast the water comes out is a simple procedure. Set a few straight-sided containers around your lawn (soup cans are best; water splashes out of shallow cans). Note the time, turn the sprinklers on, and leave them on for 20 minutes or until water begins to run off. Measure the depth of the water in all the containers.

If the least-filled can holds 1/4 inch of water, your sprinklers will take 80 minutes to deliver an inch of water to all parts of the lawn. Here's how you figure the time: Divide 1 inch by the amount in the can (1 ÷ 1/4 = 4). Then multiply the result by 20 minutes (4 × 20 = 80 minutes).

Soil can't always soak up water as fast as the sprinklers supply it. If water runs into the street after 10 minutes, that's as long as the sprinklers can operate at a time. In this case, if the water in the least-filled can is 1/10-inch deep, it will take 100 minutes to apply an inch of water (1 ÷ 1/10 = 10 × 10 = 100). And to ensure the water soaks into the lawn, run sprinklers in 10-minute cycles with a 20- or 30-minute break—or however long the water takes to soak in—between each cycle.

Recognizing Need

Pay attention to the symptoms the lawn exhibits and to the weather, and stretch the interval between waterings as much as possible. One of the best clues to whether a lawn is ready for watering is to look for footprints in the grass—a clear signal it's time to water. Subtle color changes also indicate drying grass. As grass wilts, the blades fold inward and the lawn turns gray.

Watch for dry spots. These warn you that the entire lawn is drying and will soon need watering. They may also indicate other problems (see "Dry Spots" on page 73).

Measure the amount of water your sprinkler puts out by setting soup cans randomly under the spray.

When to Water

Early morning is the most efficient time to water. Municipal water pressure is at its peak, and there's usually less wind to distort the spray from its intended target. Also the lawn will have all day to dry before nightfall. Foliage that sits wet overnight can invite diseases.

An exception to this rule is the Southwest and areas with low humidity and high daytime temperatures. In those areas, less water is lost to evaporation if you water in the evening or at night.

Variables

It's impossible to define a watering schedule that applies to every situation. Keeping the root zone moist might mean watering every three or four days or every 10 to 15 days, depending on your growing conditions and type of grass. Exactly how often and how much you should water varies according to many factors, primarily the type of soil, the weather, and the type of grass. Learn the variables and tendencies of your yard and climate; then you'll know how to apply the rule of watering deeply and infrequently to your lawn.

Soil Clay, which is composed mostly of fine, dustlike particles, holds more water than coarse, sandy soil. It may hold an inch or more of water in the root zone, whereas sandy soil rarely holds half that amount.

But clay absorbs water very slowly. Several hours or days may go by before an inch of water soaks in, compared to

Early morning is the best time to water.

Footprints in the grass are one of the first signs of wilting.

When the lawn takes on a gray cast, it is seriously in need of water. The lawn will soon go dormant.

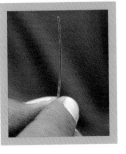

Grass blades fold inward to conserve water. A lawn that needs water then takes on a grayish cast because the back sides of the leaf are lighter colored.

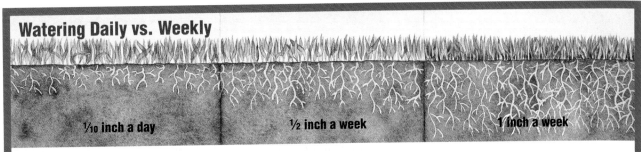

Watering Daily vs. Weekly

1/10 inch a day   1/2 inch a week   1 inch a week

Applying 1/10 inch of water daily supplies nearly 1 inch of water a week. Yet the lawn is not as healthy as it would be had you applied water in a single 1-inch or two 1/2-inch increments. The more water applied at one time, the deeper and healthier the root system grows and the more resilient the grass becomes.

A less invasive test: If you can poke a screwdriver 6 inches into the soil, there is enough moisture to supply the lawn.

30 minutes or so for sandy soil. The water is more likely to run off than to penetrate; so even though clay soil is capable of containing plenty of water, it's actually often very dry. If your soil is clay, use a sprinkler that applies water slowly. Irrigate in cycles to avoid wasting water. Sandy soil can be watered with sprinklers that apply lots of water quickly, but it will require more frequent watering.

Loam is the best soil for a lawn. It readily soaks up water and holds onto it. Any sprinkler and water regime will do.

Weather This factor plays a crucial role in the amount of water a lawn needs and the timing of irrigation. Consider two lawns at opposite ends of the United States during one particular week in September. In Southern California, Santa Ana winds prevail. These hot, dry canyon winds pull moisture from everything they touch: soil, trees, and lawns. Relative humidity dips to 5 percent. Under such conditions, a tall fescue lawn would need watering three times that week; a bermudagrass lawn would need less.

In New England, where average daily high temperatures that same week in September are in the 60s, it's cloudy and rainy, and the relative humidity is about 60 percent. The typical Kentucky bluegrass lawn, one of the thirstiest grasses, would need no additional water.

Few situations are as extreme as these examples. Even so, pay attention to how the weather shifts from week to week and season to season. To keep your lawn healthy and to avoid wasting water, account for these shifts. Use a rain gauge, and if stressful conditions develop, monitor how they affect your grass.

Grass type One of the reasons that warm-season grasses grow best in hot, dry regions and cool-season grasses in cool, moist areas is their relative dependence on water: Warm-season grasses need less, and cool-season grasses need more.

How Grasses Differ

For most people, saving water by choosing a warm- or cool-season grass is not an

Adjust watering to match your soil

Clay   **Sand**   **Loam**

- Clay holds the most water but is slow to absorb and release it. Sprinklers should apply the water no faster than it can soak in. If that's impossible, water in cycles. When runoff begins, turn off the sprinkler, let the water soak in, then repeat until you've applied the full amount your lawn requires.

- Sandy soil is porous, and water readily flows through it. To wet sandy soil 6 to 8 inches deep, water in ½-inch increments.

- Loam is the ideal soil. It is porous yet retains moisture. Follow normal watering recommendations.

option. That decision is made by virtue of location. However, there are differences within each grass type. For instance, St. Augustinegrass (one of the most popular grasses in Miami) takes more water than bermudagrass—another good choice for Florida. Some Kentucky bluegrass varieties (the most common lawn grasses in Chicago) are more drought tolerant than others.

Buffalograss is one of the most drought-tolerant warm-season grasses. It maintains a reasonably good turf where irrigation is impossible. It is not a good choice in wet regions that are occasionally dry; however, it does best in areas of consistently low rainfall, such as the Plains states.

Where the difference between warm- and cool-season grasses is most important is in the Transition Zone, that intermediate region where both warm- and cool-season grasses grow (see page 181). Here, choosing a hardy warm-season grass will reduce the amount of water you need to apply to your lawn, and the lawn will have better summer stamina.

Tall fescue is a fairly drought-tolerant cool-season grass. But there's no comparison in water requirements between it and bermudagrass, which is much more efficient at using water.

Note that the amount of water a lawn needs to grow at its best (see "How the Grasses Rank" at right) and how that same grass responds to extended drought are different. Again, warm-season grasses usually recover from extended drought better than cool-season grasses.

New lawns are susceptible to drying. They should be watered as frequently as necessary to keep them moist until the young plants have fully rooted.

Lawns in shade generally need less water than those in full sun; however, there are complicating factors. First, although grasses vary somewhat, lawns grow best in full sun, which means you're involved in a balancing act from the start if you grow a lawn in shade. Moreover, some kinds of grasses are more likely to contract moisture-related diseases in the shade.

If the shade is cast primarily by trees or tall shrubs, the roots of these plants will compete for the water applied to the lawn. In fact, lawns shaded by trees and shrubs often fail less from the shade itself or the amount of water applied than from being outcompeted by the roots of the larger plants. One of the reasons fine fescues are noted for shade tolerance is their ability to vie successfully with tree roots for moisture.

For a lawn that will be in shade, select only grasses known to be somewhat shade tolerant. In the North, the best grasses for shade are fine fescues; in the South, the choice is St. Augustinegrass.

Dry Spots

A Patches of dry grass scattered here and there suggest a problem with either the soil or the watering system.

B Probe the spot with a shovel. Buried construction debris, such as this leftover sand, is a common cause of dry spots.

C If the spray patterns of the sprinklers in your irrigation system don't overlap or the wind blows the water off track, some parts of the lawn may not be getting enough water.

How the Grasses Rank

Needs the most water

- Bentgrass
- Perennial ryegrass
- Kentucky bluegrass
- Fescues
- St. Augustinegrass
- Bahiagrass
- Centipedegrass
- Zoysiagrass
- Bermudagrass
- Buffalograss

Needs the least water

SPRINKLERS & IRRIGATION SYSTEMS

If you live where lawns occasionally need supplemental watering—or where they depend upon it for much of the year—you'll need some kind of watering system. You have two choices: portable or permanent. Water reaches portable sprinklers through hoses and permanent ones through buried pipes.

Sprinkler-and-hose setups are simplest and cheapest and the way to go if you water only occasionally. But if you water every week, a permanent inground sprinkler system saves effort over the long haul. Expensive initially, an inground system is convenient and efficient.

Both permanent and portable systems have advantages and disadvantages. Choose what best matches your lot, buy the best quality you can afford, and use the equipment correctly.

Portable Sprinklers

These sprinklers are usually inexpensive and definitely flexible, especially compared with a permanent system. To cover a large lawn, you must move them around by hand.

All portable sprinklers are designed to be supplied by a ⅝-inch-diameter hose at water pressures of 50 pounds per square inch. Even though they all start at this basic level, the amount that your water supply and hose actually deliver varies; some spread it over as little as 100 square feet, others over as much as 7,000 square feet. Generally, the smaller the area covered, the faster the sprinkler applies water; the more area covered, the slower the water is applied.

The sprinkler's packaging will tell you its maximum coverage area. Ones that cover 2,000 square feet or more do so by spreading the water thinly and slowly. Both slow and fast

types of sprinklers have advantages and disadvantages. For instance, slow sprinklers water more gently, which is useful for new seedbeds. Such sprinklers are also good to use on slopes or when soil is heavy clay—two situations where getting water into the soil can be difficult. In the case of oscillating sprinklers (see page 76), however, the slow rate of application results from the sprinkler projecting small droplets of water into the air, which wind easily blows off target. In windy areas, a sprinkler that applies water faster or in larger droplets is more practical, as is one that keeps the spray low to the ground.

Sprinkler performance has improved in recent years, but many sprinklers still apply water unevenly. Extra water may fall near the sprinkler head or at the outer edges of the spray pattern. It's likely that some portions of a yard will receive more (or less) water than others. Be aware of how your sprinkler operates; then compensate for uneven distribution.

Some sprinklers have a built-in timer or gauge. Some allow you to set the sprinkler to run for a certain number of minutes; others measure the number of gallons. Both types are useful if you know how to use the information.

It is important that you test whatever kind of sprinkler you use. Do the soup-can test described on page 70 to see how many minutes it takes to apply a specific amount of water and where any gaps in coverage occur. That's the only way you'll know how long to let the sprinkler run and where to place it and move it so the entire lawn is watered.

Five Types of Portable Sprinklers

Stationary sprinklers These most basic sprinklers are not much more complicated than putting your thumb over the end of a hose. Only the water moves with these sprinklers, sometimes through numerous small holes, other times through a flattened slot. Their chief virtue is their ability to

Retest Your Sprinkler

If you buy a new hose, especially one that is larger in diameter than the old one, retest your sprinklers (see page 70). Hose diameter affects the volume of water flowing through the sprinkler, which in turn influences the rate at which the sprinkler applies water.

quickly deliver water to relatively small, distinctly shaped areas. Some come with a revolving turret of shapes: one for a narrow rectangle, one for a square, and one for a semicircle, for instance.

On the downside, stationary sprinklers often don't distribute water uniformly and those that spray through small holes are prone to clogging. Even though you can manage the volume of water by adjusting the faucet, stationary sprinklers put out a lot of water over a small area, so runoff is likely. Best use: small areas that other sprinklers don't fit.

Impact and rotary sprinklers These sprinklers turn through the combined action of a spring-loaded counterweight bouncing off the water stream. They always water a circular area, but you can adjust a set of tabs or stops to control how much of the circle they cover, usually between 15 and 360 degrees. There's also an adjustment for the distance the stream shoots, generally between 15 and 50 feet.

Rotary sprinklers differ from impact sprinklers only in the mechanism that drives the stream. Impact sprinklers use a counterweighted lever bouncing against the stream to advance the spray; rotary sprinklers use the energy of the stream to turn gears. Impact sprinklers make the familiar "thwack–thwack" sound; rotaries are silent. Some people love the sound of the impacts and can't conceive of a summer without it; others find it annoying. If your sprinklers come on at 4 a.m., the silent rotary is a more polite choice.

Both impact and rotary sprinklers slowly cover large areas with dependable uniformity. The low angle of their stream and the relatively large drop size make them more wind resistant than other large-area sprinklers. If you plan to water in a circular pattern, check the sprinkler before buying. Some can only be adjusted to water a near circle of about 300 degrees. Best use: medium to large lawns that can accommodate a circular pattern. If overhanging trees are present, the low angle is advantageous.

Impact
Impact sprinklers have the most uniform distribution pattern and efficiently cover large areas.

Oscillating
Older models of oscillating sprinklers dispense more water over the sprinkler and at the ends of each fan. Newer models distribute water more efficiently.

Revolving
Revolving sprinklers quickly dispense lots of water through spinning arms. More water usually falls on the outer edge of the circular pattern than near the sprinkler head.

Traveling
Traveling sprinklers have fairly uniform distribution patterns. Take care when laying out their path to ensure all areas are covered.

Oscillating sprinklers This design slowly moves a fan of water over a large, rectangular area. The sprinkler shoots thin streams high into the air while a geared mechanism powered by the water stream moves the fan back and forth. Of the many varieties, the simplest are plastic with a thin aluminum tube sporting pinholes. Some are all metal with tiny removable and cleanable nozzles. Others are one-piece units made of heavy-duty plastic. Many newer sprinklers have a lever that lets you easily adjust the size of area to be watered.

These sprinklers work well for large, open areas free of overhanging trees, when the air is still. Uniformity of distribution is fair. Older models pause at both ends of the cycle, depositing more water there; newer ones are less prone to that problem.

Oscillating sprinklers apply water slowly and gently, ideal for seedbeds and clay soils. Because the water streams are thin, even a light gust of wind can blow them off course. Best use: whenever you need a low delivery rate, whether for a new seedbed or because runoff is a problem.

Revolving sprinklers One or more rotating arms shoot jets of water in a circular pattern. The nozzles sit at the tips of arms that spin rapidly due to the force of the water stream. The spinning breaks up the spray and improves distribution, so that the sprinklers can be made with large, clog-resistant nozzles. Many types of these sprinklers are available. The most flexible have adjustable arms and nozzles. Their strength is in quickly delivering lots of water to a small area with reasonably uniform coverage. Best use: watering small areas where runoff is not a problem.

Traveling sprinklers They spray like revolving sprinklers with spinning arms, but while doing so they travel along a track of hose. Water pressure turns gears connected to the wheels. Because the sprinkler moves slowly and the sprays continuously overlap, uniformity is good. Some models shut off automatically at the end of the hose. Best use: large, level lawns.

Permanent Sprinklers

Think of a permanent irrigation system as an insurance policy that protects your investment in your lawn. The greater the value your lawn has for you, the more reasonable it is to invest in a high-quality sprinkler system. Inground systems are not for everyone. They make watering lawns more convenient and efficient, but if you water only occasionally, installing one is probably not worth the expense. In areas

Tips for Watering Slopes

Watering slopes—even gentle slopes—can be difficult. Gravity pulls the water to the bottom of the slope before the soil at the top can absorb it. Here are a few techniques that might help.

- Use an oscillating sprinkler or soaker hose that dispenses the water slowly. Be sure to run the sprinklers longer to compensate for the reduced application rate.

- Set the sprinkler to water the top of the slope. Water that runs off the slope will irrigate the lawn at the bottom. Use a soaker hose in the middle.

- Design an inground sprinkler system to apply the greatest amount of water at the top of the slope, a moderate amount on the side of the slope, and little to no water at the bottom.

- Plant grass that can get by on little water, such as buffalograss. Or plant a drought-tolerant groundcover.

- Aerate the slope. This improves water infiltration into the soil (see pages 138 to 139).

where water is scarce, inground sprinklers make sense; a well-designed, well-installed, and correctly programmed system will use less water to keep a lawn healthy.

Even so, a permanent system is no guarantee of water conservation. In fact, surveys have documented that homes with an automatic system use more water than those without one. Some of the extra usage is attributable to better lawn care, but most of it is waste caused by letting the clock do the thinking. To really save water, you must operate the system correctly.

A major concern is cost. Although prices vary widely according to the size of the property and its particular needs, a typical system can cost $1,500 to $2,000. That is a significant sum to be sure, but the sprinkler system will pay for itself if it results in a healthier, more drought-resistant lawn.

The best time to install an underground system is just before planting the seed or sod for a new lawn but after the soil is level and graded. Digging trenches is relatively easy at that time. If you wait until the grass is in place, you'll damage the lawn.

Planning and installing a watering system is doable for anyone comfortable undertaking building projects. You should be familiar with plumbing, electricity, and local building codes, and be willing to take the time to research and design the system. Digging trenches is hard work, but most of the materials are lightweight and easy to manage.

The paper-and-pencil stage is where many homeowners run into trouble. Start by consulting a company that sells lawn irrigation equipment. The staff's knowledge of the types of sprinklers available and the latest designs should help you create a plan for your lawn.

If your lawn is especially large, includes significant elevation changes, or has poor drainage, consulting a professional irrigation designer is especially important. Irrigation specialists are by far best equipped to design and install an irrigation system that waters both completely and efficiently. Find a specialist who has been

Garden hoses

Buy the best hose you can afford. Hoses come in three diameters: ½, ⅝, and ¾ inch. Half-inch-diameter hoses are too skinny to deliver enough water fast enough; ¾-inch hoses deliver more water than either ½- or ⅝-inch hoses but are heavier and more expensive; ⅝-inch hoses are the most common.

Garden hoses are rated by their number of reinforcing plies. Three-ply hoses are the lightest duty. Choose four- or five-ply hoses for long-term service.

Common materials are vinyl and rubber. Vinyl is cheaper and lighter; it can also be stiff and hard to handle. Rubber is more expensive, less prone to kinking, and heavier. The best option is a combination of both materials.

certified by a professional group such as the Irrigation Society of America to ensure you're getting good advice.

Automatic sprinklers An automated sprinkler system is a boon for homeowners who travel frequently or for anyone who values the extra watering efficiency an advanced automatic system provides.

There are several degrees of sprinkler automation. Some systems do nothing more than turn the sprinklers off after a certain period of time or set amount of water. Most turn sprinklers on and off. Some have rain and soil moisture sensors that can override the programmed schedule. The most advanced of this type are satellite-dependent irrigation control boxes that adjust programs according to local conditions.

An automated system may be more precise and convenient, especially if you purchase the sensors the system needs to prevent mistakes, such as watering on schedule even after three straight days of rain. The chief drawback of an automatic system is that … well, it's automatic. Regular supervision is necessary, if only to ensure that it's getting the job done.

Many types of spray heads are available for inground irrigation systems, allowing you to match the rate of application to the variables of your lawn.

CONSERVING WATER

Mandated watering restrictions are a fact of life in many regions, especially those with cyclical droughts. No matter where you live, it's a good idea to conserve water as a habit and it's always best to plan ahead for times when water restrictions are in place.

When you can't or don't want to water, the lawn will go dormant and turn tan. Most grasses can go without water for many weeks, bouncing back as soon as the rains resume.

If water restrictions are declared, don't panic. Although it won't stay green, grass has an incredible ability to survive extended droughts. This is particularly true of grasses that spread by rhizomes, such as Kentucky bluegrass, bermudagrass, and zoysiagrass. Rhizomes have buds that, once moisture is restored, will begin to grow even after months of drought. Lawns that appear dead can be restored to a healthy, dense condition in a few weeks. This is true even of lawns that have a relatively high need for water, such as Kentucky bluegrass.

A healthy, vigorous, well-managed lawn will endure and is best able to recover from extended drought. The key to ensuring that your lawn returns after a drought is to take care of it by fertilizing, mowing, and watering regularly and aerating periodically before drought starts. Then you'll be more likely to still have a lawn once the dry period ends.

Fertilize Lawns that are starved for nutrients have smaller root systems and thus are less efficient at obtaining water from the soil. This can easily be observed during dry periods when unirrigated lawns begin to go dormant. Fertilized lawns will remain green for several days, even weeks, longer than lawns lacking nutrients.

Mow Mow at the tallest cutting height recommended for your grass (see page 40). No matter the type of grass, the higher you mow, the deeper the roots and the more water efficient the lawn. A plant with an extensive root system is better able to tap into available soil moisture than is a plant with a shallow, restricted root system.

Water Adapt your lawn to deep, infrequent irrigation before drought begins. A lawn that is used to overwatering or frequent light irrigation will suffer the most because those practices promote shallow roots. During a drought, it's often better to not water at all than to provide just small amounts of water. Small amounts can prevent the lawn from entering dormancy and will encourage weed growth.

Aerate Core aeration opens the thatch layer and improves water infiltration into the root zone (see page 138). The timing of this task is important. Spring is the best time for warm-season grasses. Aerate cool-season lawns in late summer or early fall.

Where Drought Is the Norm
Think about replanting your lawn with a native grass. Considering the energy and expense that starting a lawn from scratch requires, it makes sense to grow a species that is naturally adapted to the climate and availability of water in your area. For example, buffalograss, a native of the short-grass prairie in the United States, is a good choice for mild, dry areas from Montana to Mexico.

Mowing high helps the grass conserve water. It also protects the crown of the plant from damage and helps the grass more efficiently uses the water that is available.

Take time to find the most suitable species for your region, and learn about its maintenance needs. Not all native grasses do well with the same care you give typical lawn grasses.

If a native species isn't an option, consider switching your lawn to a more drought–tolerant species, such as tall fescue in cool areas or bermudagrass in warm ones. Whichever option you decide on, "Selecting the Right Grass," starting on page 180, will help you choose a new grass.

When Water Is Plentiful

Several devices will help you conserve water even when there isn't a drought. Rain and soil–moisture sensors override the schedule programmed into a timer. Depending on which you choose, they keep the system off not only during rains but also as seasons change or through unseasonably cool weather when the soil doesn't dry as quickly, and they turn the system on when the lawn is dry.

Sensors that monitor rainfall will shut off the irrigation system if it starts to rain while the system is running. Usually,

they measure whether the lawn has received a set amount of water before shutting off.

As their name implies, soil–moisture sensors monitor the soil. When moisture is adequate, they keep the system from turning on. When it's dry, they let the water flow.

Timers for Sprinklers

Sprinkler timers can make watering your lawn more convenient and perhaps more efficient. The simplest kinds connect faucet to hose and shut off the sprinkler after either a set amount of time has passed or a predetermined number of gallons of water has been applied. These usually cost less than $15. While their capacity and adaptability are limited, they work well, assuring that the sprinkler will not be left on all night. Some more sophisticated sprinklers have timers integrated into their design.

Battery-powered timers (costing $30 to $40) connect just as simply but turn sprinklers both on and off and provide up to four watering cycles a day. These are a big help when you must cycle water on and off to prevent runoff.

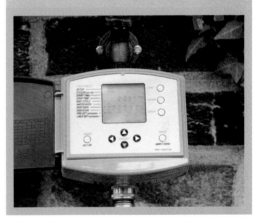

Wetting Agents

Professional groundskeepers are increasingly incorporating products called wetting agents into their watering programs. Homeowners will soon be able to follow suit. These products have a physical quality similar to shampoo. When applied to your lawn, they ensure that water doesn't languish on the soil surface and evaporate before soaking in. This way your lawn gets more water at each watering, which helps the lawn develop a stronger root system that can hold up in a drought.

TROUBLESHOOTING

Even the most glorious green lawn belies the invisible war endlessly being waged against its good health and beauty. Drought, weeds, thatch, pests, heavy foot traffic—all conspire against your lawn's inherent will to thrive. The good news is that turfgrasses are tough plants. They are hardy competitors for the sustenance they need to flourish under crowded conditions. And they're quite resilient; they're naturally inclined to heal when damaged and to spread and fill out thin or bare areas. After many years of breeding improvements, turfgrasses are even better able to stand up to foes.

But what if you have a mature lawn made up of older grass varieties? Or what if you've done everything right and dead spots or weed invasions still pop up in your new lawn?

In times like these, you're the doctor and your lawn is the patient. You must consider the symptoms, identify the problem, then choose the best treatment to solve the problem. With luck, this prevents the return of the problem. To figure out the problem, turn to Lawn Detective, which begins on page 88. After you've made your diagnosis, the rest of the chapter will help you find the best solution. To repair damage, check out Reviving Your Lawn, which begins on page 144.

TROUBLESHOOTING DIGEST

Take a Long-Range View

Looking for an easy way to control weeds? Set your lawn mower to cut at the highest or next to highest setting (at least 2¼ inches high, or 1½ inches if your lawn is bermudagrass or zoysiagrass) and mow often. The taller grass shades soil and prevents weeds such as crabgrass from germinating. Also fertilize three to five times a year. The dense lawn that results will help choke out weeds.

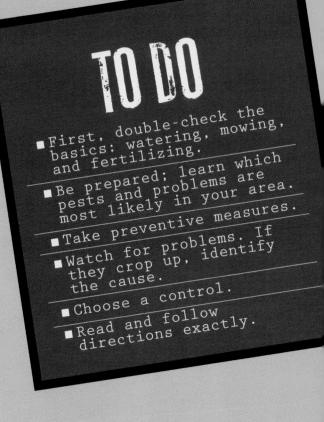

TO DO

- First, double-check the basics: watering, mowing, and fertilizing.
- Be prepared; learn which pests and problems are most likely in your area.
- Take preventive measures.
- Watch for problems. If they crop up, identify the cause.
- Choose a control.
- Read and follow directions exactly.

Q&A

Q What shrub is like an alarm clock?

A Forsythia. Wherever it grows, it's a reliable indicator of crabgrass germination. When it starts to bloom, you know it's time to stock up on crabgrass preventer. As soon as forsythia blossoms start to drop, crabgrass seeds begin to germinate, so that's when you should apply a crabgrass preventer. If forsythia doesn't grow in your region, watch the lilacs and viburnums. When they bloom, apply the crabgrass control.

Extension Agents

- Your tax dollars pay for one of the best services around: the county or state extension service. There you'll find a wealth of educational information on many subjects affecting daily life, including lawn care. With a quick call to the office, you can learn which pests are most common in your region and on your type of lawn. Look under the county government section in the blue pages of your phone book for the number of the office nearest you.

- **The Scotts Helpline**
  Scotts also offers help with your lawn questions. Call the help line at 800/543-TURF (8873), or visit the Scotts website: www.scotts.com

Did You Know?

Japanese beetles, the adult form of the white grubs that eat lawns, first arrived in North America at Trenton, New Jersey, in 1916. They stowed away in the cargo hold of a shipment of nursery plants from Asia. They've been moving westward ever since and are now common everywhere east of the Mississippi River, as far west as Dallas.

Myths, Facts & Good Advice

Myth: If a little's good, more is better.

Fact: Pest controls are studied and tested until optimum application rates for effectiveness and safety (for you, your lawn, and the environment) are established. On the other hand, it's human nature to assume that if something is good, more of it is better.

Advice: Read product labels until you understand them, and follow directions exactly, just as you do when taking prescription medicine.

Be Smart

Many lawn problems result from poor care, from too much or too little water or fertilizer, from too much shade, or from sweltering heat. Never just automatically spray a weed or pest control on a lawn. If the lawn is suffering from poor care or is weak because its needs aren't being met, these controls won't help.

The first step when treating problems is to identify the cause. Then if a control is called for, read and follow all the directions and cautions on the product label. Using either too much or too little of a product or applying it at the wrong time can make problems worse, not to mention waste your time and money. And remember, proper maintenance and good nutrition are an integral part of any pest or weed control program.

Kids, Pests & Weed Control

Most broadleaf weed controls work by sticking to the weeds' leaves, and they must stay in place for 24 hours after application. When you have kids and pets and don't want them cooped up inside all day after spreading controls, here's a solution: Spread controls on one part of the lawn at a time. Treat the backyard and let the kids play out front for the rest of the day. In 24 hours, the kids and pets can play in the backyard while you treat the front yard.

Kill Two Birds With One Stone*

Combination products serve two purposes: to feed your lawn and to rid it of insects or weeds.

- Use Scotts Turf Builder with Halts Crabgrass Preventer to keep crabgrass and other grassy weeds from sprouting.
- Use Scotts Turf Builder with Plus 2 Weed Control to kill dandelions and other broadleaf weeds.
- Use Scotts Turf Builder with SummerGuard to kill insects and protect against heat and drought.
- Use Scotts Turf Builder WinterGuard with Plus 2 Weed Control in the fall for a better lawn with fewer weeds the following spring.
- If your lawn is St. Augustinegrass, centipedegrass, zoysiagrass, or carpetgrass, use Scotts Bonus S, which is specially formulated for these grasses.

* Product recommendations may differ for your specific area and grass type. If you are unsure which product to use, check with your local retailer or the Scotts website for help and a complete product guide.

DEALING WITH PESTS

A flush test drives certain insects out of the soil. It can help you identify which pest is the problem. For more information, see page 113.

When weeds are a problem, it's usually a simple matter to learn their identity by looking through photos. Weeds are a signal of poor lawn maintenance, and they may alert you to other problems.

All lawn problems can be solved in four steps: identifying the cause, stopping its damage, changing an environmental or cultural condition that allows the problem to occur, then repairing the damage that the problem has caused.

Identifying Lawn Pests

Like any good doctor you need to use all the methods at your disposal to diagnose lawn problems. Besides using the tools and information you find in this chapter, also talk to your neighbors, to garden center staff, and to extension service personnel. You will also find help at www.scotts.com, which has more than 1,500 pages of information, along with email links to lawn experts. Or call Scotts at 800/543-TURF (8873).

Being a lawn detective means checking the grass from the tip of its blades to its roots to ferret out all symptoms and signs.

Starting Point

A good place to start identifying insect and disease problems is page 88 with the Lawn Detective. To use this feature, begin at the upper left-hand corner. Each box asks a question that can be answered yes or no. Follow the arrow from your answer to another box with a further defining question. The arrows finally take you to a box that gives a name to your problem and directs you to more information about it.

While you are isolating and identifying your lawn's problem, think about your current lawn care habits and how they compare with an ideal care regimen, as described in the first five chapters of this book. This will help you determine whether your problem is environmental or cultural, which will help you solve your immediate problem and adjust your habits to prevent similar issues in the future.

What Are Lawn Pests?

Lawns support a host of creatures, from microscopic fungi to insects to browsing rabbits and meadow mice. Although your lawn can defend against many of these creatures, mounting the defense takes energy. Strong, vigorous grass plants are the ones best able to fight off pests.

Weeds Weeds do not prey on grass directly as other pests do, but they do compete with it for sunlight, food, and water. Most weeds are pioneers. They regularly explore new territory for suitable habitat. Weeds love a poorly maintained lawn; it's easy to take advantage of grass that is too dry, too wet, shaded, underfed, or physically damaged by traffic, insects, or other pests, or incorrect mowing.

Insect pests The variety among insects is astounding. Most are not pests. Those that are can attack from many directions: the soil, the leaves, even from inside the plant. Some chew plant tissue; others pierce it and suck out juices.

Pathogens Pathogens are disease-causing organisms. Most of them are fungi; a few are other types of microorganisms. Most invade grass blades or roots and grow within the cells, causing disease symptoms.

Animal pests Because of their size, animals can do a considerable amount of damage. One mole or gopher can make a mess of a lawn in a matter of days. Most do not start out intending to damage the lawn. They usually tear it up on the hunt for insects and earthworms to eat.

Cultural and environmental problems This is a catchall that includes all problems not caused by some living creature. For example, the brown spots in a lawn could be caused by a disease or an insect or they could be the result of drought damage, salts put down to melt ice, or other environmental or cultural causes. The following are cultural and environmental factors that often lead to problems:

TEMPERATURE When it's too warm for cool-season grasses, the plants often show symptoms of drought. Blades curl, and the lawn becomes yellowish or brown.

WATER If lawns are dry during hot periods they will go into summer dormancy, turning brown or tan. They can also develop dry spots where watering is not uniform. Dry lawns are susceptible to damage from pests and overuse.

WEAR AND COMPACTION Overuse of a lawn can damage grass faster than it can grow. It compacts soil, pressing air out of the top few inches, keeping roots shallow and the grass weak. Paths develop where people walk and the ground under a child's swing becomes bare.

NUTRIENTS Both over- and underfed lawns are susceptible to problems. Underfed grass grows slowly, has a restricted root system, and can't outgrow pest damage. It lacks a healthy green sheen and is more often pale green or yellowish. Overfertilized lawns become soft, succulent and easily damaged.

MOWING Regularly removing more than a third of the leaf blade stresses grass. The root system never expands, and the lawn always looks off-color, just as it can when you mow with dull blades. On uneven ground, mower blades can dig into the dirt, damaging the grass.

LIGHT Most lawn grasses are full-sun plants and require bright light. Even shade-tolerant grasses need at least four hours of sunlight a day. Thin grass with the soil showing through or moss growing in it indicates inadequate light.

Signs and Symptoms

Lawn problems are identified by signs and symptoms, so it's important to understand the difference between the two.

A sign is the problem-causing organism itself; a symptom is the plant's reaction to the organism.

For example, the fungus that causes rust disease forms visible rust-colored spores on leaf blades—these are signs. The disease causes the leaf blade to yellow and grow slowly. These are symptoms.

Symptoms may be the actual damage to the plant. Or they may be an expression of the damage, such as the holes left in leaf blades by chewing insects, such as armyworms or slower growth caused by lawn disorders that disrupt the grass's metabolism or rob it of nutrients.

Signs may be as obvious as the armyworm chewing on a leaf or the sod webworm moths flying up from the lawn as you mow. They can also be as subtle as a bit of damp fuzz at the base of a plant. Frequently, no signs can be seen.

Some symptoms and signs are minute but important. Sometimes you must examine the grass carefully, perhaps with a hand lens or magnifying glass, so you can clearly see spots or bands on blades of grass. Some insects, such as scale insects and mites, are so small they can only be seen with magnification. You'll need to get down on your hands and knees with a 5- to 10-power magnifying glass or hand lens to really see what's going on.

Bare, brown, dead patches are symptoms of a problem. Several diseases and insects can have the same symptoms and leave a lawn looking like this.

Dig deep to find a sign of the culprit, like fungal strands *(top)*, or insects, such as the armyworm *(above)* feasting in the dead patch at left.

USING PEST CONTROLS

The subject of pest control brings out a range of attitudes in people, from the person who would "nuke 'em" to the purist who would never use anything unnatural. This book speaks to all lawn owners within that range. It describes the most effective chemicals available to home gardeners, explains how and when to change cultural practices to help the grass, and even suggests new grass varieties to help avoid pests in the first place. Some of the suggestions are chemical, some cultural, some mechanical, and yet others biological. You can select the ones that fit your approach to gardening and lawn care.

IPM

A philosophy of pest control becoming increasingly popular is integrated pest management (IPM). The heart of IPM is to solve garden problems with methods that are as harmless to the environment as possible but that are effective.

All agricultural colleges and universities in the United States as well as extension services—the community outreach arms of those colleges—have adopted IPM. In fact, the philosophy has become so popular that the schools now publish information under the title "IPM" rather than "Pest Control."

The logic of IPM is similar to the logic of medicine. If a doctor discovers you have an elevated cholesterol level during a routine checkup, you would probably be advised to change your diet and start exercising. If that doesn't bring your cholesterol down, drugs might be the next step. If your cholesterol worsens, you might have surgery to open your arteries. On the other hand, if the first time you see the doctor is while you are having a heart attack, it is unlikely that diet change and exercise will be the cure. You would probably go straight to surgery.

Similarly, IPM tries to solve problems in the least invasive way first. If a problem can be solved by fertilizing more often, you may not have to do anything else. But if the problem can't be solved any other way, IPM recommends chemical methods.

Pest Control Methods

Insecticides and fungicides are not the only ways to combat insect pests and diseases. In many cases, they may not even be the best way. Some problems can be solved by changing the environment (such as by thinning a tree to let more light reach the lawn), by changing your cultural practices, by mechanical methods, or by introducing biological agents.

Chemical Insecticides, fungicides, and herbicides fall into this category. Among them are materials derived from natural substances, such as pyrethrum. A good pest control is one that kills the target pest (insect, disease-causing organism, or weed) without any other effects. Following label directions carefully ensures the pesticide does just that.

Cultural Because poor or improper lawn care weakens grass and leads to problems, sometimes simply changing care tactics—mowing taller or watering correctly—is all it takes to cure a problem. At other times, however, once the problem has gotten a toehold, improving lawn care isn't enough.

Mechanical Many problems can be solved mechanically, for example, by pulling weeds or by trapping gophers. Sometimes these are the best ways to solve a problem. In other cases, they give the appearance of success, but the problem returns quickly, as when you pull a dandelion but fail to get all of the root.

Biological This type of pest control uses agents such as nematodes, bacteria, and other organisms to eliminate and prevent problems. Not many of these controls are available for use on lawns. Just one, endophyte fungi which protect the grass plants from within are becoming common.

Using Pest Controls

Pesticides are usually the big guns in a gardener's armory. They are effective if used properly but can cause real and lasting damage when misused.

Pesticide labels Pesticide labels are legal documents. Federal rules tell pesticide manufacturers in considerable detail what to place on them. For this reason, all labels are uniform, containing the same information in similar language.

The label is binding not only on the manufacturer, but also on you, the user. The law prohibits you from applying pesticides in ways that are not described on the label. Common sense also suggests it. Applying too little or too much makes the pesticide ineffective or harmful. You can liken using pesticides to taking medicine. Cutting the prescribed dose may extend an illness; doubling it may harm you.

When purchasing a pesticide, check the label for the pest you are encountering in your lawn. If it isn't listed, then using that pesticide for that pest is illegal and may be ineffective. Also be sure the pesticide is made for your type of grass. Some pesticides for cool-season grasses should not be used on warm-season species. Read carefully and be sure you clearly understand the instructions and cautions on the label. Refresh your memory every time you apply the pest control by reading it again.

Applying pest controls Lawn pesticides can be applied in several ways. Many are in the form of easy-to-use granules (often combined with fertilizer) that you spread across the lawn. Others are in spray form, which is good for spot-treating pests. Some sprays come in ready-to-use formulations, which eliminate any concerns about working with the concentrated material.

Clean the application equipment after using it, and wash your hands. Hose down spreaders and drain them. Rinse and drain hose-end sprayers three times; on the third rinse, pump water through the hose to clean the sprayer and the nozzle.

Keep separate sprayers for herbicides and other pesticides. Even after three rinses, herbicide residue left in the sprayer may be enough to harm ornamental plants, if you use it to, say, spray a disease control on your roots.

Spreading Pest Controls

- Drop spreaders are more accurate than broadcast spreaders. They are especially good for spreading weed controls near flowers and shrubs that you don't want affected. Use the spreader setting listed on the label, and apply the material in a single, even pass.
- Broadcast (or rotary) spreaders will be faster for large lawn areas. Look for the newer broadcast spreaders that can be easily adjusted to control the spread pattern next to a sidewalk or flowerbed.

Spraying Pest Controls

- Small sprayers are ideal for spot treatments. The different types of controls require different application techniques. With herbicides, it's important to control the spray to avoid killing the wrong plants. Use low pressure and a nozzle with a fan-shaped spray. Spray when the air is still; otherwise the pesticide could drift to and harm nontarget plants.
- When spraying fungicides and insecticides, applying the product to every part of the plant is the most important factor. Use high pressure and a nozzle with a cone-shaped pattern to cover all plant surfaces.

Using Hose-End Sprayers

- Hose-end sprayers are particularly useful for treating a large lawn. To ensure even coverage, decide on a pattern with which to cover the lawn. Then walk that pattern at a uniform speed, sweeping the nozzle in a constant, even motion.
- Be sure to follow label directions so that you apply the product at the correct rate. You may have to fill the bottle four or more times before you finish. One way to be sure you uniformly apply the right amount is to mentally mark out blocks on the lawn equal to the size each bottle is to cover. Then spray each block until the bottle is empty.

LAWN DETECTIVE: DECLINING GRASS

To detect the identity of your lawn problem **START HERE**. Each box asks simple yes-or-no questions. If you answer **YES**, follow the blue arrow leading from that question to the next box. If the answer is **NO**, follow that blue arrow. If neither answer matches exactly, select the one that comes the closest.

Is the problem a weed?
If **YES**, go to pages 96–111 and identify it from the photographs.

If **NO**, the problem is thinning, discolored, or dying lawn grass.

Does the thinning, discolored, or dying lawn grass occur in patches from 2 inches to 10 feet across?
If **YES**, go to first box on page 89.

If **NO**, the thinning, discolored, or dying lawn grass occurs generally over large areas or the whole lawn.

Is the problem across large areas a discoloration of the lawn grass (including dead brown grass)?
If **YES**

If **NO**, the problem across large areas is thinning lawn grass.

Does the thinning occur in both sun and shade?
If **YES**

If **NO**, it occurs only in shade (see page 140).

Is the discoloration brown or straw-colored, from dying or dead grass?
If **YES**

If **NO**, is the discoloration yellow, yellow-green, or yellow with a bronze cast?
If **YES**

If **NO**, the discoloration is another color

Did the browning begin as smaller patches that grew together?
If **YES**, go to first box on page 90.

If **NO**, it began over a large area

See nutrient deficiency (page 57), watering basics (page 70), or greenbug aphids (page 119). But also continue.

Thinning in any kind of lawn may be due to insufficient light (see page 140), a nutrient deficiency (see page 57), or excess thatch (see page 136). But also continue.

Do you have a St. Augustinegrass lawn?
If **YES**

If **NO**, do you have a bermudagrass lawn? If **YES**

If **NO**, does the thinning appear to be caused by grass blades that have been chewed off, and do you see moths flying from the lawn as you mow? If **YES**

See St. Augustinegrass decline (page 134), chinch bug (page 118), and sod webworm (page 122).

See bermudagrass mites (page 116).

See sod webworms (page 122), cutworms (page 119), or armyworms (page 116).

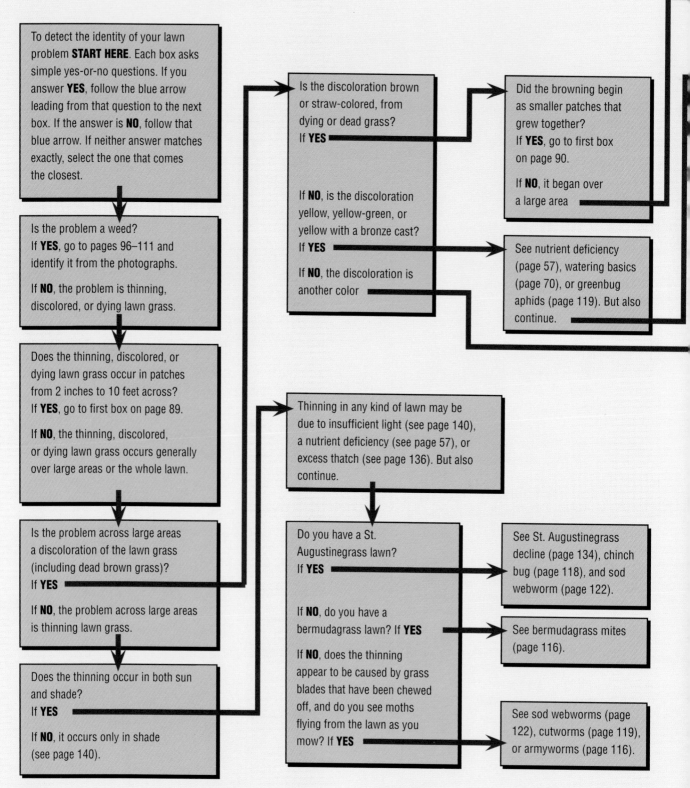

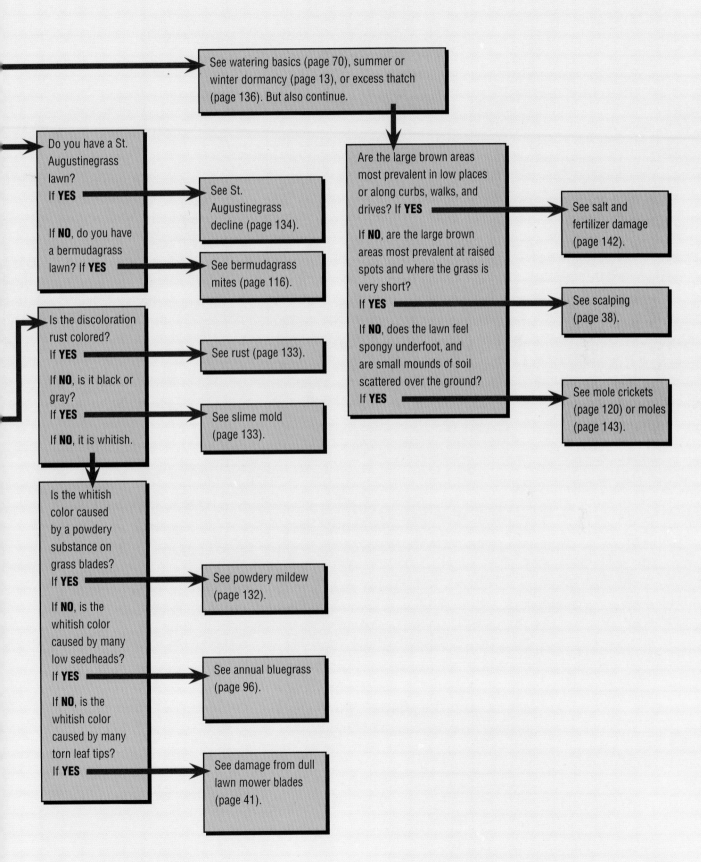

See watering basics (page 70), summer or winter dormancy (page 13), or excess thatch (page 136). But also continue.

Do you have a St. Augustinegrass lawn?
If **YES**

If **NO**, do you have a bermudagrass lawn? If **YES**

See St. Augustinegrass decline (page 134).

See bermudagrass mites (page 116).

Is the discoloration rust colored?
If **YES**

If **NO**, is it black or gray?
If **YES**

If **NO**, it is whitish.

See rust (page 133).

See slime mold (page 133).

Is the whitish color caused by a powdery substance on grass blades?
If **YES**

If **NO**, is the whitish color caused by many low seedheads?
If **YES**

If **NO**, is the whitish color caused by many torn leaf tips?
If **YES**

See powdery mildew (page 132).

See annual bluegrass (page 96).

See damage from dull lawn mower blades (page 41).

Are the large brown areas most prevalent in low places or along curbs, walks, and drives? If **YES**

If **NO**, are the large brown areas most prevalent at raised spots and where the grass is very short?
If **YES**

If **NO**, does the lawn feel spongy underfoot, and are small mounds of soil scattered over the ground?
If **YES**

See salt and fertilizer damage (page 142).

See scalping (page 38).

See mole crickets (page 120) or moles (page 143).

LAWN DETECTIVE: OTHER SYMPTOMS

If the thinning, discolored, or dying lawn grass occurs in patches from 2 inches to 10 feet across, **START HERE**.

Are the patches regular or linear in shape? If **YES**

If **NO**, they are circular or irregular in shape.

See scalping (page 38), chemical spill, or salt and fertilizer damage (page 142).

Are the circular patches a uniform dead brown? If **YES**

If **NO**, the center of the patch is a different color than its outer border (a frog-eye or doughnut pattern).

Are the patches circular in shape? If **YES**

If **NO**, they are irregular in shape.

Are the circular patches brown and dead? If **YES**

If **NO**, the circular patches are another color, such as yellow, yellow-green, gray, black, or pink.

Is the grass that borders a dead patch a healthy dark green color? If **YES**

See dog damage (page 142).

Is there a circular ring or arc of very dark green? If **YES**

If **NO**, are the patches wilting, light brown grass that mats when walked on? If **YES**

See pythium blight (page 132).

If **NO**, do the patches appear light, dark, or reddish brown due to spots on the grass blades? If **YES**

See leaf spots (page 130) or dollar spot (page 128).

If **NO**, when the dead grass in the patch is grasped and pulled, does it roll up like a carpet? If **YES**

See white grubs (page 123).

If **NO**, when the dead grass in the patch is grasped and pulled, does it break off from the crown in handfuls? If **YES**

See sod webworms (page 122) or billbugs (page 117).

If **NO**, when you dig among the grass roots under the patch, do you find small yellow-brown spheres that look like pearls? If **YES**

See ground pearls (page 121).

If **NO** and you have a bermudagrass or centipedegrass lawn, do you find hard white bumps on the grass stems, especially near the base of the plant? If **YES**

See bermudagrass scale (page 121).

If **NO**, do affected areas border a paved area or outline the shade pattern around a tree? If **YES**

See chinch bugs (page 118).

If **NO**, do the circular patches first turn pale green to yellow and then dark gray or black with a whitish gray residue? If **YES**

If **NO** and the weather is cold, do yellow patches turn grayish white, especially at the border? If **YES**

If **NO** and the weather is cold, do yellow-green patches turn pinkish white, then tan with a pinkish border? If **YES**

If **NO**, do light tan patches turn pink with pink threads binding the blades together?

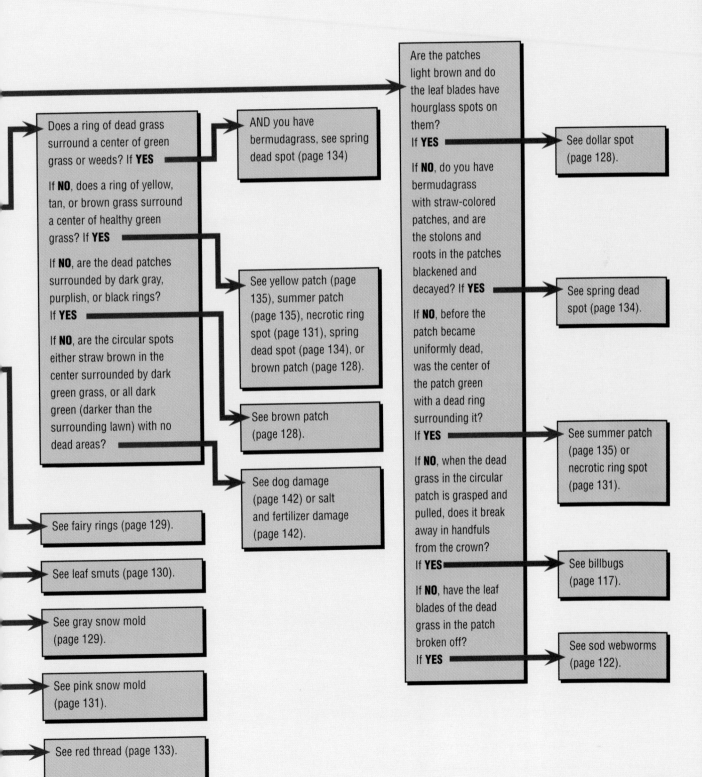

Does a ring of dead grass surround a center of green grass or weeds? If **YES**

If **NO**, does a ring of yellow, tan, or brown grass surround a center of healthy green grass? If **YES**

If **NO**, are the dead patches surrounded by dark gray, purplish, or black rings? If **YES**

If **NO**, are the circular spots either straw brown in the center surrounded by dark green grass, or all dark green (darker than the surrounding lawn) with no dead areas?

AND you have bermudagrass, see spring dead spot (page 134)

See yellow patch (page 135), summer patch (page 135), necrotic ring spot (page 131), spring dead spot (page 134), or brown patch (page 128).

See brown patch (page 128).

See dog damage (page 142) or salt and fertilizer damage (page 142).

See fairy rings (page 129).

See leaf smuts (page 130).

See gray snow mold (page 129).

See pink snow mold (page 131).

See red thread (page 133).

Are the patches light brown and do the leaf blades have hourglass spots on them? If **YES**

If **NO**, do you have bermudagrass with straw-colored patches, and are the stolons and roots in the patches blackened and decayed? If **YES**

If **NO**, before the patch became uniformly dead, was the center of the patch green with a dead ring surrounding it? If **YES**

If **NO**, when the dead grass in the circular patch is grasped and pulled, does it break away in handfuls from the crown? If **YES**

If **NO**, have the leaf blades of the dead grass in the patch broken off? If **YES**

See dollar spot (page 128).

See spring dead spot (page 134).

See summer patch (page 135) or necrotic ring spot (page 131).

See billbugs (page 117).

See sod webworms (page 122).

ALL ABOUT WEEDS

Broadleaf weeds include any plant that doesn't look like a grass, such as clover, dandelions, and chickweed.

With its rough, multicolored and textured surface, a weedy lawn detracts from the beauty of a flower bed.

In lawns, a weed is any plant that disrupts the uniformity of the turf. It could be an invader that's easy to identify, such as a dandelion, or it could be another turfgrass that stands out from the main grass, such as tall fescue in a bluegrass lawn.

Lawn weeds, like all weeds, are aggressive competitors, able to successfully compete with turfgrass. In fact, they grab more than their share of water, nutrients, and light by growing rapidly to take advantage of any weakness in the lawn grasses.

Lawn grasses are aggressive, too, and can crowd out weed seedlings if the turf is dense and healthy. But weak, thin, or slow-growing lawns are open to invasion, and many weeds will appear in them if given the slightest opportunity.

Grassy weeds subtly disrupt the uniformity of a lawn. They may grow faster than the lawn or have a different color or texture.

Weed Warriors

Think of weeds as opportunistic raiders that constantly probe your lawn for weaknesses so they can mount an invasion. Weeds that thrive in compacted soil take over where the ground is too compact for good grass growth. Where the lawn doesn't get enough water, drought-resistant weeds move in. Water-loving weeds invade overwatered and poorly drained lawns. Underfed lawns are open to weeds that thrive in poor soil.

Once weeds have established a stronghold, they invade surrounding territory. By taking more than their share of food and water, they weaken neighboring grass plants and creep even farther. Some physically crowd out turfgrasses by growing taller than the lawn, creating such a dense mat that the grass underneath, unable to get enough light, dies. (To survive in a lawn, the growing points of weedy plants must be lower than the mowing height. That is why weeds commonly found in flower and vegetable gardens rarely succeed in the lawn—mowing kills them.)

Weed seeds Seeds are among the most important weapons in a weed's arsenal. Annual weeds especially produce copious amounts of seed; one crabgrass plant alone may set thousands of seeds each year. Whenever you disturb soil, you bring weed seeds to the surface to germinate. That's why it's so important to aerate in the fall and do other soil-disturbing activities when weed seeds are less likely to germinate.

Runners and spreaders Many weeds compete with lawn grasses by spreading from a central point. They grow new plants from their crowns or send out runners either above or just below the soil surface. The runners root at intervals and form a new plant, which also sends out runners.

Underground attack Many weeds persist against all efforts to eradicate them because of their underground parts. Dandelions, for example, have deep, strong taproots dotted with dormant buds. Others, such as nutsedge, pull up easily but leave behind small tubers, the "nuts," to sprout into new plants.

Chemical warfare Some weeds, including quackgrass and johnsongrass, use a form of chemical warfare called allelopathy. They slow the growth of the lawn around them by emitting toxic chemicals from their roots.

Grouping Weeds

Weeds conveniently divide into groups that have traits in common. Weeds in a group can often be controlled with the same methods. Knowing which group a weed falls into takes you several steps toward selecting an effective control.

Grassy and broadleaf weeds One such grouping of weeds separates them into monocots and dicots. These groups are often called grassy weeds (monocots) and broadleaf weeds (dicots). In this book, we'll use both terms. Monocots include grasses such as crabgrass and foxtail and a couple of relatives of grasses—sedges and rushes. Dicots are everything else. At first glance, sedges look like grasses. You can tell them apart by their triangular stems. Sedges generally show up in low, wet areas but may occur almost anywhere lawns grow.

Annual and perennial weeds Another basic division of weeds is into annuals and perennials. Annual weeds are those that live for up to 12 months, which is not necessarily a calendar year. Perennial weeds live for at least three growing seasons.

Annual weeds can be further divided into two groups: winter and summer. Seeds of summer annual weeds such as crabgrass germinate as the weather warms in spring, and plants die with the first frost in fall. A few annual weeds die with the first

hot weather of summer. These winter annuals, which include annual bluegrass, usually germinate during the cooling weather in fall; the plants live through the winter, form seeds in spring, and then die.

Control Tactics

Mowing at a high setting helps control annual weeds. Another tactic is to prevent seed germination. Because annual seeds have a short life, keeping them from germinating stops the weeds dead.

There are two ways to do this. The first is to not let seeds form in the first place. Whenever a weed produces seed, you will battle its offspring the following year. But if you kill the weed before it can set seed, you won't.

The second method is to use preemergence herbicides. These compounds kill germinating weed seedlings but don't harm grass plants. Most preemergents stop all seeds from germinating for several weeks, long enough to prevent most annual weeds if the herbicide is put down at the right time (see page 95).

Perennial weeds can be more difficult to control than annual weeds. Most perennials don't make as many seeds as annuals do, but keeping their seeds from germinating isn't enough to kill them. Some perennials (and some annuals too) grow roots and start new plants wherever their stems touch the ground. This creeping habit allows them to form large mats that crowd out lawn grasses. Perennial grassy weeds are the most difficult to control; any control method you use on them will also affect the lawn.

(see page 95)

How Weeds Survive

■ Stolons and rhizomes creep over and under the soil surface. Weeds with such runners quickly spread through a lawn.

■ Weeds can produce thousands of seeds, which drop to the ground or blow in the wind.

■ It's nearly impossible to dig up all of a taproot; leaving even a tiny piece will ensure regrowth of weeds like dandelion.

CONTROLLING WEEDS

You can control weeds in several ways; using an herbicide or weed-and-feed is only one of them. Often, a good control plan is a mix of two or three methods.

Cultural Controls

With cultural controls you use management practices such as irrigation, fertilization, and mowing to strengthen the lawn and create conditions less to the liking of weeds.

The best weed control is thick, well-fed, healthy turf. Properly managed grass can outcompete most weeds. The instructions for management practices given in earlier chapters tell you what conditions favor the lawn grasses. The more you can create the conditions they prefer, the stronger and thicker the grass will be and the fewer weeds the lawn will have.

Mowing Mowing itself is a weed-control method; most weeds can't tolerate frequent mowing. On the other hand, mowing can also be a cause of weed problems. When you mow too low, grass becomes less competitive and weeds adapted to low mowing heights will increase. This is the case with crabgrass, which is more of a problem in lawns that are mowed short.

Fertilizing Feeding a lawn can help control weeds. Lawns established with cool-season grasses are often infested with warm-season weeds such as crabgrass, goosegrass, and foxtail. Time the feedings to favor the lawn and not the weeds. In the case of a cool-season lawn with warm-season weeds, apply most of the fertilizer in spring and fall. Fertilizer applied during the weeds' peak growth period in summer will only encourage the weeds.

Watering Correct watering is an important part of a weed control program. Watering deeply and infrequently (at least ½ inch twice weekly) is best for the lawn. It allows the soil surface to dry, which discourages germinating weed seeds. Excess, shallow watering keeps the soil surface wet and encourages germination.

Herbicides

Postemergents: Apply when the weed is actively growing in mid- to late spring (arrow 1), or to young, easy-to-control weeds (arrow 2).

Preemergents: Apply before seeds germinate (arrow) or before seedlings break through the soil. Once a weed is up and growing, it's too late to prevent its growth.

Aerating Weeds such as prostrate knotweed often invade compacted areas. Aeration discourages them by opening up the soil. The grass grows more strongly and becomes more competitive. Compaction is reduced and so is the knotweed's advantage.

Pulling or digging Removing weeds by hand works well with some weeds, especially if the lawn has only a few of them. Consider this method for annual weeds and perennial weeds that don't resprout from underground parts—taproots, rhizomes, bulbs, and the like. Hand pulling can control seedlings, even those of species that have persistent underground parts if those parts haven't formed yet.

For a lawn with many weeds, herbicides are the best approach. Once your yard is weed free, hand pulling can keep the few weeds that germinate from getting away from you. For hand removal as a control method to really work, inspect often and pull every weed that emerges.

Biological control Research is being conducted on naturally occurring biological organisms that kill certain weeds without damaging the grass. This approach is not yet ready for the market but shows promise. The biggest limitation is the selectivity with which these organisms kill plants. Cultivating organisms that kill a wide variety of weeds without killing the grass is the challenge.

Types of Herbicides

The method most often used for weed control—because it's so effective—is chemical. Chemicals that kill plants are called herbicides. Two types exist, each with its own action and method of use.

Postemergence These kill existing weeds, from small seedlings to mature plants. They fall into four categories:

CONTACT These herbicides kill all plant tissues they touch. They give a quick die-down, with the plant wilting in just a few hours and appearing dead by the next day. Unfortunately, only the tissue that is contacted actually dies, which means that the weed can resprout from the roots.

SYSTEMIC Systemic means the herbicide moves throughout the plant before killing it. Every part of the plant dies.

SELECTIVE These herbicides take advantage of differences in the biological makeup of the plants to kill some plants and not others. For example, they kill broadleaf weeds but not lawn grasses.

NONSELECTIVE These herbicides kill every plant they are sprayed on—lawn grasses as well as weeds, so apply them carefully. Nonselective products are sold as ready-to-use sprays and in containers that shoot jets of foam that mark which weeds you've sprayed already. Products are also available in concentrated form.

Preemergence This type of herbicide kills seeds as they germinate but has no effect on growing plants. It gets its name from the fact that it kills weeds before they emerge from the ground. Preemergents are effective against annual weeds; it's possible to control annual weeds with preemergence herbicides alone. You may also see some reduction in the number of perennial weeds that grow from seed.

Selecting Herbicides

Herbicides generally work on one class of weed, with most weeds in the group controlled by the same type of herbicide.

Annual grasses Apply preemergence herbicides before the weed germinates to control annual grasses. Timing is critical because these herbicides are not effective once the seed germinates and forms a root. Their activity lasts from a few weeks to three to four months, depending on the herbicide, soil type, and weather conditions.

Perennial grasses Perennial grasses are the most difficult weeds to control. Once established, you generally must use nonselective herbicides to control them. Spot-treat individual patches of these weeds. Glyphosate is the herbicide most widely used to control perennial grasses.

Broadleaf weeds Both perennial and annual broadleaf weeds can be controlled with selective postemergence broadleaf herbicides.

Making timely applications of pre- and postemergents effectively controls weeds in lawns.

When there are only a few weeds digging is an effective control.

Preemergents must be applied before weed seed germinates. The dates on the map indicate the best time period for applying them in each region.

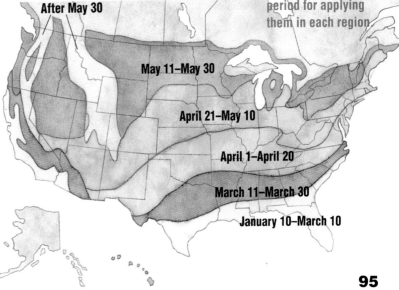

After May 30

May 11–May 30

April 21–May 10

April 1–April 20

March 11–March 30

January 10–March 10

WEED PROFILES

Annual Bluegrass *(Poa annua)*

Cool–season winter annual; some strains are perennial. Seed germinates from late summer to late fall and grows rapidly in spring, especially if the lawn is fertilized then. This weed is most serious in cool, wet climates where lawns are mowed low and in poorly drained, overwatered, and compacted soils. It usually dies in early summer when temperatures rise.

Immediate control Apply preemergence herbicides.

Prevention Best control is to mow at a height of 2½ inches or higher. Aerate compacted areas. Time irrigations to allow the surface of the ground to dry. If you use a preemergence herbicide, apply it in late summer or early fall, about the time the nights turn cool; avoid using it if you plan to reseed the lawn in fall.

Annual bluegrass

- Pale green, lighter in color than Kentucky bluegrass
- Turns yellow and dies with onset of hot weather
- Abundant seedheads that are at same height as the grass; give whitish cast to the lawn
- North America, especially cool, wet regions; Hawaii

Barnyard Grass *(Echinochloa crus-galli)*

Summer annual with shallow root system. It reproduces by seed. Although its natural growth habit is upright, it forms ground–hugging mats when mowed. This weed is usually found in poorly managed lawns of low fertility.

Immediate control Kill mats by spot–treating with a nonselective herbicide. Repeat the treatment two more times at intervals of 7 to 10 days, until plants die.

Prevention Apply a preemergence herbicide in early spring, two weeks before the last expected frost. Improve soil fertility and maintain a dense, healthy lawn; barnyard grass is not in well–maintained lawns.

Barnyard grass

- Distinctive seedhead, with seeds on six to eight segments
- Reddish purple stems 1 to 3 feet long
- Smooth leaves, prominent midrib
- North America

Crabgrass *(Digitaria* spp.)

Summer annual. Crabgrass outcompetes cool–season lawns during hot weather. Plants spread rapidly, by seed and by rooting stems. Seeds lie dormant over winter and sprout in spring. When a lawn thins from insects, disease, low fertility, drought, low mowing, or poor drainage, crabgrass is one of the first weeds to invade.

Immediate control Preventive measures are best, but you can use postemergence weed killers. Older plants are harder to kill; repeat the treatment twice at four- to seven–day intervals.

Prevention Apply preemergence controls in late winter or early spring. Follow good cultural practices; crabgrass is less of a problem in thick, healthy lawns. If seeding a cool–season lawn in spring, use a control containing siduron to prevent crabgrass.

Crabgrass

- Thick, heavy stems
- Seedhead like a crow's foot or fingers, thus the name *Digitaria*
- Light green leaves
- Stems may root at joints
- Rolled vernation
- North America

Crabgrass cont.

Smooth crabgrass (D. ischaemum)
- Smooth leaves without hairs
- Often found in lawns along with large crabgrass
- Seedheads branch from multiple locations on leafstalk
- North America

Southern crabgrass (D. ciliaris)
- Similar to large crabgrass but occurs in warmer regions
- Warm regions from the Midwest to Mexico

How to distinguish crabgrass from goosegrass
- Goosegrass survives in high traffic areas better than crabgrass.
- Goosegrass stems do not root at the stem joints; those of crabgrass may.
- Leaves of goosegrass are usually darker green than those of crabgrass.
- Goosegrass seedheads are thicker and its stems are flatter than those of crabgrass.

Large crabgrass (D. sanguinalis)
- Leaves covered with fine hairs
- Seedheads branch from multiple locations on the leaf stalk

Dallisgrass (Paspalum dilatatum)

Warm–season perennial. This deep-rooted bunchgrass spreads by seed and by short rhizomes left in the soil after pulling. It begins growth in early spring and prefers warm, moist areas and high-cut lawns. It often infests bermudagrass and other warm–season lawns.

Immediate control Dallisgrass is hard to control. Spot-treat actively growing plants with glyphosate; repeat the treatment two more times at seven–day intervals. The area must be reestablished with a turfgrass after control is achieved.

Prevention Dallisgrass is usually less of a problem in lawns mowed frequently at a short height than in rarely mowed lawns.

Dallisgrass
- Distinct clumps with 2- to 6-inch-tall stems that radiate in a starlike pattern
- Coarse 4- to 10-inch-long leaves
- Three to five fingerlike segments on seed stalks; grow from top of stems
- Seeds covered with fine, silken hairs
- Ranges through the southern states and into the tropics; Hawaii

Fall Panicum and Witchgrass
(Panicum spp.)

Summer annuals with shallow roots. Seeds sprout in spring. When seeds mature, seedheads break off and tumble about, scattering the seeds. Plants thrive in moist soil. They often take root in compacted areas along curbs. Stems root wherever nodes touch the ground. These weeds usually do not become established in well–maintained lawns.

Immediate control Hand pull weeds. Spot-treat existing plants with nonselective herbicide.

Prevention Apply a preemergence herbicide in early spring, about two weeks before the last expected frost. Use good lawn management practices to maintain a healthy, dense lawn.

Fall panicum (P. dichotomiflorum)
- 4- to 10-inch-long gray-brown seedheads on the tips of 1- to 4-foot-tall stems from June to October
- 4- to 8-inch-long, rough leaves, with an obvious midrib
- No hairs
- North America, except the northern plains

Witchgrass (P. capillare)
- 4- to 10-inch-long gray-brown seedheads on the tips of 1- to 4-foot-tall stems from June to October
- 4- to 8-inch-long, rough leaves, with an obvious midrib
- Profuse covering of hairs on foliage
- North America

Fall panicum

Witchgrass

WEED PROFILES continued

Foxtail (Setaria spp.)

Summer annual. Seedheads appear from July to September; seeds sprout when soil temperatures reach 65°F. Plants grow vigorously through the summer and die with the first killing frost. Foxtail is less tolerant of mowing than crabgrass and goosegrass. It is found in yards with rich soil bordering unmaintained areas such as fields and roadways.

Immediate control Foxtail can be successfully controlled by hand pulling. Bag and remove lawn clippings when seedheads are present. Spot-treat with a selective or nonselective herbicide.

Prevention Apply a preemergence herbicide in early spring, two weeks before the last expected frost. Maintain a regular mowing schedule and other good lawn management practices. Foxtail is rarely a problem in well-maintained lawns.

Foxtail
- Seedhead like a fox's tail
- Clumps 1 to 2 feet tall or low mats in mowed lawns
- Leaves narrow, flat, and sometimes twisted
- North America, especially central states and provinces

Green foxtail

Green foxtail (S. viridis)
- Smaller than yellow foxtail
- Light green seedheads

Yellow foxtail (S. glauca)
- Larger than green foxtail
- Yellowish to brown seedheads

Yellow foxtail

Goosegrass (Eleusine indica)

Summer annual. It reproduces by seed that begins germinating in spring two to three weeks later than crabgrass and continues germinating into midsummer. Frequently mistaken for crabgrass and sometimes called silver crabgrass, it has an extensive root system that is difficult to pull. Goosegrass most often invades thin areas of the lawn where the soil is compacted and infertile.

Immediate control Kill clumps by spot-treating with a nonselective herbicide. After seven days, remove the weed. It will still be green, but the roots will have been killed and will not resprout. Reduce soil compaction, then reseed or resod.

Prevention Apply a preemergence herbicide in late spring or early summer. Use good practices to maintain a healthy, dense lawn.

Goosegrass
- Low rosettes like the spokes of a wheel
- Smooth, flat-stemmed, 2- to 10-inch long, dark green leaves, silvery and hairy at the base
- Stems do not root at the stem joints
- Folded vernation
- The United States (except the Intermountain West); Hawaii

Johnsongrass (Sorghum halepense)

Perennial. Johnsongrass reproduces by seed that ripens all summer and germinates in spring, and by stems that root at their lower nodes, and by creeping rhizomes that can penetrate 3 to 6 feet deep. It grows in areas with rich, moist soil, along roads, and in fields, lawns, and gardens. It does not tolerate low mowing.

Immediate control Extensive rhizomes make johnsongrass difficult to control. Spot-treat with a nonselective herbicide; repeat treatments if new growth appears. Hand pulling is not practical; new plants will sprout from any rhizomes left in the soil.

Prevention Apply a preemergence herbicide in spring, about the time of the last frost. Dense, healthy turf helps prevent this weed. Avoid introducing it in new sod or the root balls of new trees and shrubs. Use only high-quality seed mixes.

Johnsongrass
- Broad, coarse-textured 1- to 2-foot-long leaves, conspicuous midvein
- Grows 1 to 6 feet tall in unmowed areas; forms dense clusters that crowd out a lawn
- Hairy, 4- to 16-inch-long purple seedheads
- Central and south United States; a serious problem in the South and the Southwest

Nimblewill *(Muhlenbergia schreberi)*

Warm-season perennial with shallow roots. Reproduces by seed and by stems that root at the lower nodes. Seeds are produced from August to October and lie dormant over winter to sprout in late spring. Plant tops become dormant in fall and begin growth again the following spring. The weed invades moist lawns, gardens, and unplanted areas with rich, gravelly soil in cool- and warm-season regions.

Immediate control Use a control labeled for nimblewill in lawns. The plant is easiest to kill from late spring to early summer while it is a seedling. To eradicate nimblewill from a lawn, kill the entire area with a nonselective herbicide and replant with sod. If you use seed, the nimblewill will reinfest the area before the new lawn can become established. Sod keeps its seeds from sprouting.

Prevention Before it has a chance to produce seeds, hand pull nimblewill from garden beds and other areas of open soil near the lawn.

Nimblewill

- Spreading habit, wiry appearance
- Wiry stems grow out and then up (to 10 inches tall)
- Bluish green leaves turn whitish tan with the first fall frost
- Each seed has a small hair (an awn) at its tip
- North America, east of the Rockies

Orchardgrass *(Dactylis glomerata)*

Cool-season perennial. It often shows up in tall fescue or Kentucky bluegrass lawns that are started from bargain seed. It is a bluish green, coarse-textured bunchgrass common in the cooler parts of the Midwest and Northeast. Orchardgrass grows quickly, rising an inch or more above the lawn within a few days of mowing.

Immediate control There is no selective chemical control. Small patches can be removed by digging out and replacing the soil. Or spot-treat with glyphosate. If the infestation is extensive, kill the entire lawn, then reestablish it.

Prevention Dense, healthy turf is the best guard against orchardgrass becoming established. Avoid introducing it in sod, the root balls of new trees and shrubs, and inexpensive seed mixes.

Orchardgrass

- Long, membranous ligule
- Wide, smooth leaves
- Faster growing than the lawn
- North America; Hawaii

WEED PROFILES continued

Quackgrass (Elymus repens)

Cool-season perennial. It reproduces by seed that is formed from May to September and by rhizomes. Seeds may lie dormant for up to two years. Small parts of a rhizome left in the soil when the weed is pulled or hoed will grow into new plants. Pulling or cutting off the top of the weed stimulates the rhizome to form new plants. Quackgrass tolerates nearly all types of soil and competes with all plants. It can quickly take over fertile, newly planted lawns.

Immediate control Quackgrass is difficult to kill. All parts of the rhizome must be killed or it will reinfest the lawn. Trying to remove the plant by tilling, hoeing, pulling, or cutting off the top only spreads the plant to a greater area.

If the entire lawn is infested, the lawn must be killed and another reestablished. If only isolated areas are infested, kill them and patch those spots with sod. To kill, let the quackgrass grow 4 to 6 inches

tall, then spray it with a nonselective systemic herbicide. Regrowth is likely; if it occurs, repeat the treatment. Patches of quackgrass can also be killed by covering them with black plastic for one year. Reestablish the lawn with sod rather than seed; quackgrass rhizomes have difficulty surfacing through dense, newly laid sod.

Prevention Dense, healthy grass discourages quackgrass. Avoid introducing quackgrass in your yard. Before laying new sod or planting trees and shrubs, check the soil and roots to be sure no quackgrass roots have hitched a ride. When seeding new lawns, purchase high-quality seed.

Quackgrass

- Hollow stems with wheatlike spikes at the tips
- Narrow bluish green blades, rough on upper surfaces
- Pair of long, clawlike, clasping auricles
- North America, except the South; most prevalent in cool climates, especially in the East

Sandbur (Cenchrus spp.)

Summer annual. Seed germinates in spring. Many burrs and seeds are produced from July to September and spread by clinging to clothing, animal fur, and bare feet. Most troublesome in fields and lawns with light, sandy soil.

Immediate control Spot-treat plants with a selective herbicide labeled for sandbur in early to midsummer, before burrs and seeds are produced. Plants can be removed by hand; be sure to wear sturdy gloves. Where the weed is most troublesome, kill the area with a nonselective herbicide and reestablish a new lawn.

Prevention In early spring, apply a preemergence herbicide. Keep the grass properly watered and fertilized, and take care to mow at the correct height.

Sandbur

- 6 inches to 2 feet tall; forms low mats in mowed lawns
- Narrow yellow blades, may be rough on the upper surface
- Abundant burrs with sharp spines
- Southern United States from the East Coast to the Rockies and the Southwest

Sedges *(Cyperus spp.)*

Perennials and annuals with narrow, grasslike leaves. Sedges include yellow and purple nutsedge (also called nutgrass), annual sedge, and hurricanegrass.

Yellow and purple nutsedges are perennials that reproduce by seed, underground stems, and tubers the size of popcorn kernels that sprout in late spring and early summer. Their top portions die back in fall, leaving new tubers in the soil to repeat the cycle the following year. Tubers and underground stems are firmly anchored and remain in the ground to resprout into new plants if the plants are pulled. The tubers store food and are drought tolerant.

Hurricanegrass and annual nutsedge reproduce by seed and by extensive underground rhizomes that stay in the soil if the plants are pulled.

All four sedges prefer poorly drained, rich soil and thrive in frequently watered lawns. In summer, they grow faster than the lawn and quickly stand above it.

Immediate control Sedges are difficult to control. Treat with a selective herbicide labeled for nutsedge when the plants become active in spring. Repeat two or three more times 10 to 14 days apart. If you miss a treatment, the weeds will recover and take longer to control. Treat again the following spring to kill persistent tubers.

Herbicides may temporarily discolor turfgrasses (for two to four weeks). On centipedegrass and St. Augustinegrass lawns, apply the herbicide in January, February, or March, before the weeds germinate.

Prevention Hand pull small patches early, before they get established. Improve drainage and avoid overwatering. Maintain a dense, healthy lawn.

Purple nutsedge
(C. rotundus)
- Purplish seedheads
- Southern United States; West Coast; Hawaii

Yellow nutsedge
(C. esculentus)
- Branched seedheads are yellow or straw colored
- North America; Hawaii

Annual nutsedge *(C. compressus)*
- Long leaves in a whorl just below the seedhead
- Eastern United States from New York south to Florida and west to Illinois and Missouri; also Texas and New Mexico

Hurricanegrass *(C. spathacea)*
- Seedhead is a dense cluster on an unbranched stalk
- Southern Florida and the tropics

Is It a Grass or a Sedge?
- Roll a stem between your fingers. Sedges have triangular stems; grasses have round stems.
- Examine the arrangement of leaves on the stem. Sedge leaves are always arranged in threes; grass leaves are arranged by twos along the stem.

Smooth Brome *(Bromus inermis)*

Cool-season perennial with shallow, fibrous roots and short rhizomes. Common in seed mixes used for roadside establishment, smooth brome produces many seeds that are spread to lawns by birds or wind. Seeds germinate in fall or early spring. The plants grow faster in early spring and late fall than Kentucky bluegrass and perennial ryegrass. Smooth brome is most troublesome in areas with dry, sandy, or gravelly soil.

Immediate control Individual plants may be pulled by hand. No selective chemical control is available; the entire lawn must be killed to eliminate the weed. Use a single application of glyphosate before reestablishing the lawn.

Prevention Weed early and frequently to prevent smooth brome from becoming established in the lawn.

Smooth brome

- Smooth 6- to 24-inch-tall stems
- 2- to 6-inch-long, light green leaves
- Sheath like a V-neck sweater
- Drooping purple seedheads in spring
- Plants purplish tan at maturity
- Most noticeable in spring and fall
- North America, especially the Intermountain West

Smutgrass *(Sporobulus indicus)*

Perennial. Tufted bunchgrass forms deep-rooted clumps in lawns. Smutgrass has blades that are less than ½ inch wide, tapering to a point. This weed is a problem, particularly in bahiagrass lawns.

Immediate control Apply a postemergence herbicide.

Prevention Use a preemergence herbicide. Dense, healthy turf discourages establishment of this weed. Ensure that any new sod or the root balls of new trees and shrubs don't harbor smutgrass. Use only high-quality seed containing no weed seeds.

Smutgrass

- Coarse-textured clumps
- Black fungus covers ripening seeds
- Leaf blades are flat at the base and rounded toward the tip
- Southeastern United States into the tropics; Hawaii

Tall Fescue *(Festuca arundinacea)*

Warm-season clumping perennial. Coarse blades originate from a central point. Although some types of tall fescue have short rhizomes, most are bunchgrasses that form clumps in the lawn.

Immediate control Spot-treat with glyphosate. Or have a professional treat your lawn with a restricted herbicide, not available to homeowners, that selectively kills tall fescue (Kentucky bluegrass lawns only).

Prevention Spot-treat with glyphosate whenever a clump appears. New clumps will not resprout after pulling.

Tall fescue

- Coarse blades to ½ inch wide, ribbed on top and smooth on the bottom
- The United States, except far south Texas and Florida; most of Canada

Wild Onion and Wild Garlic (*Allium* spp.)

Perennials. The slender dark green leaves look like those of grasses and sedges, however, wild onion and wild garlic are members of the lily family. Both reproduce underground from soft or hard bulbs and bulblets. Soft bulblets sprout in autumn; hard ones are dormant over winter and sprout the following spring or summer. Both species also form seed and bulblets at the tips of their leaves, which fall to the ground and sprout. Wild garlic and wild onion spread rapidly, especially in poorly kept thin, open turf.

Immediate control Wild garlic and wild onion are hard to control. Hand digging is impractical; any bulbs left behind sprout into new plants and quickly multiply. Apply a selective broadleaf herbicide as the leaves emerge in spring or anytime the plants are actively growing; repeat the application in two weeks. Repeat the treatments annually for two or three years.

Prevention Frequent mowing in spring helps reduce the vigor and spread of these weeds.

Wild onion (*A. canadense*)
Wild garlic (*A. vineale*)
- Leaves join at the lower half of the stem just above the bulb; pungent odor when crushed
- Greenish purple or white flowers, the same height as the leaves
- Canada and much of the United States, except Southwest

Wild Onion or Wild Garlic?
- Wild onion leaves are solid, flattened, and have a strong onion odor. The bulb has a fibrous skin.
- Wild garlic leaves are round and hollow and have a strong garlic odor. The bulb has a membranous skin.

Broadleaf Weeds

Black Medic (*Medicago lupulina*)

Summer annual with a shallow taproot that forms mats. Black medic reproduces by seed formed in mid– to late summer. It usually invades lawns with poor, infertile soil in which turfgrasses grow poorly or not at all. Ideal sites for black medic are hillsides and compacted areas where water does not readily penetrate.

Immediate control Black medic can be successfully hand pulled. Or treat the lawn with a selective postemergence broadleaf herbicide from late spring to early summer or early to midfall, preferably before seeds form. Hold off watering for 24 hours after treatment.

Prevention Improve soil porosity and water retention; also fertilize and water regularly.

Black medic
- Forms ground-hugging, trailing mats
- Slightly hairy stems
- Cloverlike leaves with three leaflets slightly toothed at the tips; central leaflet has a stalk (clover doesn't)
- Small bright yellow flowers in May and June
- Black kidney-shape seedpods
- North America

Broadleaf Plantain (*Plantago major*)

Broadleaf perennial. Broadleaf plantain forms a rosette, with rounded leaves lying along the surface of the ground. A slender seed stalk protrudes above the lawn. There are many local names for broadleaf plantain, among them black seed and Rugel's plantain.

Immediate control Broadleaf plantain is easily controlled by standard selective postemergence broadleaf herbicides.

Prevention Treating broadleaf plantain in fall usually prevents it from returning.

Broadleaf plantain
- Central rosette of 2- to 10-inch-long oval leaves
- Small flowerheads held high above the lawn
- North America

Buckhorn Plantain (Plantago lanceolata)

Broadleaf perennial. Buckhorn plantain is closely related to broadleaf plantain. It differs by having narrow, pointed leaves and seeds that develop just at the tip of the seed stalk rather than extending 2 inches or more down the stalk. Buckhorn plantain takes a long time to become established and is usually associated with older turf areas, like cemeteries or older parks.

Immediate control Treat the whole lawn or spot-treat it with a selective postemergence broadleaf herbicide. Don't mow for five days before treatment or two days afterward. Late fall is the best time to control plantain; spring is the second best.

Prevention Even the best herbicides or mix of herbicides may fail to kill buckhorn plantain. Persistence is the best approach.

Buckhorn plantain
- Central rosette of long narrow leaves
- Flowers rise a foot above the leaves, forming at the tip of the flower stalk
- North America; Hawaii

Canada Thistle (Cirsium arvense)

Broadleaf perennial. This large spiny-leaved plant spreads by rhizomes and seed. Several thistles occur in lawns, but Canada thistle is the most common throughout the United States and Canada. When mowed, it takes on a rosette growth pattern like that of a dandelion, with its deeply lobed leaves growing along the ground's surface.

Immediate control Spot-treat with a selective postemergence broadleaf herbicide or paint glyphosate on the leaves. If necessary, repeat after six weeks. Treatments are most effective in early spring or in late summer.

Prevention Spot-treat with glyphosate if seedlings appear.

Canada thistle
- Close-cropped rosettes form in mowed lawns
- Deeply lobed leaves with spiny edges
- Dies back to the ground with the first frost
- North America, except central and southern areas

Carpetweed (Mollugo verticillata)

Summer annual with a short taproot. Seeds lie dormant over winter and sprout slowly in spring, then the plants grow rapidly in the heat of summer. Carpetweed prefers fertile, dry, sandy or gravelly soil in lawns and gardens and along walkways. It is commonly found in shaded areas in the lawn and may be a problem in new lawns seeded in spring.

Immediate control Hand-pull carpetweed or treat with a postemergence broadleaf herbicide in early to midsummer.

Prevention Apply a preemergence herbicide in midspring, about the time of the last expected frost. Keep the lawn vigorous through good fertilizing and mowing practices.

Carpetweed
- 20-inch-diameter mats
- Smooth stems
- Whorls of five or six leaves at nodes of each stem
- Small white flowers from June to November
- North America, especially along the coasts; most prevalent east of the Rockies

Common Chickweed *(Stellaria media)*

Winter annual. Seed germinates in late summer through fall. Plants have smooth, oblong leaves and tiny white flowers. The prostrate stems root at their joints, forming an intertwined mat that covers open areas in the turf. Chickweed does not compete with well–maintained turf; proper management will usually prevent it. Chickweed favors shady, moist areas of the lawn and often appears in graveled areas and along driveways and walks.

Immediate control Hand–pull common chickweed or treat the lawn with a selective postemergence broadleaf herbicide while chickweed is growing.

Prevention Apply a preemergence herbicide in late summer or when nights begin to cool.

Common chickweed
- Small teardrop-shape leaves
- Starlike white flowers
- Single row of white hairs along one side of the stem
- North America, especially the East; Hawaii

Corn Speedwell *(Veronica arvensis)*

Winter annual. Also called veronica, corn speedwell reproduces by seed, which germinates in fall, and by creeping stems that root at their joints. Mowing distributes pieces of cut stems, which root to start new plants. As many as 43 species of speedwell are weeds. They are among the earliest of lawn weeds to appear, often greening up in late winter. Speedwell thrives in cool, moist soil where turf has thinned, especially in shady spots, but it also grows in sunlight if the soil is moist. It seldom invades well–fertilized, well–drained, sunny areas of the lawn.

Immediate control Corn speedwell can be hand pulled; remove all parts of the plant so new plants do not emerge. Treat with a selective postemergence broadleaf herbicide while plants are flowering or actively growing. Plants die slowly, so repeated applications may be necessary.

Prevention Use good cultural practices. Especially improve drainage and thin overhanging trees to increase the amount of sunlight reaching the lawn.

Corn speedwell
- Small, hairy, rounded leaves with toothed margins
- Ground-hugging mats
- Tiny light blue flowers
- Heart-shape seed capsule
- North America, except the South

Curly Dock *(Rumex crispus)*

Broadleaf perennial. Curly dock has large reddish leaves with rippled surfaces that grow from a central point. Its deep taproot makes cutting or pulling plants ineffective.

Immediate control Curly dock is susceptible to most of the standard broadleaf weed controls, and it is easily killed with a single application.

Prevention Mowing prevents curly dock from setting seed in lawns; spot–treating any plants in adjoining gardens or waste areas or odd plants that move into the lawn is all that is necessary.

Curly dock
- Rosettes of large, 6- to 12-inch-long leaves
- Leaves have rippled surfaces and wavy margins
- North America

WEED PROFILES continued

Dandelion (Taraxacum officinale)

Broadleaf perennial. Reproduces by seed. With its yellow flowers in spring followed by fluffy white seedheads, dandelion is one of the most universally recognized lawn weeds. Its deeply lobed leaves radiate from a central growing point forming a rosette. However, dandelions are highly variable plants. Plants with rounded leaves and a few pointed extensions at their base that turn back into the center of the rosette are not uncommon. Dandelions are competitive with lawns, and even the best-managed lawn may have some. A long taproot makes them difficult to control by pulling; the plant generally comes back quickly if the root is not completely removed.

Immediate control Dandelions are easy to control with selective postemergence broadleaf herbicides. You can keep lawns dandelion free with one single, well-timed application. The best time to treat dandelions (and many other broadleaf perennial weeds) is in the fall, when they are storing carbohydrates, or food, in their roots for next spring's growth. In fall, the plants readily translocate the herbicide to underground plant parts. The second best time is in late spring.

Prevention Be vigilant; spray dandelions as they appear.

Dandelion
- Bright yellow flowers
- Rosette of jagged leaves
- White puffball seedheads
- North America; Hawaii

Field Bindweed (Convolvulus arvensis)

Broadleaf perennial. Field bindweed is common in and around lawns in the Midwest and into central Canada. This spreading vine is related to morning glory; its leaves are pointed and shaped like arrowheads, and it has pink or white funnel-shape flowers.

Immediate control Because of its deep root system, field bindweed is hard to control, especially as plants grow older. Herbicide applications will seem to kill them, but they return in a few weeks. Repeat applications of selective, postemergence broadleaf herbicides over a two-season period may be needed. Fall applications are most effective.

Prevention Seedlings are most easily controlled. Spot-treat them with a postemergence broadleaf herbicide whenever you seem them.

Field bindweed
- Long, twining stems with leaves shaped like arrowheads
- Small white morning glory-type flowers in summer and fall
- North America, especially the Midwest and central Canada

Ground Ivy *(Glechoma hederacea)*

Persistent broadleaf perennial. Also called creeping charlie, ground ivy has rounded leaves and extensive runners that can outcompete most lawn grasses. It spreads rapidly and readily becomes a serious weed problem. It is well adapted to shade and in fact was once recommended for shade gardens, from which it moved into the lawn. Ground ivy also grows in full sun.

Immediate control Treat with a selective herbicide; the best time to apply it is fall.

Prevention If ground ivy grows in the neighbors' lawns, it will probably take regular treatments to keep it out of yours. Its aggressive, spreading runners quickly reinfest the lawn, and the problem usually returns within a year of treatment. The best approach is persistence, and convincing your neighbors to follow your lead.

Ground ivy
- Nickel- to quarter-size, scallop-edged round leaves
- Leaves paired opposite each other along square stems
- Purplish blue flowers in spring and early summer
- Distinct odor when crushed
- North America, except southern Texas and Florida

Henbit *(Lamium amplexicaule)*

Winter annual. Henbit sprouts from seed in September, then grows rapidly through autumn and into the following spring, when it blooms and then dies. It also reproduces by stems that root easily wherever the stem joints touch the soil. Henbit most frequently invades thin areas in lawns where soil is rich. It can be a problem in fall seedings of cool–season grasses.

Immediate control Treat lawns with a selective postemergence broadleaf herbicide in late fall or early spring; do not water for 24 hours after treatment. If only a few small plants infest your lawn, you can hand–pull them.

Prevention Follow good turf management practices to maintain a healthy, dense lawn. Control henbit in nearby planting beds and around trees and shrubs by applying preemergence herbicide in fall before the seeds sprout.

Henbit
- 1-inch leaves on a square stem
- Lavender flowers in spring and fall
- Upper leaves directly attached to central stem; lower leaves on stalks
- The United States, especially the Transition Zone; Hawaii

Mouse-Ear Chickweed *(Cerastium vulgatum)*

Broadleaf perennial. Mouse–ear chickweed has small, rounded leaves covered in fine hairs. The plant spreads by short runners but not as far as prostrate spurge or knotweed. It is especially troublesome in well–watered lawns in full sun.

Immediate control Mouse–ear chickweed is difficult to control, primarily because the hairs prevent herbicides from contacting the leaves' surface. Adding a wetting agent to herbicide sprays improves penetration and, in turn, control. Apply a selective postemergence broadleaf herbicide; hold off watering for two days after applying the herbicide. (Postpone spraying if rain is forecast within two days of application.) Spot–treat with glyphosate.

Prevention Fertilize and water your lawn properly.

Mouse-ear chickweed
- Mat forming
- ½-inch-long or shorter, hairy, fleshy leaves
- Starlike white flowers
- North America; Hawaii

WEED PROFILES continued

Pineapple Weed (*Matricaria matricarioides*)

Summer annual. Pineapple weed reproduces from seed that lies dormant over winter and germinates the following spring. Plants grow along roadsides and in fields, waste places, and sometimes landscaped beds. It tolerates many kinds of soil and frequently grows where other plants do not survive. It has shallow roots and is not competitive with well-maintained turf, usually showing up in compacted areas, such as along sidewalks.

Immediate control Spot-treat with glyphosate. Pineapple weed can be hand pulled, especially when it's young and the soil is moist.

Prevention Healthy, thriving lawns crowd out this weed; it is best controlled by using proper turf management techniques, especially good fertilization, regular mowing, and core aeration that reduces soil compaction.

Pineapple weed
- Crushed stems, leaves, and flowers have pineapple scent
- 6- to 18-inch-tall plant with many stems growing from its base
- 1- to 4-inch-long finely dissected leaves
- ¼-inch greenish yellow flowers shaped like pineapples appear from May to September
- North America, except central states and provinces; especially along West Coast

Prickly Lettuce (*Lactuca serriola*)

Summer annual. Prickly lettuce reproduces by seed that falls to the ground or is blown by wind from nearby waste areas. Seeds sprout in fall or, in cold areas, the following spring. The plant prefers sites with dry or light soil and is troublesome along roadways and unmaintained areas, from which it can invade lawns. Dense turf will crowd out prickly lettuce and prevent it from becoming established. Plants have a thick taproot.

Immediate control Kill prickly lettuce with a selective broadleaf postemergence herbicide or spot-treat with glyphosate. It's best to apply either herbicide before plants bloom and form seeds.

Prevention Keep the lawn healthy and thick by fertilizing and mowing properly.

Prickly lettuce
- 2 to 3 inches tall in mowed lawns; 1½ to 6 feet tall, unmowed
- Spiny leaves and lower plant parts
- Bluish green leaves
- Milky white sap oozes from broken leaves, stems, and taproot
- Small yellow flowers at ends of side branches from July to September
- North America, especially northern regions and West Coast to northern California

Prostrate Knotweed (*Polygonum aviculare*)

Summer annual. Prostrate knotweed reproduces from seeds that germinate as soon as soil warms in early spring. Seedlings may be mistaken for crabgrass seedlings, but knotweed emerges six to eight weeks before crabgrass. It is a problem in infertile lawns and compacted soil, especially along driveways and in paths cut through lawns. It sometimes occurs in newly established lawns.

Immediate control Treat the lawn with a selective broadleaf herbicide in early spring when the seedlings are still young. Repeated treatments may be necessary.

Prevention Alleviate soil compaction by aerating, diverting traffic from the grass, or placing stepping-stones or making paths where people walk. Follow sound management techniques to produce a healthy, vigorous lawn.

Prostrate knotweed
- Low mats to 2 feet wide
- Tiny greenish white flowers from June to November
- Smooth 1-inch, oval leaves
- Leaves alternate along wiry stems
- No milky sap from cut stems
- Southern Canada and all of the United States

Prostrate Pigweed *(Amaranthus blitoides)*

Summer annual. Pigweed reproduces from seed that forms throughout summer and germinates the following spring. It prefers hot, dry weather and dry soil and is often found in fields and vacant lots and along roadways. Shallow roots make it difficult to become established in dense turf.

Immediate control Control pigweed before flowers and seeds form. It can be pulled by hand; wear gloves to guard against the prickles. Spot–treat with a selective, broadleaf postemergent.

Prevention Apply a preemergent two weeks before the last expected frost. Good turf management practices that maintain a dense, healthy lawn are the best way to keep the weed in check.

Prostrate pigweed
- Mats of heavy, prickly runners
- Oval or egg-shape leaves
- Inconspicuous green flowers
- Produces many seeds
- North America

Prostrate Spurge *(Euphorbia humistrata)*

Shallow–rooted summer annual. It sprouts from seed in late spring and early summer and dies with the first frost. Seeds germinate later than goosegrass, which germinates later than crabgrass. Seeds begin to form when plants are only two weeks old. Spurge invades thin areas of the lawn, as well as flowerbeds and cracks in paved areas. It commonly infiltrates lawns that are dry and infertile but can also be found in well-maintained lawns.

Immediate control Treat with a postemergence broadleaf herbicide in late spring or early summer. Or hand–pull plants; wear gloves since the sap can irritate skin.

Prevention Germinating seedlings can be killed with a preemergence herbicide applied in spring. However, if the herbicide is applied early enough to control goosegrass and crabgrass, it may lose its effectiveness by the time spurge seeds sprout. Keep the lawn well watered to discourage prostrate spurge from invading. Weed lawns regularly, as well as flower–beds and cracks in paving, from which spurge might infest the lawn. Weed early while plants are young, before they set seed.

Prostrate spurge
- Low-growing mats to 2 feet across
- Small, oval, dark green leaves
- Leaves arranged opposite one another on stems
- Broken stems ooze milky white sap
- North America, especially east of the Rockies and the West Coast

Purslane *(Portulaca oleracea)*

Summer annual. This weed reproduces by seed that may remain viable in the soil for many years and sprout in warm weather when brought to the surface by aerating. It forms thick mats; the stems root wherever they touch soil. The plant thrives in hot, dry weather and is seldom found in spring; it dies with the first frost. Purslane has difficulty becoming established in healthy, vigorous lawns. The stems and leaves store water, enabling the plant to survive drought and to grow in cracks in sidewalks and driveways. Any plants pulled and left to lie on the soil will reroot.

Immediate control Kill purslane with selective postemergence broadleaf herbicides. Wait for three to four weeks before reseeding

Prevention Follow good lawn management practices to maintain a healthy, vigorous lawn.

Purslane
- Low-growing mats
- Thick, succulent reddish brown stems
- Thick, fleshy, wedge-shape leaves
- Occasionally the plant forms small yellow flowers
- North America; most prevalent east of the Rockies

WEED PROFILES continued

Red Sorrel (*Rumex acetosella*)

Broadleaf perennial. Also known as sheep sorrel, red sorrel has lance-shaped leaves, a deep taproot, and rhizomes. Its reddish flowers protrude above the lawn on long stalks. Red sorrel grows throughout most of the United States and is common in lawns in the Midwest and the Northeast.

Immediate control Treat the lawn or spot-treat with a selective postemergence broadleaf herbicide. Don't mow for five days before treatment or two days afterward. It may take more than one application to kill all plants.

Prevention Sorrel is a sign of acid soil and low fertility. Fertilize regularly. Apply lime to raise soil pH to between 6 and 7.

Red sorrel

- Dense, 4- to 14-inch-tall rosettes of 3-inch-long, arrow-shape leaves
- Greenish flowers in midspring
- North America

White Clover (*Trifolium repens*)

Broadleaf perennial. Has white flowers from spring to fall. In the 1940s and 1950s, white clover was often added to Kentucky bluegrass seed mixes. This has resulted in it being one of the most widely distributed weeds in cool-season lawns. It attracts bees, which can pose a hazard to bare feet. Wet conditions encourage its growth.

Immediate control Treat the lawn with a postemergence broadleaf herbicide or a weed-and-feed labeled for clover. Fall is the best time to control white clover.

Prevention Once cleaned out of a lawn, white clover is unlikely to return. Spot-treat any invaders.

White clover

- Shamrock-shape leaves with three round leaflets at the top of 2- to 4-inch-tall stalks that sprout directly from the base of the plant
- ½-inch clusters of white or pinkish flowers from June to September
- Attracts bees
- North America; Hawaii

Wild Violet (*Viola* spp.)

Broadleaf perennial. Violets have an attractive blue flower and are not always objectionable in a lawn. The plants have shiny leaves with a waxy coating that makes penetration by herbicides difficult. They often survive when all other weeds in the lawn have been controlled. Violets are usually associated with shaded areas where the turf is thin from lack of light, but they will also grow in full sun in a well-watered lawn.

Immediate control Apply a postemergence broadleaf herbicide that is labeled for wild violet.

Prevention Hand-pull or spot-treat seedlings with glyphosate. Spread a preemergence herbicide in early spring. In mild-winter areas, repeat the treatment in late fall.

Wild violet

- Grows from a central point to form broad, low rosettes
- Rounded, 2-inch-long, heart-shape leaves
- Violet, sometimes yellow or white, flowers in spring
- North America, especially the Northeast and Northwest

Yarrow *(Achillea millefolium)*

Broadleaf perennial. Yarrow reproduces by creeping under–ground rhizomes and by seed. Most common in lawns bordering roads, fields, and vacant lots, yarrow thrives in poor, dry soil, where little else survives.

Immediate control Eliminate yarrow from lawns with a postemergence broadleaf herbicide. Treat anytime from spring to fall.

Prevention Yarrow seldom becomes established in dense, healthy turf. Follow good lawn management practices, and water properly during dry periods.

Yarrow
- Forms a low rosette in mowed lawns
- Ferny leaves covered with fine, gray hairs, aromatic when crushed
- White flat-topped flowers bloom and produce seeds from June to November
- North America, especially the Transition Zone

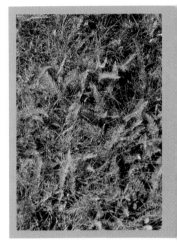

Yellow Wood Sorrel *(Oxalis stricta)*

Annual or broadleaf perennial. Yellow wood sorrel (also called oxalis) reproduces by seed that forms and germinates throughout the growing season. Dry seedpods explode under a light touch, shooting their seeds several feet in all directions.

Although the stems root wherever they touch the soil, new plants do not form at these spots. Plants thrive in dry, open places but may also be a problem in moist, well–fertilized lawns. They often invade lawns that are beginning to thin from insect, disease, or maintenance problems. In the South yellow wood sorrel can be perennial; in the North it does not survive harsh winters.

Immediate control Apply postemergence broadleaf herbicides in spring or late summer to fall. Several treatments are usually needed. Yellow wood sorrel can be pulled by hand, although this will be an ongoing task because of its many seeds.

Prevention Because the seed germinates throughout the growing season, a preemergence herbicide may not control late–germinating seeds. Water and fertilize properly, and follow other sound management steps that keep the lawn healthy.

Yellow wood sorrel
- A three-part leaf; the leaflets are heart-shaped
- Small five-petaled, bright yellow flowers from May to September
- Small, light green, cucumber-shape seedpods
- 4 to 12 inches tall, growth habit is prostrate to erect
- North America

ALL ABOUT INSECTS

Damage from insects may be localized in one spot or spread across the lawn. Look for insects in the grass and for signs of chewing on leaves and roots. Heavy use and poor lawn care can increase your lawn's susceptibility to damage.

Plants and insects have amicably coexisted throughout the history of the natural world. How they get along in your lawn today is another story. The lawn—an orderly mass of carefully tended grass plants—is a concept that's been around only since the Victorian era. So while grass plants and insects played nice for millions of years, homeowners changed the rules and have been trying to boss them around for only 100 years or so. Managing that relationship isn't always easy.

While a well-maintained lawn is the best defense against invasive weeds, the same well-irrigated, well-fed, and properly mowed grass is like catnip to pests. That's because good management results in rapidly growing grass, which is supremely attractive to insects.

Although the rapid growth afforded by good care attracts pests, it also enables lawns to outpace damage from these creatures, growing new blades and roots faster than insects can destroy the old ones. It helps the lawn muster strong defenses against the pests. Even so, you sometimes have to take action. To do so effectively, it helps to understand how insects in general grow and live.

Anatomy

Insects are built differently from higher animals. For one thing, their "skin" is their skeleton. It's a lightweight exoskeleton—a flexible outer covering that is stiff enough to support their bodies. Also, insects have no lungs; oxygen enters their bodies through pores in their legs and exoskeleton.

You don't need to be an entomologist to battle pests in your lawn, but knowing a bit about a particular insect's mouthparts and life cycle helps you select the best pest control method and timing.

Mouthparts Some insects—beetles, for example—have chewing mouthparts. They take bites of things and chew, like people do. If the plant is coated with a contact pesticide, the insects will ingest it while they are feeding on the plant.

Other insects—such as aphids and scales—have piercing-sucking mouthparts (called stylets). These parts work like a hypodermic syringe. The insect pierces the plant's outer tissues and sucks out the juices inside. Controlling insects with stylets requires a systemic pesticide, one that is present throughout the plant's system.

Life cycle Understanding the insect's life cycle helps you predict when damage can be expected and when the pest is vulnerable to controls. Rather than simply enlarging over time as humans do, insects go through a series of abrupt changes, or molts. At each molt, they shed their exoskeleton and grow a new, larger one. Each period between molts is a growth stage called an instar. Some insects go through five or six instars before reaching the adult stage.

The insect's life cycle determines how it will proceed through these stages. Depending on the insect, the next stage may simply be a larger version of the previous stage—incomplete metamorphosis. Or it might be completely different from its predecessor, such as a grub changing into a beetle; this more dramatic change is called complete metamorphosis.

An incomplete life cycle begins with an egg that hatches into a nymph. The nymph and each of its instars look like wingless versions of the adult. Wings develop as the insect changes into an adult. Lawn pests with incomplete life cycles include chinch bugs and greenbug aphids.

Most of the insects that attack lawn grasses have a complete life cycle. They include white grubs, billbugs, sod webworms, and armyworms. Insects with a complete life cycle hatch from an egg into a larva; the larval stage is the one that usually does the most damage. The larva grows through a few instars, then pupates, entering an inactive stage in which the body changes radically. After a period of time, the adult, which is the most visible stage, emerges from the pupa—for example, a butterfly emerging from a cocoon.

Insect Damage

Insects usually damage lawns by their feeding. Grubs eat roots, billbugs the crown, and sod webworms the grass blades. Greenbugs and chinch bugs suck the juices from grass plants, sometimes injecting a toxin as they feed. This is direct damage.

Indirect damage occurs when animals such as skunks, raccoons, or armadillos dig up areas looking for insects to feed on. Indirect damage can be worse than direct damage and can occur even when you have no idea your lawn is playing host to such a critter-attracting insect population.

Diagnosing insect damage The damage caused by insects may look similar to that caused by drought, disease, or other harmful conditions. The surest way of diagnosing the problem when you suspect insect damage is to look for the insects themselves. Get down on your hands and knees and examine the turf, perhaps with a hand lens. (The profiles beginning on page 116 explain exactly what to look for and where to look.)

It's not unusual for insects to do their damage, then leave. When that happens, the damage from their feeding may be the only way to identify the culprit. For example, grubs sever the root system; if you pull on the grass, it will easily break away

below the crown, where the roots have been cut. Billbugs feed on the crown of the plant. You'll see hollow leaf blades near the crown and a sawdustlike material around the exit holes.

Monitoring insects In sunny areas, insect damage tends to recur at about the same time each year. If you have problems with an insect one year, mark your calendar to start looking for it at the same time the following year. This will help, especially with insects that are hard to spot before they cause damage. Then you can take action against them before any significant damage is done, when the insects are still young and easier to control.

One way to monitor lawn insects is with a flush test, which uses soap to drive the insects to the surface, where you can see them. This test helps detect cutworms, mole crickets, armyworms, sod webworms, chinch bugs, and billbug adults, but not white grubs or billbug larvae, which live well underground.

Mix 2 tablespoons of dish detergent (lemon-scented works best) in 2 gallons of water in a watering can. Sprinkle the mixture on a square-yard section of lawn where you suspect there might be insects. If present, they'll come to the surface within 5 to 10 minutes, irritated by the soap. Look carefully for them.

Another way to test for chinch bugs is to float them out of the grass. Remove the bottom of a large can. Press the can a couple of inches into the soil at the edges of the area where you suspect insect activity. Pour water in the can until it puddles over the grass; maintain this water level for five minutes. Any chinch bugs will float to the surface. Sample several spots in your lawn.

Billbug adults can be monitored with pit traps made from empty cans. In early April, set out several traps where you expect damage. To make a trap, bury a can so that its rim is flush with the soil or thatch layer. Pour an inch of soapy water into it. (Leave the bottom on the can.) Check the traps for billbugs once a week until June; refill the traps as necessary.

Skunks, raccoons, and other animals destroy lawns while digging for soil-dwelling insects. This indirect damage may be worse than that of the pest.

Starlings, crows, and grackles flocking to a lawn are usually feeding on sod webworms and other insect pests. Take a cue from them. Another sign of sod webworms, cutworms, and armyworms is moths fluttering over the lawn as you mow.

CONTROLLING INSECTS

A healthy lawn is a good defense against insect pests. To a certain extent, it protects itself against insect damage, although it doesn't do as good a job against insects as it does against weeds and diseases. However, a healthy lawn can endure a lot of insect feeding without showing it. And once the insects are gone, a healthy lawn makes a quicker recovery from insect damage than a lawn that is struggling.

Insecticides offer the most effective control of insect pests in lawns. Certain bacteria and nematodes are effective parasites or predators of insects that feed on lawns, according to research, but these agents have not proved practical for use as comprehensive pest controls in lawns.

Whichever material or control method you choose, the most important aspect of achieving success is to apply it when the insect is most vulnerable. For example, as insects mature and grow larger, thicker exoskeletons, they are better able to tolerate pesticides (it takes more pesticide or stronger pesticides to kill them) and become more difficult to control. The first and second instars are often the easiest to eliminate.

With other insects, timing is not so much about size as about the point in their life cycle. For example, insects feeding on grass blades are relatively easy to control, but many insects spend portions of their lives in protected locations within the plant or in the soil. To control a pest that burrows into the soil involves understanding exactly where the pest resides, when it will be in a spot that is easy to reach, and when it is most vulnerable to the insecticides.

Insecticides

These control agents fall into several categories or chemical families. Members of each category have features in common, both in the way they affect insects and the hazards they pose.

Two groups of pesticides, the organophosphates, which include materials such as diazinon, and the carbamates, including carbaryl (Sevin), used to be the most commonly used insecticides. These materials, however, are being replaced by newer, safer, and more efficient pesticides.

One replacement involves a group of chemicals derived from pyrethrum, a naturally occurring pesticide found in the flower of a type of chrysanthemum. Another group includes insect growth regulators (IGRs).

Pyrethrum Insecticides derived from pyrethrum include pyrethrins and synthetic pyrethroids. They are less toxic to humans than organophosphates and carbamates, but have little residual activity. Many newer pyrethrins have a longer residual effect.

These materials must come in contact with the pest shortly after application, so they are generally not very effective against soilborne insects such as white grubs. They are quite effective against surface feeders, though. Pyrethrins are harmful to fish and must not be applied in the vicinity of lakes and streams, or water gardens.

Insect growth regulators Insect growth regulators don't kill pests directly, as do the older classes of insecticides. These hormonelike compounds interfere with insect development. Most prevent the insect from molting, the process of casting off the exoskeleton to develop a new instar. Because only insects molt, IGRs are safe for people and the environment. Another group of IGRs, molt-accelerating compounds (MACs), interfere with the insects' normal molting process. IGRs are especially effective at controlling grubs, fire ants, mole crickets, and billbugs.

Biological Controls

Insects' natural pathogens and predators, such as bacteria and nematodes, are becoming popular alternatives to synthetic insecticides, especially in gardens. However, several problems have kept biological controls from being practical for use on lawns.

Helpful Fungi

Endophytic fungi (*Neotyphodium* spp.) are another weapon against lawn insects. Endophytes are naturally occurring fungi that live within some grasses in a symbiotic relationship. The grass is a source of food for the endophytes, but rather than harming the grass, they benefit it. While an endophyte lives and grows, it produces chemicals that repel insects such as chinch bugs and sod webworms. Grass breeders have learned to breed grasses containing endophytes. Several endophyte-enhanced grasses are on the market, including varieties of creeping red fescue, chewings fescue, perennial ryegrass, and tall fescue. To find one, look for *endophyte* on the seed label. More grass varieties may follow as interest in this approach increases.

First, most are more expensive than traditional pesticides, and when using them on the scale you need to with lawns, they can be prohibitive in price. Second, biological controls tend to be highly selective, only attacking one stage of one species of pest. And they are not effective at all if you are unable to treat during the insect's susceptible stage.

Third, it's difficult to keep these biological materials alive long enough to be effective. This has been especially true of parasitic nematodes. Several attempts have been made to create a commercial product using parasitic nematodes, but the logistics of keeping them from dying during shipping, in storage on the garden center shelf, and in your home have not yet been worked out.

Many advances have been made in this technology in the last few years, and several new products have recently appeared on the market. Turfgrass researchers continue to focus their efforts on these types of products, so it is likely that other products will be released in the future.

Nontraditional controls Other nontraditional materials include insecticidal soaps. More commonly used in gardens, these are a potassium salt of a fatty acid, a soaplike product that kills by disrupting insect cell membranes. Soaps are most effective against aphids, caterpillars, and mites. They are contact insecticides and must come in direct contact with the insects. They have no residual action; insects not hit by the spray are not hurt.

Life-Cycle Clues to Control

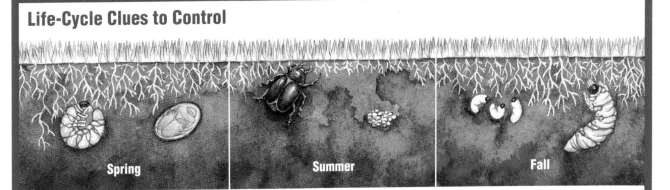

Spring **Summer** **Fall**

In late summer, adult Japanese beetles lay eggs in the lawn. The eggs hatch into white grubs, which tunnel into the soil and eat grass roots. They continue feeding until cold weather forces them deep underground, where they spend the winter. When spring arrives, the grubs move back up to the roots and resume feeding for a short period. They then pupate and in a few weeks emerge as adult beetles that start feeding on ornamental plants. The adults lay eggs; the cycle continues.

In fall, the grubs are small, active near the soil surface, and doing their most severe damage, although it may not be apparent until the next spring. When using older pest controls, fall is the time to treat because the grub is most vulnerable at this stage. Newer materials on the market offer more flexibility. They let you treat in May, June, or July to prevent egg laying.

INSECT PROFILES

Armyworms

Armyworms generally do not overwinter in the North but ride winds from the South each spring. Several generations can occur in a growing season. If conditions are right, they can achieve very high populations in lawns and cause severe damage. The larvae damage turf by feeding on stems and leaves. Outbreaks of armyworms may occur over large areas—100 square miles or more—and are often the subject of local television news coverage.

Armyworm larvae have green, yellow, and brown stripes on the length of their bodies. The adults are brown to tan moths with a white spot in the middle of each forewing. They are less than 1 inch long.

Control Armyworms are surface feeders and are easily controlled by insecticides when identified early enough. Monitor for them with the flush test (page 113). The crown is not damaged by the feeding and can recover if the area is kept well watered. The most severe damage occurs when feeding takes place during hot, dry weather.

Armyworm diagnosis

- Grass blades look tattered from moths feeding at the edges
- Larvae population may be in the thousands; the lawn can undulate as they feed
- Larvae are green with yellow and brown stripes the length of the body
- Adults are brown to tan moths less than 1 inch long, with a white spot in the middle of each forewing
- Primarily the South

Bermudagrass Mites

Related to spiders, mites are major pests of common bermudagrass. Hybrid bermudagrass is resistant, and the mites do not attack other grasses. They damage lawns by sucking sap from the base of the leaves and from under leaf sheaths and stems. While feeding they inject a toxin that causes the plant to form short internodes (space between leaves) so that the plants grow in tight rosettes, or knots, called witches'-brooms. When the mite population is large, no new green growth occurs.

The mites are most numerous on well-fertilized lawns in humid, 75°F or warmer weather. They reproduce rapidly and by midsummer build up to tremendous numbers.

Control Apply a pesticide when the grass turns green in spring, and repeat whenever damage appears. Before treating, mow the lawn low and remove clippings. Fertilizer sometimes increases the mite population but ultimately will aid in the lawn's recovery.

Bermudagrass mite diagnosis

- In spring, areas of a bermudagrass lawn fail to begin normal growth, remaining yellow or brown
- Swollen leaf sheaths form tufts or rosettes that turn yellow, then brown, and die
- Large clumps of distorted stems die; grass loses vigor and thins, allowing weeds to enter
- Shake a rosette over a sheet of dark paper, and look for nearly microscopic specks, smaller than grains of pepper, that drop to the paper and begin to crawl around
- Primarily the South and the Southwest

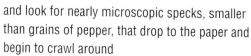

Billbugs

Adult billbugs are weevils about ½ inch long. A type of beetle, a weevil has a long, curved snout that digs into plant tissue and eats holes in it.

Female billbugs burrow into sheath tissue just above the grass crown to lay eggs. The hollow sheaths protect the eggs until they hatch. Billbug larvae, which look like tiny white grubs, feed in the crown for a while, then move into the soil, where they feed on roots. Later they pupate in the soil and become adults.

Billbugs damage lawns in midsummer when the grass is under stress from heat and drought. The damage is often not apparent until later, when lawns normally begin to recover from the stresses of a hot summer.

Among the several species is bluegrass billbug, a pest of cool-season grasses, especially Kentucky bluegrass. The adults overwinter in brush piles and window wells. Hunting billbug is a pest of warm-season grasses.

Use a tug test to identify billbugs. If they are the cause of the damage, dead grass will break away at the crown as you pull on it. The severed ends of the stems have a sawdustlike material (it's the insects' excrement, called frass). Digging near the damage may reveal billbug larvae or pupae, although damage lasts long after the insects are gone. Older larvae are sometimes found with white grubs.

Control The key to controlling billbugs is to kill the adults before they can lay eggs. By the time damage becomes noticeable, the eggs are in the sheath, where most insecticides will not penetrate. After mid-July, the grubs have moved deep into the soil to pupate and can't be killed.

Adults are much easier to control than grubs, and a single insecticide application at the right time usually gives good protection. However, seeing the adults and deciding when to treat can be difficult, even for experts. Begin monitoring for adults in late April to mid-May. The slow-moving adult weevils may be seen crossing driveways after dark; look for them with a flashlight. Or set pit traps (see page 113). Extension service personnel can also tell you if the adults are active.

Apply a grub control that is also labeled for billbugs. Mow the lawn before treating, then irrigate with ½ inch of water to flush the insecticide down to the root level.

Billbug diagnosis

- Grass turns brown and dies in expanding, often circular patches
- Damage may not become apparent until nearby lawns recover from summer stress
- Dead grass breaks away at the crown when grasped and pulled
- The hollowed-out stems have a sawdustlike material at their ends
- Digging near damaged crowns may reveal billbug larvae or pupae; damage remains long after the insects are gone
- In May and October, ⅛- to ¼-inch-long, slow-moving black weevils may be seen crossing sidewalks and driveways
- North America

Billbug larvae

- White, fat, and humpbacked
- ⅛ to ¼ inch long
- Brown heads, no legs

Chinch Bugs

Chinch bugs suck juices from grass plants. As they feed, they inject toxins into the plant. It takes many chinch bugs to damage a lawn, but they have an incredibly high reproductive rate. Populations can grow to hundreds—even as many as 1,000—per square foot.

They prefer to feed on grass growing in full sun; they avoid shady spots. Often their damage outlines the shade patterns of trees in the lawn.

Eggs hatch into tiny reddish nymphs with cream-colored bands around their midsection. The nymphs go through a number of instars before becoming winged adults. The adults are tiny, and it is easy to overlook them in the lawn, although they may be present in huge numbers.

Chinch bugs may be found throughout the season, depending on location. Their numbers may peak twice: in June and again in August. In warm climates, they may even be active in winter.

They sometimes disappear suddenly. You could search a lawn a few days after first noticing damage and not find one.

Control Chinch bugs are surface feeders and are easily controlled if diagnosed early. The most severe damage occurs when the problem is not noticed until large sections of the lawn have died. If you suspect chinch bugs, inspect the lawn closely or use the float test or the flush test (page 113) to monitor them. Or get down on your hands and knees and pull back the grass. You might see red nymphs scurry near the base of the plants.

Use granular or liquid insecticide labeled for chinch bug control. Mow and water the lawn before spraying a control, applying ½ to 1 inch of water to bring the insects to the surface.

Chinch bug diagnosis

- In sunny areas and along pavement, the grass wilts, turns yellowish brown, dries out, and finally dies
- Damaged areas often outline the shade pattern of trees in the lawn
- When you pull back the grass in a sunny spot at the edge of a damaged area, you may see tiny reddish nymphs
- Nymphs are tiny pink to brick red with cream-colored bands around their midsection; adults are ⅛ to ¼ inch long and black to brown with white wings
- Chinch bug adults are black to brown, ⅛ to ¼ inch long, with white wings. The nymphs are tiny pink to brick red insects with cream-colored bands around their midsection
- North America through southern Canada

Cutworms

Like sod webworms, cutworms are moth larvae. They hide in thatch during the day and emerge at night to feed, chewing off grass blades close to the ground. Severe damage on mature lawns is rare, but cutworms may damage newly seeded lawns to the point that reseeding is necessary.

Cutworms are primarily a problem in early and late summer but can cause harm all growing season. Once established in spring, several generations can hatch in one season and damage lawns before they die out in the fall.

Black cutworm adults are dark moths, which you often see fluttering around lights in summer; they have bands or stripes on their forewings.

Cutworm larvae are 1½- to 2-inch-long, thick-bodied gray, brown, or black worms. Larvae curl up and lie still when they are disturbed.

Control Because cutworms are surface feeders, insecticides easily control them. Use a granular product or a spray in the evening when cutworms are most active. Repeat if the damage continues. Monitor for cutworms with the flush test (see page 113).

Cutworm diagnosis

- Grass blades are chewed unevenly along their edges in early or late summer
- Seedlings may be chewed off near the ground
- When a section of turf is peeled back, larvae may be found in the thatch
- Bird damage may be evident where birds scratch to feed on the larvae
- North America

Greenbug Aphids

The insects are tiny and often overlooked, but they cause damage by sucking juices from leaf blades. Because the grass turns bronze, homeowners frequently water the damaged area, thinking the damage is from drought. Examining the leaf blades with a hand lens is the best way to identify aphids.

Females can make exact copies of themselves through asexual reproduction, or they can produce eggs through sexual reproduction. In northern regions the eggs survive over winter and hatch in spring; adults may also arrive in spring on winds blowing from southern regions.

Adults reproduce rapidly all summer, and their populations can increase to large numbers. They damage lawns throughout the Midwest and the East and have been observed in California.

Control Greenbug aphids are surface feeders and are easily controlled with standard insecticides.

Greenbug aphid diagnosis

- The lawn develops a bronze discoloration, which looks like drought damage
- Discolored areas usually develop in shaded spots under trees but can appear in sunny areas
- A single blade of grass may carry dozens of greenbug aphids
- The Midwest primarily, but possible in all of North America

Mole Crickets

Mole crickets feed on grass roots, but the major damage they do is from their movement through the soil. They tunnel near the soil surface with strong forelegs, loosening the soil and uprooting plants, which dry out. The insects eat at night and may tunnel as many as 10 to 20 feet. During the daytime, they return to burrows deep below the soil surface.

They are most prevalent in the Southeast, from North Carolina to eastern Texas. Bahiagrass and bermudagrass are the preferred targets, but the insects also feed on St. Augustinegrass, zoysiagrass, and centipedegrass.

Adults migrate to new burrows twice a year, from March to July and again in November and December. They lay eggs from April to midsummer; the eggs hatch in June or July. The nymphs feed from midsummer into October or through the winter in some regions.

Control Chemical control of mole crickets is difficult because they burrow deep into the soil where insecticides cannot reach them. The key is to saturate thoroughly with insecticide.

Treat the lawn in June or July, after the eggs hatch and before the young nymphs cause much damage. Water the lawn well if it isn't already wet. Treat late in the day, then follow label directions as to how much water to use to wash the insecticide into the soil. Wait 36 hours before watering again.

To time the treatment more precisely, monitor for mole crickets with a flush test (page 113) to bring nymphs to the surface. Flush weekly beginning in early June. Treat when the largest nymphs are about ⅜ inch long. By that time, most of the eggs are hatched but little damage has been done. Treatments are effective for a couple of weeks, killing new nymphs that hatch during that time. If damage continues, treat again in late summer to early fall. Keep the lawn watered to encourage the growth of new roots.

Mole cricket diagnosis
- Small mounds of soil are scattered on the soil surface
- Lawn feels spongy underfoot
- Large areas of the grass turn brown and die
- North Carolina, through Florida, to the Texas Gulf Coast

Observation Pays Off
Watch for symptoms of damage to your lawn or—even better—the egg-laying adults themselves. With insects, as with other things that damage a lawn, solving the problem early is easier and ensures less damage is done. Look for moths flying from your lawn as you mow. Watch for billbugs crossing a sidewalk or driveway in the evening. Keep an eye out for other pests. If you can eliminate the adults before they lay eggs, the lawn may never suffer damage.

Scale Insects

These insects are related to aphids and feed like them, by sucking plant juices. Their feeding causes the lawn to yellow, as if damaged by drought. Scale insects move around during their first instar, when they look like tiny, almost microscopic aphids. Later they settle in one location, secrete a waxy shell to enclose their bodies, and never move again.

Bermudagrass scales settle down near the base of the plant or on stolons. The scales are tiny, only $\frac{1}{16}$ inch long, and shaped like clamshells. Large numbers of them look like white mold on the stems and crowns of the plants. You can see the scales with a hand lens.

Ground pearls—the "pearls" are actually the waxy shell—are also scale insects. Immature nymphs secrete a spherical shell as they feed on the roots of centipedegrass, bermudagrass, zoysiagrass, and St. Augustinegrass in the Southeast and the Southwest. Their feeding causes the grass to turn yellow, then die by fall.

Control No pesticides are labeled for control of scale insects of lawns, although the insects might be controlled by insecticides applied for other pests. The best defense is to maintain a vigorously growing lawn.

Ground pearl symptoms

- During dry periods, irregularly shaped patches of grass turn yellow, then brown, then die in fall
- Among the roots in these patches you'll find yellow brown spheres that look like pearls and range in size from a grain of sand to $\frac{1}{16}$ inch in diameter
- Southern states, especially Florida

Bermudagrass scale diagnosis

- In late summer, irregular patches turn yellow, then brown, and may die
- Grass appears drought damaged
- Look for hard white bumps on the grass stems, especially on or near the base of the plant
- Primarily the South and the Southwest

Ground pearls

Bermudagrass scale

Sod Webworms

Sod webworms chew on grass blades just above the crown—in effect, scalping the lawn. They get their name from web-lined tunnels, where the larvae (worms) retreat during the day.

The worms are smooth green or light brown caterpillars about 1 inch long with rows of spots on their bodies. They emerge from their tunnels at night to feed on the grass. Birds eat them, and flocks are sometimes seen on infested lawns. The adult webworms, also called lawn moths, fly up from the lawn as you mow.

The adult stage of the sod webworm is a white to tan moth with a snoutlike projection from its head. The wings wrap around the body when folded.

Webworms spend the winter as larvae, turning into adult moths as the weather warms in spring. The adults fly over lawns in a zigzag pattern, dropping their eggs in flight. There are two egg-laying peaks—one in June and one in August, the exact date varying by location. Eggs hatch in two weeks.

A similar species, the tropical sod webworm, feeds on warm-season grasses in the southern states. The adults are darker than their northern cousins. The larvae are similar but have smaller spots on their body segments.

Control Watch for flights of moths in June and August. Treat two weeks after their flight peaks—their numbers will dwindle, with fewer moths observed one evening than the night before. This is when the larvae are just hatching from eggs and before they begin to do any serious damage. For more accurate timing, use the flush test to monitor for larvae (see page 113).

Webworms are surface feeders and are easy to kill with insecticides if the problem is diagnosed early enough. However, they often go unrecognized until considerable damage has been done. Apply a granular insect control, with or without fertilizer, to provide control for up to six weeks.

As an alternative, spray with a contact insecticide labeled for sod webworms as soon as you see damage. Mow and water the lawn the day before treating. Treat in the evening, as the larvae become active, taking care to apply as much insecticide as the label directs. Hold off on watering for a couple of days after spraying.

Sod webworm diagnosis

- Small brown patches of grass that initially look like scalped grass. If worms are numerous, patches may merge into large, irregular shapes; later the spots eventually turn yellow and die. The lawn has a moth-eaten appearance
- On close inspection, you may see small green pellets of excrement
- Nestled in the root area under the soil surface are silk-lined white tubes with larvae inside
- You may see birds feeding on the lawn or following you as you mow
- North America, especially the West Coast and the East

Sod webworm adults

- Night-flying
- White to tan or brown
- Snoutlike projection from the head
- Wings wrap around the body of moths at rest to form a tube

Sod webworm larvae

- Black spotted, ¼- to ¾-inch-long light brown, green, or gray worms
- Found in silky white tubes nestled in the soil during the day

White Grubs

White grubs are the larvae of several species of beetles. The adults do not feed on grass but may damage other ornamental plants.

Extensive damage occurs when grubs feed on grass roots in the top layer of soil, 1 to 3 inches below the crown. The grass wilts and dies from lack of water. Birds and other animals are likely to further damage the lawn as they search for grubs to eat.

If you suspect grubs, grasp the grass and lift. It will break away at the roots. It almost rolls up like a rug. If the damage is recent, you may see grubs on the soil surface. More likely, they have burrowed deep into the soil where they are out of sight. Sift through the soil to find them.

The species of white grubs that attack turf occur throughout North America. They include June beetles (also called June bugs or May beetles) and masked chafers, which are especially prevalent in the Midwest. Japanese beetles predominate in the east but are moving south and west. Midwest. Other species, including the European chafer, Asiatic beetle, and green June beetle, are less common but do significant damage where they are found.

Control White grub control can be difficult. You often don't know they are a problem until the lawn starts to die. Also, thatch protects them from insecticides. Once you see the damage, it's often too late to control the current population, but you can prevent future damage.

Newer grub controls, such as imidacloprid, have a season-long residual effect, so one application should take care of all grubs, no matter when in the summer they feed. Apply the control in May, June, or July. It does not affect the adults but ensures you have a layer of protection in place before the eggs hatch and the grubs start to feed.

Grub Tip
Grub feeding does not directly kill the lawn. Drought stress brought on by their feeding kills it. Grub damage is most apparent during dry periods after the grubs have already done their damage.

White grub diagnosis
- Irregular patches of wilted brown turfgrass
- Damaged areas can be pulled up like a carpet, exposing fat ¼- to 1-inch-long white grubs with six legs. If you don't see them, sift through the top 2 inches of soil, because they may have burrowed deeper
- The first indication of grubs may be holes in the lawn from birds, skunks, or raccoons digging; all make triangular holes with sod pulled aside
- North America

Japanese beetles, masked chafers, and Asiatic beetles are referred to as fall grubs because their damage is most apparent in fall. They lay eggs in spring. The eggs hatch in summer, and the grubs feed from August to October. They burrow 6 inches or more into the soil to overwinter, then emerge as adults the next spring.

Japanese beetle

- June beetle grubs are larger than those of Japanese beetles and masked chafers. They also have a three-year life cycle. They are called summer grubs because they damage the lawn in midsummer. Green June beetles lay eggs in June and July and damage lawns in late July and August.

- European chafers lay eggs in July. The grubs are a problem in September and October.

June beetle

ALL ABOUT DISEASES

The spores that infect grass plants are easily spread across a lawn on your shoes, on mower blades, as well as by wind and water.

Diseases are caused by both living and nonliving factors. Nonliving factors—which include nutritional imbalances and drought—weaken plants and allow the living disease agents to move in. Among the living disease-causing organisms are bacteria, fungi, viruses, phytoplasmas, parasitic plants, and nematodes. Of these, only fungi are a major cause of disease in lawns. Viruses cause many plant diseases but only one major lawn disease: St. Augustinegrass decline (SAD).

Fungi

Fungi are everywhere. As with insects, the vast majority are benign. They serve the useful purpose of breaking down dead organic matter into basic chemicals that are recycled as plant nutrients.

Mushrooms are the "flowers"—the reproductive organs—of some fungi. They're the only part of a fungus that is easy to see. The rest of the fungus exists as microscopic threads called hyphae. These threads mat together in a mass called a mycelium. You've probably seen mycelia as the white strings covering rotting leaves. Another example is the dusty covering over a leaf with mildew.

There are three types of fungi. The first type—saprophyte—feed only on dead plant or animal tissue and do not cause disease. Most fungi are saprophytes.

The next type—pathogens—are disease-causing fungi that grow in living organisms. This type includes parasites, which depend on a living host for sustenance. Pathogens are specialists in invading plants in spite of the plant's defenses, and they thrive in the rich mix of nutrients within a plant's body. Most pathogens can't grow outside a plant. Only a few fungi fall into this group.

The final category are the facultative saprophytes. In other words, these fungi are saprophytes most of the time, but in the right circumstances—usually when the plant is weakened by stress or by a pathogen—they can invade plant tissue.

Many plant diseases are caused by a combination of fungi; often a pathogen first weakens the plant, then is joined by one or more facultative saprophytes. Frequently, a sick plant may host so many different fungi that pathologists have difficulty figuring out which one is responsible for the condition.

Disease Spread

Fungi reproduce by spores, dust-size particles that sprout into new hyphae. Although spores serve the same purpose as seeds, they are far simpler and less efficient. Many live only for hours, and if they don't land on a suitable host in that time, they die. But if they do find a host and conditions are right, they can grow rapidly.

Spores may be carried by wind or water. Wind-borne spores are dry and dustlike. They are so small that they float for great distances on the wind, landing on and eventually infecting plants. The spores that are spread in water are moist and easily picked up by running water. Raindrops splashing on the ground carry the spores to new plants.

Animals, people, and tools may also pick up and carry spores. Because plant pathogens live in the soil, on the host plant, and in plant debris, they can be carried from one place to another on plant material. For example, they could be found on sod, in the soil, or in the grass.

In winter, fungi persist in the soil or dead plant material or stay within the grass plant. Many fungi also form tough masses of mycelia called sclerotia, which can last for months or years in the soil or on dead plant tissue. They are small but may be large enough to be visible to the naked eye. When the climate is right, they invade plant roots, sometimes growing up into the crown. This type of disease-causing fungus spreads in the soil attached to sod. Because it lives in the soil, it is difficult to eradicate.

Lawn Diseases

Like other plant diseases, lawn diseases occur when three ingredients come together:

- a susceptible plant
- a pathogen
- the right conditions

Without the presence of all three, no infection takes place.

It's easier to prevent lawn diseases than to cure them. Prevention focuses on avoiding one or all of the three ingredients for infection. Although there's little you can do to prevent a pathogen from being in your lawn, you can do something about susceptible plants and conditions that invite disease.

First, grow only resistant grass varieties. Learn which lawn diseases are prevalent in your area, and select the seed or sod of a grass that isn't affected by the diseases. Or plant seed mixtures or blends, which enable lawns to resist damage better than lawns composed of a single, possibly vulnerable variety. If a disease attacks one grass in the mix, the others carry on. (Note: Most Scotts grass seed mixtures contain disease-resistant varieties.)

Most lawn diseases require specific conditions to infect grass, and homeowners are often responsible for creating some of those conditions. To avoid disease, provide the best lawn care you can, giving the grass just the right amount of water and fertilizer and keeping the soil open and loose. Avoid soil compaction, overwatering, or fertilizing too much or too little.

Identifying Lawn Diseases

Diseases can be difficult to identify. Many, especially patch diseases, look the same. And from a distance, many disease symptoms resemble those caused by poor lawn care or insect damage. The yellow area in your bluegrass lawn could be caused by a disease, an insect, or hot weather.

So you have to dig deeper to determine the presence of a disease. Look for distinctly shaped patterns in the lawn or lesions and spots on leaf blades. The color and shape of spots in the lawn and on blades hold clues to the disease. Sometimes the way the spots are distributed across the lawn is an important indicator. The disease profiles starting on page 128 describe the signs and symptoms for each disease. For more help, take a sample to your local extension service for identification.

Extension staff will supply directions for collecting and delivering the sample. Usually you need to dig one or more grass plants from the edge of the damaged area, where the fungus is most active. You'll also need to provide some roots and soil with the plant. Put the sample in a plastic bag and deliver it to the office rather than mailing it. (In the few days it takes for a sample to arrive in the mail, saprophytic fungi can turn the sample into a slimy mess, destroying the necessary clues for identification.) The staff will culture the disease in a laboratory, so getting a definite id may take a few weeks.

The size, shape, and color of patches give clues to the identity of a disease. Irregular brown spots like this are symptoms of pythium blight.

To come up with a more definitive identification, delve deeper. Look for spots on the leaves and check their size, shape, and color. This is grey leaf spot on St. Augustinegrass.

Water deeply, applying at least 1/2 inch of water at a time for a total of 1 to 2 inches of water per week. Water in the morning so grass blades are dry by nightfall.

Use a fertilizer program that provides steady, season-long growth. Feed three to five times a year, depending on the grass and the region. Use fertilizer that is formulated for lawns.

Some slow-growing leaf spot diseases can be controlled by bagging or raking clippings and disposing of them.

Preventing Lawn Diseases

The most important principle of preventing lawn diseases is to keep the grass healthy. Although plants have evolved chemical and physical defenses against diseases, they need energy to deploy them. The vigor they develop from good care is your first and most important line of defense.

Watering Many fungal diseases infect plants only when moisture abounds. If grass blades are wet for long periods or you water daily so the soil never dries out, your lawn is more likely to be infected. Follow the rules laid out in the chapter starting on page 68: Water properly (at least 1/2 inch twice a week) in the early morning so that the grass blades can dry during the day.

Mowing Cutting the grass helps further the spread of some diseases by wounding the plants and giving pathogens easy points of entry into the leaves. As explained in the chapter on mowing, starting on page 34, routinely mowing too short weakens the grass plant, making it more susceptible to infection. Lawns are healthiest when no more than a third of the blade is cut off at a time.

Some slow-growing diseases that affect leaf blades, such as rust, can be controlled with mowing. Fertilize the lawn to spur growth, then mow regularly and bag the clippings. By removing the clippings, you eliminate one source of possible new infection.

Fertilizing Unlike most other plants, grasses have the ability to store excess nitrogen in their tissues. To pathogens, a healthy grass blade looks like a bank full of money waiting to be robbed. On the other hand, nitrogen deficiency weakens grass, leaving it vulnerable to infection.

Managing your lawn's nutrition is an important step in preventing many diseases and aiding recovery. Follow a balanced fertilizer program for your type of grass to keep the lawn healthy without promoting disease (see the chapter starting on page 52).

Potassium strengthens grass plants against disease. If the soil supporting your lawn is low in potassium, the feeding you apply just before a period of environmental stress (such as summer heat or winter cold for cool-season grasses) should contain a good dose of potassium.

Turfgrass selection You probably inherited your lawn and must deal with whatever grass is growing there. If it is susceptible to disease and breaks out in spots every year, consider renovating it. That involves killing the existing grass and replanting with a better variety (see the chapter starting on page 144). Before renovating or installing a lawn, ask your local extension service about the best turfgrasses for your area. The staff will know which grasses succeed in your climate and resist the prevalent diseases.

Thatch and aeration Thatch is a breeding ground for pathogens. Take the steps described later in this chapter (see page 136) to prevent thatch from growing thicker than 1/2 inch. Aerate to reduce thatch, relieve compaction, and improve drainage—all conditions that favor disease (see page 138).

Drainage Because it's difficult to improve drainage after a lawn is in place, it's important to fix it before installing the lawn. Aerating an existing lawn with poor drainage helps somewhat. If drainage is really bad, consider installing drain lines under your lawn. While this is difficult and somewhat expensive, doing so offers an opportunity to renovate your lawn and upgrade the grass.

Soil pH In many regions, you know whether your soil is naturally acid or alkaline. Applying lime or sulfur every few years is a normal practice. However, pH levels are not so clear-cut in some regions. To ensure that the lime or sulfur you apply is needed, test your soil every few years.

Fungicides

Diseases in home lawns rarely require fungicide treatment. They should be controlled with cultural techniques whenever possible, but situations may arise where you need to use fungicides, chemicals that kill fungi or prevent spores from germinating.

Types of fungicides Turf fungicides fall into two general categories: contact and systemic. Contact fungicides form a protective barrier on the plant's surface that prevents the fungus from penetrating the plant's defenses. Once the disease enters a plant, contact fungicides will not help that plant but will stop the spread of the disease to nearby healthy plants.

Like contacts, systemic fungicides control fungi on the outer surface of the plant. They also enter plants through roots or leaves and kill fungi within the plant—in effect, curing the disease.

Rain and irrigation will wash contact fungicides off of the blades. New blades that grow after the application are unprotected. Systemic fungicides are inside the plant, so they are not washed off. As the grass grows, these fungicides are carried into the new leaf blades and continue to protect the plant. But even systemic herbicides gradually fade from the plant and need to be reapplied.

Contact fungicides and some systemics control most lawn diseases, such as leaf spot, dollar spot, and brown patch. Only systemics are effective against systemic diseases such as the patch diseases.

Applying fungicides Select a fungicide labeled for the disease, then apply it following all the directions on the label. Fungicides are more effective at preventing disease than curing it, so it's important to apply them at the right time. Schedule fungicide applications when they will be most effective against the disease. The profiles that follow point out the timing, and fungicide labels offer guidance as to when and how often to apply the product.

Fungicides are available as granules, liquids, and wettable powders. They are applied with the same sort of equipment used to spread or spray other lawn products. When treating thatch or soil, follow irrigation directions carefully to wash the fungicide down to where it is needed.

DISEASE PROFILES

Brown Patch

Brown patch is caused by the fungus *Rhizoctonia solani* and is sometimes called rhizoctonia blight. Affected lawns develop large, blighted patches that often have dark halos around them in the early morning. It is one of the most prevalent diseases in warm, humid areas, attacking all types of grass: Kentucky bluegrass in the Midwest and the East, St. Augustinegrass in Florida, Texas, and the Gulf Coast. It can devastate tall fescue lawns in the Transition Zone during hot summers. Damage may show up late in the season and continue into fall. The halo pattern usually does not occur on St. Augustinegrass, but the fungus may move quickly and blight large sections of the lawn.

Lush, tender growth resulting from use of quick-release nitrogen fertilizer is most susceptible. Sometimes only the blades are affected, and the grass recovers in two to three weeks. When infection is severe and warm weather continues, the disease attacks plant crowns and kills the grass.

Immediate control Apply a contact fungicide when you first notice the disease and at least three more times at 7- to 10-day intervals. Repeat for as long as warm, humid weather continues.

Prevention Keep the grass as dry as possible to slow the spread of brown patch; water properly (one or two times a week) only in the morning. To reduce recurring infections, control thatch and follow a balanced fertilizer program. The heaviest feeding for cool-season grasses should be in late summer and fall.

Brown patch diagnosis

- Circular patches of dead grass, a few inches to a few feet across, appear during periods of high humidity and warm (75°F–85°F) temperatures
- Dark gray, purplish, or black halos may surround the brown patches at night and persist into early morning
- After two to three weeks, the brown grass in the center may recover and turn green, giving the circular patch a doughnut shape
- The United States, primarily east of the Rockies, especially in the Southeast

Dollar Spot

Dollar spot is caused by the *Sclerotinia homoeocarpa* fungus. On golf greens affected areas start out the size of a silver dollar; on home lawns, they are more often softball size. Spots can merge into large, blighted areas. Active during moist, mild days and cool (60°F to 80°F) nights, dollar spot occurs in spring and fall. Infections may linger through the summer. The disease is most severe on Kentucky bluegrass, bentgrass, and bermudagrass, but it also attacks bahia, zoysia, fescue, and ryegrass. Lawns under stress from lack of moisture or low fertility are most susceptible. Excess thatch may also contribute. Dollar spot seldom damages permanently, although a lawn can take several weeks or months to recover. Dollar spot is spread on the shoes of people walking over the lawn and by hoses, mowers, and other equipment.

Immediate control Apply a contact fungicide twice, 7 to 10 days apart, beginning when the disease is first evident. Grass recovers quickly if treated promptly.

Prevention Maintain proper nutrient levels. Applying fertilizer helps the lawn recover if it is nutrient deficient. Control excess thatch. Water only in the morning, one or two times a week.

Dollar spot diagnosis

- Circular light brown to straw color spots the size of a silver dollar to 6 inches across form in spring or fall
- Spots may merge into large, irregular patches
- Leaves have light brown, hourglass-shape blotches edged in reddish brown; tips may remain green
- In early morning before dew dries, a cobwebby white growth may cover infected blades
- North America

Fairy Rings

The fungi responsible for fairy rings are saprophytes that grow on organic matter in soil. Most don't harm the grass but rather compete with it for water or inhibit water flow into the soil.

A ring of dark green grass develops in the lawn as the fairy ring fungus breaks down organic matter, releasing nitrogen. If the lawn is pale and low in nitrogen, the greener area will be more pronounced in contrast. The fungus grows from a central point outward at a rate of 1 to 2 feet per year. Mushrooms, which are the fruiting bodies of the fungus, appear in the morning when weather conditions are right.

Fairy rings may grow in any type of lawn. The disease often starts on wood buried in the soil, such as rotting trunks and roots of dead trees, as well as grade stakes and other wood debris buried in the soil during construction.

Immediate control No fungicides control fairy ring.

Prevention Mask the effects by fertilizing. If the grass in the ring is pale green or yellow, aerate the lawn and water thoroughly so that water penetrates the soil. The grass in the ring may be lost, even in well-irrigated lawns. Using a tree-root feeder to keep the ring soaked for four weeks or more may provide some relief, although the rings may return when you stop. If you're building a new home or having grading work done on your yard, make sure the contractor doesn't bury wood debris.

Fairy ring diagnosis

- Circles or arcs of dark green grass as small as 1 foot or as large as hundreds of feet across appear
- Mushrooms may grow in the ring
- Areas of dead grass may develop in the ring, or in the case of smaller rings, the entire center of the circle may be dead
- North America

Gray Snow Mold

Also called typhula blight, gray snow mold is caused by *Typhula* fungi. Active only in cool (30°F to 40°F), moist weather, gray snow mold is most likely to occur when snow stays on the ground for several months. Like pink snow mold, it grows under snow but may continue to grow after snow melts. Prolonged cold weather worsens the symptoms; turf recovers quickly when warm weather arrives. Gray snow mold primarily affects cool-season grasses.

Immediate control For serious infections, treat with a fungicide labeled for the disease (generally, it is different from what is labeled for pink snow mold). Rake dead patches thoroughly, then reseed them. Lightly infected turf usually recovers on its own.

Prevention Do not apply excess quick-release nitrogen in early fall as the lawn goes into dormancy. Once the grass is dormant, it's OK to fertilize. Rake and remove leaves before snow falls. Mow until the grass stops growing in fall; tall grass is most susceptible. Reduce thatch.

Gray snow mold diagnosis

- Yellow-green spots a few inches in diameter appear in cold, wet weather
- Spots grow in size and become covered with grayish white mycelia; they can grow into 2-foot-diameter patches and have a grayish white border
- Affected grass is matted and turns light tan
- Circular patches grow outward; several patches may eventually join together
- Leathery, raised dots (sclerotia) on affected grass blades may be half the width of the blade
- Northern United States and Canada

DISEASE PROFILES continued

Leaf Smuts

Two diseases fall under the label of leaf smut: stripe smut (*Ustilago striiformis*) and flag smut (*U. agropyri*). They primarily attack Kentucky bluegrass but can also affect fine fescue and perennial ryegrass. Spores infect the plant's crown and adjoining underground stems, then grow throughout the plant's tissues. The disease is most active in cool weather (50°F to 60°F). Affected plants die when the weather heats up. Excessive fertility, watering, and thatch encourage leaf smuts.

Immediate control Leaf smut is difficult to eliminate completely, but its severity can be lessened. Treat the lawn with a systemic fungicide in October or early March, with two applications 14 to 21 days apart. Water thoroughly afterward to carry the fungicide to the roots, where the plant can absorb it.

Prevention Avoid overwatering. Follow a balanced fertility program. Reduce thatch.

Leaf smut diagnosis

- Grass turns pale green to yellow in cool spring and fall weather
- Long yellowish streaks appear on leaf blades, later turning gray to black; blades curl, wither, and shred in thin strips from the tip down
- Affected plants occur singly or in spots from a few inches across to more than a foot in diameter; these areas grow more slowly and are shorter than the surrounding healthy grass
- North America

Melting Out Leaf Spot

The most common leaf spot disease is melting-out, caused by *Bipolaris sorokiniana*. It affects cool-season grasses, especially common Kentucky bluegrass, and bermudagrass. Most improved grass varieties resist the disease. Lesions form on blades in cool spring and fall weather but may be seen any time of year. As weather warms, the fungus kills the blades, spreads to the base of the plant, and kills entire plants. Lawns that are excessively lush from quick-release nitrogen fertilizer or are under stress from short mowing, thick thatch, and over- or underwatering are most susceptible.

Immediate control Apply contact fungicide when you first notice leaf spotting and again at least three more times, 7 to 10 days apart.

Prevention Keep your lawn healthy and vigorous. Mow at the proper height and control excess thatch. Avoid overfertilizing. Water thoroughly once or twice a week. Try to keep the grass dry at night; do not water in late afternoon or early evening. When establishing or reseeding a Kentucky bluegrass lawn, use only improved resistant varieties.

Melting-out leaf spot

- In cool weather grass turns light, dark, or reddish brown in 2-foot-plus irregular patches of thin grass
- Small oval spots with straw-colored centers and dark borders mark leaf blades
- As the summer warms, leaves and sheaths may be covered with spots; entire plants may die
- North America

Necrotic Ring Spot

Necrotic ring spot (*Leptosphaeria korrae*) shows up during cool, wet weather in spring and fall. The main symptom is a frog-eye pattern in which a ring of dead grass surrounds living grass. The frog-eyes may merge into large blighted sections of lawn. This disease is most prevalent in compacted soil, and on exposed sites and steep slopes, and in dense turf with excessive thatch. It is common on Kentucky bluegrass, fescue, and perennial ryegrass but can attack any cool- or warm-season grass.

Immediate control Apply a systemic fungicide. Replant with a resistant variety. Fertilize to help the lawn to fill in.

Prevention Regular dethatching and core aeration help prevent necrotic ring spot. Avoid drought stress and provide adequate fertilizer. Raise the mowing height during hot summer months.

Necrotic ring spot

- Symptoms appear in cool, wet weather and subside as weather warms; they last all summer in cool areas
- Frog-eyes—rings of straw- or red-colored blades around a patch of healthy grass—develop; dead parts fade to tan
- Patches are 6 inches to several feet across; they spread outward, join to form a large blighted area
- Area can look pockmarked
- North America, especially in the East and West

Pink Snow Mold

Also known as fusarium patch, pink snow mold is caused by the fungus *Microdochium nivale*. It develops in wet weather below 65°F and can be destructive under snow, especially if the grass was growing when the first snow arrived. Pink snow mold is most likely to occur after snow has been on the ground for several months or after prolonged rainy periods. Prolonged cold worsens symptoms; turf recovers quickly if warm weather follows snow melt. Serious infection leads to crown and root rot. Pink snow mold mainly affects cool-season grasses, although it may attack bermudagrass and zoysiagrass in the right conditions.

Immediate control For seriously affected areas, apply a fungicide labeled for pink snow mold according to directions. Lightly infected turf usually recovers on its own. To encourage recovery, rake matted spots in early spring to improve air circulation to the crowns of the plants.

Prevention Reduce shade in affected areas. Avoid excess fertilizer in fall. Mow until the grass stops growing; overly tall grass is susceptible to pink snow mold. Reduce thatch buildup.

Pink snow mold

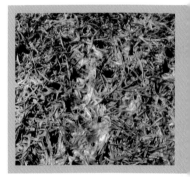

- Favored by cool, wet weather especially after snow melts
- Circular yellow-green spots start small and grow into 12-inch-wide, pinkish white patches with a rusty pink border; patches may merge
- Affected blades are matted and light tan but have no leathery, raised dots
- Northern United States and Canada, especially in the West

Powdery Mildew

Caused by the fungus *Erysiphe graminis*, powdery mildew occurs when nights are cool (65°F to 70°F) and damp and days are warm and humid. It is most severe on Kentucky bluegrass but also attacks bermudagrass and fescue. It is especially common in shady lawns, but can be found in open areas during extended wet, overcast conditions. Powdery mildew is more unsightly than damaging. It slows growth of leaf blades, roots, and underground stems, causing gradual weakening and thinning of the lawn and making it more susceptible to other problems. Some cultivars are highly susceptible, and in shade, readily thin out. Excessively fertilized, rapidly growing lawns are susceptible to attack. The fine white coating develops powdery spores that spread in the wind.

Immediate control Treat the lawn with a systemic fungicide when you first see mildew. A second application 7 to 10 days later may be needed in severe cases.

Prevention Prune surrounding trees and shrubs to reduce shade and improve air circulation. Fertilize and water moderately in shaded areas. If the grass is badly thinned by powdery mildew, reseed with more shade-tolerant grasses such as fine fescues.

Powdery mildew diagnosis

- Whitish gray mold develops on upper surfaces of leaf blades in cool, rainy weather, especially in shady areas
- Lawn looks as if it is dusted with flour
- Leaf tissue under the mold turns yellow, then tan or brown
- Severely infected plants may wither and die
- North America, especially the Northeast and the Northwest

Pythium Blight

Pythium blight (*Pythium* spp.), also called grease spot or cottony blight, attacks heat-stressed lawns when temperatures are above 85°F. Poorly drained soil, excessive moisture, and low mowing also promote it. Pythium blight is one of the worst diseases on golf courses, where it can kill the dense, lush, closely mown grass overnight. It is rarely that bad on home lawns, which generally have taller grass.

All cool-season turfgrasses are affected, with ryegrass the most susceptible. Pythium blight can also attack bermudagrass under the right conditions. The fungus spores spread easily in free-flowing water, on lawn mower wheels, and on the soles of shoes. The disease is difficult to control because it spreads so rapidly, killing large areas in hours. Pythium blight is common in fall on winter-overseeded ryegrass.

Immediate control Keep traffic off the diseased area to avoid spreading spores. Treat the lawn during hot, humid weather with a contact fungicide as soon as you notice the disease. Usually the fungicides that control pythium blight don't control other diseases and vice versa. Repeat treatments every 5 to 10 days until either the disease stops or cooler weather resumes. Severely infected areas often do not recover, and you will need to reestablish the lawn. Wait until cool weather to overseed.

Prevention Don't overwater. Improve drainage. Mow at the highest setting possible. Fertilize moderately. Control thatch.

Pythium blight diagnosis

- Irregular ½- to 4-inch spots of shriveled, light brown grass develop in hot, humid weather from April to October
- Spots grow rapidly into 1- to 10-foot-across patches
- Affected blades mat together
- Thin white threads bind blades in the morning before dew dries
- Grass can die within 24 hours
- United States east of the Rockies (the Southeast especially), and Southern California

Red Thread

The red thread fungus (*Laetisaria fuciformis*) is most serious on fine fescue and perennial ryegrass lawns, but bentgrass, Kentucky bluegrass, and bermudagrass lawns are also susceptible. It attacks only leaves and leaf sheaths and is seldom serious enough to kill a lawn. The disease is most active in cool, wet weather. Slow-growing, nitrogen-deficient lawns are most severely affected. Potassium deficiency may also make a lawn more susceptible to attack by this disease.

Immediate control If the weather conditions that favor the disease continue and the disease worsens, treat the lawn with a contact fungicide. Repeat the treatment two times at intervals of 7 to 10 days.

Prevention Fertilizing with nitrogen and potassium may improve mildly diseased lawns.

Red thread diagnosis

- Light tan to pink, 2- to 36-inch round patches appear in cool, wet weather
- Pink webs bind the grass blades
- As blades dry, ¼- to ¾-inch-long pink threads protrude from the tips
- Patches may grow together to blight large areas of the lawn if cool, wet weather continues
- Northeast to north central North America

Rust

Rust (*Puccinia* spp.) covers the surface of grass blades with a powdery, orange-brown growth composed of millions of microscopic spores. It attacks all cool- and warm-season grasses but favors Kentucky bluegrass, ryegrass, tall fescue, and zoysiagrass. Rust appears in summer and persists into fall, but where winters are mild, it can appear in late summer or early fall and be active all winter. Moist, warm weather (70°F to 75°F) and heavy dew favor its development. Grasses stressed from nitrogen deficiency or lack of moisture are most susceptible. Lawns with severe infections are likely to suffer winter damage.

Immediate control Treat severe infections with a systemic fungicide. Repeat the application every 7 to 14 days until the lawn improves. Fertilizing helps the lawn recover.

Prevention Rust often develops more slowly than the grass grows. Fertilize routinely, mow frequently and remove clippings.

Rust diagnosis

- Lawn turns orange-yellow or reddish brown and thins out
- Rusty orange powder coats blades and rubs off on fingers, shoes, and on clothing
- Color comes from reddish brown lesions on blades
- North America, except the Southwest; Canada only along the coasts

Slime Mold

Slime mold fungi are not pathogens but rather feed on decaying organic matter in the soil. Like powdery mildew, they coat grass blades with a powdery covering. A heavy coating may shade grass leaves from sunlight, causing them to turn yellow. Slime mold occurs on dichondra, all turfgrasses, and some weeds.

Slime mold starts as a slimy white, gray, or yellow mass on the soil. When it reproduces, it forms powdery balls of spores on the blades of grass. This is when slime mold is noticeable. Slime mold usually disappears in the warmer, drier conditions of summer.

Immediate control In most cases, control is not necessary because slime mold does not harm the grass. Hose off the mold with a strong stream of water or sweep it off with a broom.

Prevention Rake leaves and debris from the lawn, but other than that, there is little you can do to prevent slime mold.

Slime mold diagnosis

- Symptoms appear in spring, summer, or in fall, following heavy rains or watering
- Pinhead-size bluish gray, black, or white balls that feel powdery appear on grass blades
- Affected areas may be a few inches to several feet across
- North America

Spring Dead Spot

This disease of bermudagrass is caused by *Leptosphaeria korrae*, sometimes in conjunction with other fungi. It rots stolons and roots. Blighted dead spots develop as the grass emerges from dormancy in spring. Symptoms generally fade with time, but they may persist into summer. Bermudagrass lawns that have excess thatch or have been overfertilized or fertilized late in the growing season are more likely to be affected.

Immediate control Replace the sod and soil of badly diseased areas. Apply a systemic fungicide in late summer or early fall. Keep the lawn healthy and vigorous to encourage growth into dead areas.

Prevention Follow a moderate fertility program; maintain adequate potassium levels. Don't fertilize too late in the season. Don't let the thatch get more than ¾ inch thick.

Spring dead spot diagnosis

- Circular dead spots, up to several feet across, develop as spring growth begins
- The dead grass is sunken and straw colored; stolons and roots are blackened and decayed
- Weeds and green grass may form a frog-eye pattern; the bermudagrass that fills in is shorter than the surrounding healthy grass
- Affected areas of winter-overseeded bermudagrass lawns appear as light green spots
- Lawn may slowly recover over several months in summer
- The Transition Zone to Texas and the Gulf Coast

St. Augustinegrass decline (SAD)

Little is known about the spread of SAD except that it is caused by panicum mosaic virus. Like many viruses, it can be carried by insects that suck sap from infected plants, then transmit SAD to the next grass they feed on. The disease also spreads to healthy turf from infected grass clippings. Affected leaf blades develop a mottled yellow appearance that may spread over large sections of the lawn. Centipedegrass may also be susceptible to the disease.

Immediate control There are no chemical controls, and most cultural practices provide little relief once the disease has developed.

Prevention Replace infected grass and a few inches of topsoil. Replant with grasses known to have some resistance to SAD, such as 'DelMar', 'Floratam', and 'Raleigh'. Do not cut a healthy lawn with a mower that has recently trimmed an infected one. Do not mow wet turf.

St. Augustinegrass decline diagnosis

- In the first year after planting, the lawn grows poorly and looks weak for no apparent reason
- Leaf blades are blotched or stippled; pale green mottling eventually appears
- Symptoms mimic those of mite damage or iron deficiency
- In the second year, grass is bright yellow, stunted, and thin; dead sections develop
- Diseased plants may die before the third season
- The Gulf Coast

Summer Patch

Summer patch (*Magnaporthe poae*) infects grass roots during cool weather (60°F to 65°F), usually in late spring. Symptoms show up from June through September, when hot, dry weather follows a wet period. When hot weather arrives, the roots cannot provide enough water, and the grass blades die.

The disease is most prevalent in compacted soil and lawns with excessive thatch, especially on exposed sites and steep slopes. It is worsened by quick–release nitrogen applications and, unlike most other diseases, by infrequent watering. It can affect many types of grasses, including bentgrass, Kentucky bluegrass, and fescue—especially when cultivars are unsuitable for local conditions. The symptoms of summer patch are so similar to those of necrotic ring spot that the two diseases cannot readily be distinguished without culturing them in a lab.

Immediate control Apply a systemic fungicide to infected areas, following label directions; once this disease has developed, it may take several months for complete recovery. Reseed seriously damaged areas with resistant grasses adapted to your climate.

Prevention Any cultural practices that minimize thatch (see page 136) help prevent summer patch, as does a balanced fertilizer program. Light watering to prevent the thatch layer from becoming dry will help prevent initial development of the disease.

Summer patch diagnosis

- Scattered 4- to 8-inch-wide patches of dead turf appear in hot summer weather
- Patches may reach 1 to 2 feet across and are usually circular or crescent shaped; occasionally they are serpentine
- Frog-eye pattern develops
- If hot weather persists, the center of the patch dies
- The patches may grow together and blight large sections of lawn
- East of the Rockies in southern Canada and the United States

Yellow Patch

This disease appears in early spring as the lawn is emerging from dormancy. *Rhizoctonia cerealis*, the fungus that causes it, is especially destructive to Kentucky bluegrass and creeping bentgrass. It can also attack most cool–season grasses, including tall fescue and perennial ryegrass, as well as bermudagrass and zoysiagrass. Affected warm–season grasses turn yellow for several weeks but usually recover. Wet weather between 40°F and 60°F favors yellow patch. Symptoms disappear when temperatures are below 40°F or above 75°F. Yellow patch is easily mistaken for necrotic ring spot.

Immediate control Apply a systemic fungicide. In severe cases, you may need to renovate the lawn, resowing a resistant grass variety in affected areas.

Prevention A balanced fertilizer program and proper management steps to reduce thatch will help with prevention and recovery from damage once it has occurred.

Yellow patch diagnosis

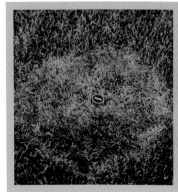

- Symptoms develop in early spring, as the lawn breaks dormancy
- Irregular circular, light green to yellow-green patches start out 2 to 3 inches across and can grow to 3 feet in diameter
- Patches are distinctly sunken and may have a frog-eye pattern
- Diseased blades develop tan lesions with dark brown borders that eventually fade to tan
- A reddish purple tint on the outer edge of the patch is possible
- Symptoms are most obvious on closely mown turf
- North America

MANAGING THATCH

There's a word for the tangled mat of organic matter that tends to accumulate in your lawn. It's called thatch and it's perfectly normal. In fact, a small amount of thatch is good for lawns. A shallow layer around the base of grass plants acts as a natural mulch to retain moisture and lower soil temperature. It cushions the plants' crowns and discourages germination of weed seeds. The decaying plant material even adds nutrients back into the soil.

A little thatch is good. But too much can cause a host of troubles in your lawn, from shallow rooting to nutrient imbalances to invasions of insects and diseases.

Two procedures will help keep thatch under control. Aeration (removing plugs of soil from the lawn) and dethatching (removing accumulated thatch) open channels for water, air, and nutrients to get through to the soil below. Both are minor procedures that help you avoid more serious complications in the future.

A little thatch, up to ½ inch thick is good. Any thicker than that and you will need to take action to maintain the quality of your lawn.

Thatch

Excess thatch—an overly thick layer of dead organic matter and living plant parts—is a common problem. Just as people slough dead skin cells and pets shed fur, grass plants cast off dead rhizomes, stolons, and crowns. Organisms in the soil—microbes, earthworms, and insects—feed on the dead matter and break it down. Thatch develops when this organic matter accumulates faster than the organisms can deal with it, which is what happens when you overfertilize and water frequently and shallowly. (Contrary to popular belief, however, leaving clippings on the lawn does not cause thatch.)

With an excess of nitrogen, the grass grows too fast for the organisms. Excess water drives oxygen out of the soil. Very high or very low soil pH may also negatively impact the organisms' ability to do their jobs and thus lead to thatch.

In thatchy lawns, the grass crown rides on top of the thatch, rather than under it, where it's insulated from heat and cold. Roots may grow into the thatch but not the soil, so the lawn is more susceptible to drought. The lawn also needs more fertilizer because thatch isn't a good source of nutrients. Thatch harbors pathogens and insect pests and impedes water infiltration. Thatchy lawns tend to be puffy or uneven, and are easy to scalp as you mow.

How do you determine whether your lawn is excessively thatchy? Look for dry and dead patches of grass and an unusual sponginess or springiness when you walk on it.

Remove a wedge of grass with a knife or trowel or remove a core with a soil probe. Dig deep enough to get some of the soil below. Carefully examine the plug so you can identify the soil, the grass, and the spongy thatch layer in between. Then measure the depth of the thatch. Thatch ½ inch or less is generally not a problem. If there is more than that, your lawn is ready for a thatch management program.

Tips for Preventing Thatch

- Resist planting vigorously growing grasses and those that produce large amounts of tough, fibrous tissue.
- Minimize activities that compact the soil.
- Avoid frequent, shallow irrigation.
- Follow an annual fertilizing program, and don't exceed recommended rates.
- Mow frequently—before the grass becomes excessively tall.

Controlling Thatch

Prevention is key. Your lawn may never have a thatch problem if you follow an annual fertilizing program, water properly, and apply lime or sulfur when a soil test indicates the pH is too high or too low.

Mechanical methods of getting rid of thatch include dethatching and core aerating. Of the two methods, core aerating is most effective, and it also helps to break up soil compaction. If thatch is a problem, you may need to dethatch or aerate once a year until it is corrected. Most home lawns will need dethatching or aerating every four or five years, as part of routine care.

Dethatching

This process involves cutting through the thatch layer and ripping out the debris. You can use a special dethatching cavex rake. It has sharp knifelike blades instead of tines and is best for small lawns and people who enjoy hard, physical work. More practical are gas-powered vertical mowers and power rakes. These are essentially the same machine with a choice of different, rapidly spinning vertical reels. Blades on vertical mower reels are solidly attached; those on power rakes swing loosely. The blades of power rakes are designed to give when they hit rocks and debris in the lawn, so the machine is less likely to suffer damage.

A word of caution Power raking and vertical mowing can damage St. Augustinegrass, centipedegrass, and others that spread by surface runners. Take care when dethatching lawns made of these grasses. Use a machine that has the knives correctly spaced for these grass plants.

Timing When to dethatch depends on the type of grass in your lawn. The ideal time for cool-season lawns is late summer or early fall. The grass readily recovers and doesn't have to compete with weeds because few germinate at this time. Dethatch at least 30 days before the end of the growing season, before the ground freezes, so the grass will have time to recover. You can also dethatch cool-season grasses in spring, before they green up. The lawn will be more susceptible to weed invasion then, however.

For warm-season lawns, late spring is the best time to dethatch. Dethatch after the turf greens up but before the hot, dry summer months set in. A good rule is to dethatch after the second mowing. Follow with a preemergence weed control to discourage crabgrass.

Step by Step For best results, dethatch after a light rain, or water the lawn beforehand. Avoid dethatching when the soil is saturated; the equipment will tear and pull the soil instead of slicing and lifting out the thatch.

Get your lawn in shape for dethatching by mowing at the lowest recommended height for your grass. Remove the clippings. If using power equipment, locate and mark all sprinkler heads, shallow irrigation pipes, and any utility lines that might be near the soil surface. Then dethatch.

The power rakes and vertical mowers available to homeowners are generally lightweight and low powered. You will need to make several passes to bring up the thatch. Make each subsequent pass perpendicular to the previous one. Don't attempt to remove the entire layer in one day; multiple passes may damage the lawn, and the raking action tends to dry the soil, which can thin the lawn. Be aware that it's possible to pull up several garbage bags of thatch from a small but heavily thatched lawn. For medium to large lawns, expect a couple of pickup-truck loads.

After you've finished raking, fertilize and irrigate. This prevents excessive drying out and helps the grass recover from injury.

Thatch-Prone Grasses

Zoysiagrass and St. Augustinegrass are thatch-prone species, but they are also easily damaged by dethatching. For maximum recovery, dethatch these grasses in the spring, as the lawn emerges from dormancy.

Use a cavex rake to dethatch small areas by hand. The tines are actually sharp blades and are more effective than a garden rake.

Whether using a power rake or a vertical mower, dethatching pulls up lots of dead organic matter.

AERATING HOW-TO

Also called coring or aerifying, aeration is the best way to reduce thatch. This simple process improves drainage and opens the thatch so water and oxygen reach roots. This helps microorganisms thrive and break down the thatch. The holes eventually fill in and grow over, but the permeability of the soil remains vastly improved. Coring aids root growth and is particularly helpful on lawns with heavy foot traffic. It's also considerably easier on the lawn than power raking.

Core aerators pull out plugs of soil, which makes them more effective at opening air channels in the ground than aerators with solid tines.

Equipment

Use a core aerator, which punches holes into the ground and removes small plugs of grass and soil. The cores create a topdressing as they crumble, further enhancing thatch breakdown. Core aerator tines make 2- to 3-inch-deep holes 2 to 4 inches apart. Some have drum-mounted tines that dig into the soil. Others have vertical tines that move up and down at a high rate of speed. Still others use solid tines or blades that poke holes into the soil without removing cores. These are the least effective.

Timing

Coring has drawbacks. It is hard on plants if you aerate when the grass is not actively growing. And bringing soil that holds weed seeds to the surface encourages weeds such as crabgrass to grow. Proper timing will help eliminate potential problems.

As with dethatching, aerate during the grass's peak growth period: late summer or early fall for cool-season grasses and spring for warm-season species. It's best not to aerate either type of grass during high-temperature stress periods.

Plan the fall project early enough that your lawn has time to recover before winter dormancy sets in, at least 30 days before the ground freezes. Avoid the primary germination period of the main weeds in your area (for example, crabgrass, goosegrass, and other summer annual weeds germinate in spring). Applying a preemergence herbicide after aerating the lawn will help keep them in check.

Step by Step

Lightly water the lawn the day before you aerate so the tines easily enter the soil and pull out plugs. (Don't overwater, though. You'll create a muddy mess that will form a hard compacted layer under the soil surface.) Be sure to flag all sprinkler heads and shallow pipes and wires.

Make two passes if the thatch is thick. The second pass should be at a right angle to the first to ensure even spacing between the holes. Let the cores dry, then use a garden rake or drag a section of chain-link fencing across the lawn to break up the cores and work some of the material back into the holes. Any remaining material will disintegrate after mowing.

Tip
Feeding the lawn after aerating or dethatching helps the grass recover and improve more quickly.

Slowing Compaction
- Reduce the negative effects of foot traffic by creating walkways in areas that receive constant use.
- Avoid driving vehicles on your lawn.
- Establish designated play areas, including access paths to them.
- Mow as often as necessary to follow the one-third rule.

For small jobs, up to 1,000 square feet, consider using a handheld corer. These tools have the same hollow tines as the powered units and perform the same function at a fraction of the cost. As when using a cavex rake, plan on getting some hard exercise doing the job. Plunge the tines into the ground, rock the corer back and forth, and pull out the tines.

Remedy for Compaction

Besides helping to reduce thatch, aeration also improves compacted soil. Compaction occurs naturally over time. Foot traffic, mowing, heavy rain, and parked vehicles all mash down your soil, compressing the top 2 to 3 inches into a dense, hard layer that seriously restricts the free movement of air, nutrients, and water into the soil. The result: stunted roots and weak grass.

You may need to aerate high–traffic areas and heavy clay soil every year or two. But even in areas with normal use, it's a good idea to aerate every three to five years.

Are there easier solutions than aerating? Consider redesigning your landscape to keep traffic to a minimum. Where the family is starting to wear a path in the grass, try installing a paved walk. Put mulch under playground equipment. In public areas you can redirect traffic with fences or walls.

Make one pass with the aerator, then make a second pass at right angles to the first. Leaving the cores where they lie helps to break down thatch because they carry microorganisms that decompose organic matter.

Root growth

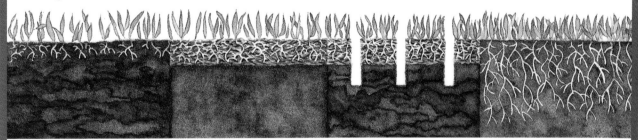

Dense, compacted soil (far left) and thick layers of thatch (center left) restrict rooting and, in turn, impair the health of the lawn. Compacted soil has no pore space for oxygen, moisture, or roots to move through; thatch forms a physical barrier. Aerating eases both conditions by creating openings in the soil, allowing air and water to enter. Microbes begin to flourish and break down the thatch. Roots again proliferate, growing thick and deep.

LAWNS IN SHADE

Using a seed mixture composed of shade- and sun-tolerant grass species ensures that all parts of a lawn will be beautiful.

Chances are good that if your yard is shady, you don't have the best lawn. Turfgrasses are full-sun plants. The lawn you established when your landscape was young and unshaded has thinned out as the trees grew.

Getting grass to grow as lush and dense in a shady yard as in a sunny one may not be possible. But there are ways to grow a better lawn. Changing your management practices will help. You can also renovate the lawn, sowing a more shade-tolerant grass that will thrive as long as the lawn receives at least four hours of filtered sun a day.

Fertilizing

Overfertilizing—whether in shade or in sun—stimulates shoot growth over root growth. The resulting succulent leaves are easy prey for pests. Because grass in shade tends to be fairly succulent anyway, overfertilizing can put the lawn at even greater risk. Always follow label directions.

It's important to fertilize shaded lawns in early spring and fall, before trees leaves emerge or after they drop. Fertilizing while the lawn has light maximizes its ability to photosynthesize and build up reserves for the shady times.

For the last feeding of the year, consider using a winterizer fertilizer, which contains greater amounts of potassium, the third number of the fertilizer analysis, than the other nutrients. Potassium aids stress tolerance and helps plants weather pest attacks and poor growing environments.

Watering

Lawns in shade often are able to get by with less water; because the shade slows soil drying. On the other hand, they could require more water if the tree's roots are particularly competitive. Keep an eye on the grass and watch for signs of wilting. Then water properly, as you would a sunny lawn, applying at least ½ inch of water twice weekly.

Mowing

If you're already mowing at the tallest recommended height for the grass, your lawn is off to a good start. If you're mowing shorter than that, raise the height. The additional leaf surface provides more area for photosynthesis so roots grow deeper and plants are healthier. Mow cool-season grasses at 3 inches tall and warm-season ones at 2 inches. Never remove more than a third of the grass blade.

Thatch and Compaction

Thatch isn't a common problem in shaded lawns. In fact, lawns in shade may not have enough thatch to cushion the crowns of the plants. That, along with the succulent grass blades, means the plants are easily damaged. If possible, limit the foot traffic and activity in shady areas of the lawn to help protect the plants and reduces compaction.

Weeds and Insects

The good news about shady lawns is that they should have little crabgrass. However, broadleaf weeds, such as ground ivy and violets, can be problems, as can greenbugs and sod webworms. See the beginning of this chapter, starting on page 80, to learn about controlling pests.

Renovate

If your shaded lawn has thinned so much that it is less than half grass, or is half weeds, it is beyond saving. At this point, you should consider overseeding with a more shade-tolerant grass, such as fine fescue or St. Augustinegrass. The chart "Shade Grasses" ranks the grasses by their tolerance for shade.

Before going to the trouble of renovating your lawn, though, assess whether your effort will be worth it. If the site receives less than four hours of sun each day and thinning the trees or raising the canopy won't substantially increase the light, plant a shade-tolerant groundcover such as pachysandra or vinca instead.

When grass gets this bad, assess how much light the area receives and replace the grass with a shade-tolerant grass species or a groundcover.

Moss

Moss moves in when a lawn thins out. It's a symptom of several problems and not necessarily the one that most homeowners assume: acid soil.

While it's true that moss thrives in soil with a pH of 5.0 to 5.5 (too acid for grass to grow), it can also be a problem where the pH is 7 or higher. Excess shade, wet soil, poor drainage, poor fertility, and compaction—which hinders drainage as well as grass growth—all can lead to moss in a lawn. Moss can even be a problem in unirrigated sites. When rains return after a drought, the moss will grow faster than the lawn.

Moss cannot invade a vigorous, healthy lawn. However, once it is there, the grass will not come back without your help.

Immediate control Apply a moss control that contains ferrous sulfate (a type of iron) following all label recommendations. Let the moss die (it will turn black), then rake it out and aerate the soil. Patch, renovate, or

reestablish your lawn depending on the size of the problem area.

Prevention Modify your yard to favor the grass instead of the moss. Prune nearby shrubs and overhead trees to let in light and air. Add drain tiles or rework the soil to eliminate drainage problems. Aerate as needed to break up compaction. If the area receives more than four hours of sunlight, you should be able to replant the lawn with a mixture of shade-tolerant grasses. In shadier spots, plant shade-tolerant groundcovers. Fertilize and water correctly for your grass and mow high.

Shade Grasses

Cool-season
- Fine fescue
- Tall fescue
- Kentucky bluegrass (some varieties)
- Perennial ryegrass

Warm-season
- St. Augustinegrass
- Zoysiagrass
- Bahiagrass
- Buffalograss
- Centipedegrass
- Bermudagrass

OTHER PROBLEMS

Chemical Spills

Pesticides, gasoline, hydrated lime, and fertilizer burn grass if overapplied or spilled. Excessive amounts of these materials dry out and kill leaf blades. Gasoline also contaminates the soil, preventing anything from growing in the area for years.

Immediate control Immediately scoop or soak up as much of the spilled material as possible (use a wet-dry vacuum for granular materials), then flush the residue through the soil. For water-soluble chemicals, irrigate thoroughly—three to five times longer than usual. For water-insoluble materials, such as gasoline or oil, flood the area with dish soap diluted in water (about the same strength as for dishwashing), then irrigate thoroughly. Some materials such as preemergence herbicides can't be washed from the soil; replace the top several inches of soil in the spill area.

Prevention Fill spreaders, sprayers, and gas tanks on a hard surface, such as a driveway. Apply chemicals according to label instructions. Push spreaders up and down slopes; a top-heavy

Chemical spill diagnosis

- Grass dies and turns yellow in irregular patterns
- Grass bordering the area is healthy
- Affected areas don't spread or enlarge
- Damage appears two to five days after a chemical has been spilled on the lawn

spreader can tip as you move sideways across the hill. If label directions recommend doing so, water after making the application. Close spreader openings when stopping or turning.

Salt and Fertilizer Damage

Salt desiccates plant tissue, drawing water out of the plant. It may come from materials put down to melt ice on sidewalks or it may be splashed from treated streets. In some locales, soil and water are naturally salty. Because fertilizer is made up of chemical salts, overfertilizing or spilling fertilizer results in the same symptoms.

Damage occurs when too little rain or irrigation water occurs to wash the salt out of the lawn. Poor drainage exacerbates the situation by keeping water from moving through the soil. As the water evaporates, the salts dissolved in it accumulate near the soil surface. In some cases, a white or dark brown crust forms.

Immediate control Wash salts out of the soil with water. Fill in low spots to aid drainage. Applying gypsum may also help; it dislodges sodium from soil particles.

Prevention If the entire lawn drains poorly, improve drainage by aerating or installing a drain-tile system. If the soil drains well, increase the amount of water applied at each watering by

Salt and fertilizer damage diagnosis

- Grass slowly dies, especially in the lowest areas of the lawn
- A white or dark crust may be present on the soil surface

50 percent or more, so that excess water can leach salts below the root zone of the grass. Fertilize properly according to label directions. Grow a salt-tolerant grass.

Dog Damage

Salts in dog urine burn grass and cause varying degrees of damage, from slight discoloration to outright death. The urine contains nitrogen, so the grass around the spot grows rapidly and turns dark green. Hot, dry weather exacerbates the damage.

Immediate control Mow high. Flush the urine from affected areas with water; this reduces but does not eradicate the damage. Let surrounding grass grow into the spot or patch with sod.

Prevention Train your pets to go to one section of the lawn. Create a mulched area at the back of your lot for the dogs.

Dog damage diagnosis

- Circular tan spots often surrounded by deep green fast-growing grass
- No spots or webbing appear on leaf blades, and grass does not mat

Moles

Moles are small rodents that have strong forelegs with long claws. They live underground and use their claws to dig their way through the soil, leaving raised ridges in their wake. Earthworms are their favorite food, but moles will feed on other soil-dwelling insects. As they mine their way through the soil, moles sever grass roots and raise the sod. These raised areas quickly dry out. The ridges also give the lawn an uneven surface that is easily scalped when you mow.

Immediate control Tamp the ridges into place and water well.

Prevention The best control is to trap the moles. Poison baits are available, however, they are not always effective and you must take great care when using them around children and pets. Applying insecticides to eliminate the moles' food source does not help, and it's best not to eliminate earthworms from the soil.

Set up the traps in active tunnels. To learn which tunnels are active, roll or tamp the ridges in early morning. Those that are raised back up by afternoon are active. Several types of traps are available. Among the most effective and easiest to use are skewer- and scissor-type traps.

Mole diagnosis

- 3- to 5-inch-wide raised ridges irregularly crisscross the lawn
- Grass in the ridges may turn brown because the soil is loose and dry

Fire Ants

Fire ants may be the worst lawn nuisance, even though all they do is build nests in a lawn. They are aggressive insects that first bite then sting their victims. The resulting white, itchy, burning pustules can send people and pets to the doctor. At one time fire ants existed mainly in the southern United States. Now, they infest lawns from eastern Texas on the west to the Carolinas on the east and as far north as Oklahoma. And they are still on the move.

Fire ants are small, red to dark orange to black or brown ants about ¼ inch long. They build conspicuous, 8- to 12-inch-tall and 18-inch-diameter dome-shaped mounds of loose soil in sunny areas. The absence of the mounds, however, does not necessarily mean fire ants do not infest your yard. Their nests can extend 3 feet into the soil and only rise above the ground in the warm, moist weather of spring and fall.

Immediate control Treat mounds with an insecticide containing bifenthrin or acephate and labeled for fire ant control. Apply it when the ants are most active: in the morning or late evening. Avoid disturbing the mound before or while treating it. If disturbed, the ants will move the queen to another location before the insect control has a chance to work. Two to three days after treating the mound, apply fire ant killer to your entire lawn.

Prevention Work with all your neighbors to ensure all nearby lawns are treated. Otherwise, stray ants will move back and forth between yards and continue to be a problem. You can also apply a feed-plus-insect control for your first feeding of the year.

Fire ant diagnosis

- 8- to 12-inch-tall mounds of loose soil dot the lawn
- Ants become extremely aggressive when they or their mound are disturbed.

REVIVING YOUR LAWN

Even lawns get tired. Sometimes you inherit a tired lawn when you buy a house. Sometimes you help wear it out yourself because you're too busy to give it the time or attention it needs over the years. Even a single season of extreme heat and drought can push your lawn to permanent fatigue.

There are many reasons why lawns deteriorate and stay that way. This chapter will help you get your lawn back in shape. In most instances, you'll find that it's remarkably easy: a little fertilizer and water, and you're back in business. In other cases, it's not that simple but can be done. The following pages will walk you through the steps of reviving your lawn.

REVIVING YOUR LAWN DIGEST

A Renovating Experience

- Exactly how you improve your lawn depends upon your assessment of the current situation and, to a degree, upon your own standards.

- Repairing the lawn is a partial renovation. It means sowing new seed or patching with sod but beyond that, you're essentially working with what you've got. Choose this route to reinvigorate a thin or weak lawn that is otherwise okay.

- Renovation starts with killing all the weeds and grass in your lawn with a nonselective weed control, and then sowing seeds. Renovate if a good weed-and-feed isn't enough to improve the lawn, or if you don't need to till amendments into the soil or grade the soil.

- Reestablishment means starting over. It's stripping off existing sod—or whatever is left of it—then tilling and amending the soil as necessary, just as you would when installing a new lawn. You might have to take measures this drastic if the soil grade or drainage is wrong or if the soil needs lots of lime or sulfur tilled into it to correct the pH.

TO DO

- Assess the damage.
- Determine the underlying problem, then fix it.
- If things aren't too bad, fertilize (or use a weed-and-feed), and fill in bare spots. If there's little left to work with, renovate.
- If you need to make major changes, such as regrading the lot, plan on starting from scratch. Turn to the next chapter, starting on page 156.

Start With Simple Measures

Water and fertilizer may be all it takes to improve your lawn. Put your lawn on a good feeding and watering regime and see how it responds. If your lawn is in very bad shape, however, spray with a nonselective herbicide and start over.

After Drought

Grass is quite resilient. Even though it may appear dead after prolonged drought, it may simply be dormant. When watering restrictions end, irrigate well. As the grass resumes growth, evaluate the extent of its injuries before taking any action.

Why Renovate?

- More than half of the lawn is weeds.

- Hard-to-kill perennial weeds such as quackgrass are taking over.

- Summer drought, insects, or a flood has killed the lawn.

- You want to convert to a better-looking and better-performing grass.

- The lawn is more than 10 years old. Older grasses are more susceptible to diseases and insects than are new, improved varieties.

What to Do After a Hurricane

After the storm, you'll find uprooted trees, standing water, and silt and mud deposits on the lawn. The worst damage may come from salt-laden seawater, which can be blown inland or carried in on a tidal surge.

Remove all debris, mud, and silt covering the lawn. Then irrigate to wash away salts. If using water from a well, have it tested to be sure it's not contaminated with salt. Core aerate so that water and salts move through the soil. Applying gypsum helps remove the salts. Water frequently and deeply until you're sure all the salt is washed beyond the root zone.

After a Flood

Flooded lawns are likely to survive under these conditions:

- They are submerged for fewer than four days to as many as six days.

- Temperatures are below 60°F during this period.

- The water is flowing, not stagnant, so it is supplying grass roots with adequate oxygen.

- The later of silt is 1 inch deep or less.

- No erosion has occurred.

- In warm-season regions, the grass is bermudagrass or zoysiagrass.

- Petroleum products haven't contaminated the soil.

Repairing the damage

- Remove the debris. Core aerate to help dry out the soil surface and break up crusty soil. Hose off as much silt as possible. Break up the remaining silt crust with a rake. Fertilize.

- If the grass died, reestablish the lawn. Remove as much of the silt as possible. Till the soil, taking care to mix flood deposits with the dead grass and soil and to break up the old sod layer. Replant with an improved grass variety.

Myths, Facts & Good Advice

Myth: It's spring and time to renovate your lawn.

Fact: True for renovating warm-season grasses, but false for cool-season grasses.

Advice: Timing is everything. Get it right for the kind of grass you grow. In the North, renovate cool-season grasses in late August, September to mid-October in the mild-winter West, and early spring in the South.

Myth: For a new lawn, just scatter seed over the old lawn and water.

Fact: The odds are against seeds sown on top of old grass and weeds. They may sprout, but their roots won't reach the soil.

Advice: Scalp or slice the old lawn so that the seed is in direct contact with soil. For best results, rent a slit-seeder.

Myth: Seed is the only way to fix a lawn.

Fact: Patches of sod are a quick fix for dead or weedy spots.

Advice: Cut a section of sod to fit with a heavy-duty knife or other cutter. Tamp the sod in place. Water daily until the sod starts to root.

PATCHING VS. RENOVATING

A lawn with only a few damaged patches, totalling less than 30 percent of the area, will require only simple repairs. Determine the cause of damage first so that you won't need to repeat repairs in the future.

If more than 50 to 70 percent of your lawn is damaged, you will need to renovate it.

Weedy, thin lawns can often be salvaged or brought back to life without starting from scratch. Often, it's simply a matter of getting on a regular fertilizing and watering schedule and mowing at the correct height.

However, you can't begin to fix your lawn until you know how bad off it is. Then you will have a clear idea of how big the job is and what it will involve, whether it's a matter of a few simple repairs or starting from scratch.

Evaluating the extent of the damage involves determining what caused the lawn to deteriorate in the first place. Lawns go bad for many reasons: lack of care, disease or insect attack, poor drainage, thin topsoil, or growing a grass species unsuited to your region, to name a few. Correcting the cause of the problem must be part of the overall repair process; otherwise any improvements you try to make to the lawn may suffer the same fate.

Once you've figured out the problem with your lawn, economics will certainly play a role in deciding how to fix it. What level of imperfection is acceptable to you? If you demand absolute perfection, the cost will be much higher than if you can live with a few minor problems. The following guidelines will help you determine the size of the job ahead.

Repair Repairing a lawn involves patching bare spots or changing maintenance practices. Repairs are appropriate if more than 70 percent of the lawn is in good shape, if the lawn consists of improved varieties of a well-adapted grass, and if only easy-to-control weeds such as crabgrass infest it.

Renovate Renovating involves killing and replacing the existing lawn without tilling, grading, or any of the other tasks involved in installing a new lawn. It's easier and less expensive than installing a brand-new lawn. It's also generally the best solution when you don't need to work on the soil, but the grass is in such bad shape that simply changing your maintenance practices, starting an annual lawn program, or patching a few bare spots can't improve it. For example, renovation is the answer if more than 50 percent of the lawn has thinned, the lawn was established with an unsuitable grass species, or it is infested with aggressive perennial grass weeds.

Reestablish This means starting from scratch. If the soil on the site is unacceptable—is poorly drained, has thin topsoil, needs to be graded, or requires modification with organic matter, lime, sulfur, or other material—the area will likely require complete reestablishment. The chapter starting on page 156 will walk you through the process.

Evaluating the Lawn

An easy first step in determining whether you need to repair, renovate, or reestablish is to fertilize the lawn. The most common reason lawns deteriorate is that they lack nutrients. If the soil is nutrient deprived, the longest a lawn can last without being fertilized is two seasons. After five years, the lawn may look so bad that you may think the only solution is to replace it. Actually, such a lawn has a good chance of responding quickly to fertilizer. The easiest way to find out whether fertilizing will revive your run-down lawn is to try it.

Following label directions for timing and quantity, apply a good-quality fertilizer. If broadleaf weeds are also a problem, as they often are in nutrient-starved lawns, also apply a postemergence broadleaf weed control or use a weed-and-feed to save a step. If the grass responds in two to four weeks with new, vigorous growth, you're on your way; resolve to give your lawn good care regularly and to follow an annual fertilization program. If it doesn't improve, look more closely, starting with the soil—the key to a healthy, vigorous lawn.

Soil Dig into the upper 6 inches of soil. Is there sufficient topsoil for proper rooting? Check its depth; there should be a minimum of 4 to 6 inches of topsoil. Send a soil sample to a laboratory for testing. See page 166 for more information.

Check whether rocks or debris are buried in the topsoil by poking a long screwdriver into problem spots. Although it may seem odd that you might find debris in the soil, it's a common practice among building contractors to bury rocks, bricks, leftover stakes, and other construction debris rather than haul them from the construction site. Problems resulting from this practice may not show up for years, then become apparent during dry weather, when the grass over the buried material wilts because its root system is restricted. Wood debris also may lead to circles called fairy rings.

Also pay attention to low areas in the yard where water stands after a rain or watering. When surface drainage is poor or nonexistent, debris is buried, or the top soil is shallow or of poor quality, you'll need to remove the existing grass, replace the topsoil or add amendments to it, regrade

the site, and replant—in other words, reestablish the lawn.

Grass Try to determine the predominant type of grass in the lawn. Many poor lawns are the result of grass struggling to survive where it is not adapted to the conditions on the site. If it's a remnant of an old pasture grass, nothing can be done to improve it except renovation. But if it's a lawn grass, such as Kentucky bluegrass, some fertilizer and a little care may quickly restore it to good shape.

Many older lawns suffer because trees have matured and now shade the grass. Or the lawn was established before insect- and disease-resistant varieties were available, and the older variety can't stand up to attack. Here again, renovation is required.

Identifying the grass species can be difficult, especially in a neglected lawn. Many older lawns are made up of a hodgepodge of grasses, a result of random attempts to reseed over the years. For clues, see the section describing individual turfgrasses beginning on page 180.

Weeds Neglected lawns are likely to have a variety of weeds. Knowing which ones thrive in your lawn is important in determining a course of action.

Perennial broadleaf weeds such as dandelion and plantain are easily controlled with a selective herbicide. Annual grasses are more of a problem but can generally be handled without killing the entire lawn. Perennial grass weeds are the hardest to eliminate; if they infest a large part of your lawn, you will need to kill them (and the lawn they infest) with a nonselective herbicide, and then renovate.

The perennial grass weeds that cause the worst problems in cool-season lawns are quackgrass, coarse-textured tall fescue, and smooth brome. Those in warm-season lawns are johnsongrass and torpedograss. All have rhizomes (underground stems) that allow them to regrow even after their tops are removed. The chapter starting on page 80 will help you identify which weeds infest your lawn.

See page 166 for more information.

Evaluate the Lawn

Checking the health of your lawn is a three-step process.

1 First evaluate the soil. Check the depth and quality of the topsoil.

2 Next evaluate the plants. Look closely at the roots, noting their depth and health.

3 Also try to identify the grass to learn whether it can take the conditions in your yard.

PATCHING

Areas of minor damage can develop in lawns for a variety of reasons, from the moving van leaving tracks in the yard to the kids wearing a path between the back door and the swing set to a dog digging in a favorite spot. Every lawn suffers some

For medium-sized spots—saucer-sized to a few feet across—patching is a viable repair method.

kind of damage at one time or another. Luckily, most readily repair themselves. But sometimes a dead or damaged spot is too large or too prominent to assume it will heal on its own. And if you let it go, weeds have a nasty habit of creeping in. That's when you need to get involved. With just a few basic techniques, you can repair the damage, using seed, sod, sprigs, or plugs.

How To Patch

The first step in patching a lawn is ensuring that the damage doesn't recur. You can assume a moving van won't be back, but if the kids still play on the swing, it may be smarter to install a walkway to the set than to patch

Tip
Use a bulb planter or golf cup cutter to cleanly dig up a patch of grass that needs repair, such as the spot the family dog uses.

the grass. Likewise, if damage resulted from insects or disease, you must take corrective action so another attack won't damage the new grass.

Begin by squaring uneven sides and cutting away ragged edges around the area. If you need to bring in soil to raise the area to the level of the undamaged lawn surrounding it, be sure it matches the existing soil. Major changes in soil type can cause growth variations because of moisture or fertility differences.

Plant a grass species or variety in the patch that matches the existing lawn so the repaired area won't be visible. Grasses show surprising variation in their green color. These color differences occur regardless of how much you fertilize, and simply fertilizing will not mask them. Textures also vary greatly and may be readily apparent when different grasses are combined.

After making the patch, give it a dose of starter fertilizer. Later, feed the entire lawn so that the patched area blends in as quickly as possible.

Take care when mowing a recently patched lawn. Riding mowers can damage areas that are not yet mature. Sodded patches will stabilize in 10 to 14 days; seeded patches may require several weeks before you can run a mower over the area.

Products that combine fertilizer, seed, and mulch, such as PatchMaster, make it possible to put down seed at the right rate, keep it moist until it germinates, and meet the germinating grass's nutritional needs in one step.

Making Repairs

The steps for patching a lawn are fairly simple. They apply to whatever you use to patch with—seed, sod, sprigs, or plugs.

1 First, square off the damaged area. This makes for a tidier patch. You'll also find it easier to cut a piece of sod to match the damaged area. Use a spade to do the work.

2 Rough up the soil surface. This helps the seed, sod, sprigs, or plugs make good contact with the soil. If repairing tire tracks, loosen them with a garden fork. Insert the tines into the tracks and pull back. If you will be seeding, sprigging, or plugging, use bagged lawn soil to bring the soil up to the level of the existing lawn. If you're going to use sod to patch the area, establish the new soil level about ½ to ¾ inch below the existing lawn grade to make room for the layer of soil under the sod.

3 Sprinkle seed or sprigs over the prepared soil. Dig holes for plugs and insert them. Cut a section of sod that roughly matches the size of the damaged area; lay it on the prepared soil and finish trimming it to size. Use a heavy-duty knife, an old butcher knife, or a small hatchet to cut sod.

4 Make sure the seed, sod, sprigs, or plugs make good contact with the soil. Carefully press the area with the back of a garden rake.

5 Water the patched area thoroughly. Apply a starter fertilizer, following label directions. Water in the fertilizer, then keep the patch moist until the seed germinates or the sod, sprigs, or plugs root. To check rooting, tug on the grass. If it resists, its roots have begun to grow.

RENOVATING

Renovating calls for vigorously cultivating the soil with a power rake—the same equipment used for dethatching—or a slit-seeder (see page 147), then sowing seed or installing plugs or sprigs into the existing lawn. Choose this solution when the soil is in good shape—loose, well drained, and level—but your grass is not and fertilizing doesn't improve it. This is also the method to use when you need to eliminate perennial weeds or to switch the lawn from an older, disease-prone grass species to an improved or better-adapted variety.

Because you are sowing seed or installing plugs or sprigs, the best time to renovate is the same as the best time to start a lawn for your particular type of grass. Sow cool-season grass seed in late summer to early fall; seed or set out plugs or sprigs of warm-season grasses in late spring, as soon as soil temperatures are warm enough for seed germination and root growth.

When seeding, use the rate listed on the seed package for new lawns. You can also increase the rate slightly, up to 20 percent, to compensate for the seeds that are lost in the dead grass and never germinate. However, if you prepare the seedbed well to ensure good seed-to-soil contact, you can probably get by using the normal rate.

How to Renovate

Spray a nonselective herbicide, such as glyphosate. Glyphosate is especially good for this job because it moves into and throughout all the underground plant parts, including rhizomes. It will kill most grasses and broadleaf plants. In addition, it has no soil activity, so it will not leave a residue to damage future germinating seedlings.

Where rhizomatous perennial grass weeds, such as smooth brome, quackgrass, johnsongrass, or torpedograss, infest the old lawn, wait at least 10 days after spraying before planting, depending on the product you use. This allows time for the herbicide to move into the rhizomes and for you to ensure that the entire weed is dead. If you start work before the weeds are completely dead, cutting off their dead tops but leaving living rhizomes in the soil, the weeds will grow back after the new lawn is planted and your efforts will have been for naught.

With especially persistent weeds, it's a good idea to spray a second time 10 to 30 days after the initial application. This will ensure the weeds are gone before you replant so that they can't overrun your new lawn. For the best results, follow all label recommendations for the product you use.

Once the existing vegetation is dead, set your mower to its lowest setting ($\frac{1}{2}$ to $\frac{3}{4}$ inch) and scalp the grass, mowing it as low as possible. If too much dead vegetation remains, the new seeds will have difficulty reaching the soil to germinate. The goal is to leave a modest amount of dead grass to serve as a natural mulch and protect the new seedlings. However, it shouldn't be so tall that it blocks sunlight.

Next, cultivate the soil. Use a power rake to further thin the existing vegetation and expose the soil. For this purpose, set the height of the blades lower than you would for dethatching. The blades should reach through the thatch and slightly into the soil. Cutting through the old lawn and into the soil is an important step that ensures new seeds make contact with soil. Power rake the old lawn in one direction, then go back over it at a right angle.

If your soil is heavy clay or seriously compacted, core aeration at this stage

Winter Overseeding

Throughout the southern United States, the Southwest, and the mild-winter West, warm-season lawns are overseeded with a cool-season grass in winter so that lawns remain green year-round. When the warm-season grass is dormant and straw brown, the cool-season grass thrives. Then the warm-season grass takes over again in spring.

The process of winter overseeding is similar to renovating. But when winter overseeding, you must take care to not kill the existing vegetation. Also the amount of seed you use is much greater than the normal amount recommended for either establishing a new lawn or renovating an older one, up to 30 or more pounds per 1,000 square feet. Extra seed is necessary because much of it will fall on top of the dormant grass and die before the roots of the germinating seedling reach the soil.

How to Overseed
After the warm-season grass goes dormant, or nearly dormant, mow it closely. Then, using a slit-seeder, sow the cool-season grass. Water well until the seeds germinate and take hold. Maintain the overseeded grass throughout the winter as you would any other lawn, mowing and watering as needed.

Grasses for Overseeding
Not all cool-season grasses are suited for winter overseeding. The grass must die out in spring, about the time the warm-season grass is coming alive again. Many cool-season grasses are too persistent to be effective. Rough bluegrass and perennial ryegrass are the ones most commonly used to overseed, with perennial ryegrass the preferred choice because it has better color and mowing characteristics. Fine fescues are also sometimes used.

is beneficial (see page 138). It brings additional soil to the surface and opens holes to air out the soil below. After you rake out the cores, you have a good location for seed germination. Make sure to rent a core aerator and not one with solid tines.

Next, apply the seed over the site as described for standard lawn establishment on page 173. Then go over the lawn area one more time lightly with the power rake. Although it seems this might damage the seeds, it actually helps work them into the soil and improves germination. You could also work the seed into the stubble with a leaf rake. Finish with a final raking—power or leaf rake—to smooth out uneven areas.

You can combine cultivating and seeding into one step by using a slit-seeder (also called a renovator). A heavy, power machine, it combines the functions of a vertical mower and a seed spreader, dropping the seed onto the soil behind the spinning blades. It is most appropriate where compaction is not a problem. Place half the total amount of seed needed in the hopper and seed the lawn in one direction. Add the rest of the seed and go back over the lawn at a right angle to the first pass.

After seeding, make an application of starter fertilizer, which is higher in phosphorus than in nitrogen or potassium.

Keep the seedbed moist until you can see the green of the new seedlings; gradually lengthen the time between waterings as the roots establish and grow more deeply.

Renovation Step by Step

1 Kill the existing lawn with a nonselective herbicide. Spray on a calm day, following all label directions. Be sure to apply the herbicide evenly, leaving no missed spots or strips.

2 Once the weeds and the old lawn are completely dead (in 10 to 40 days), scalp the grass. Mow low, as low as ½ inch if your mower allows. This helps ensure the seed reaches the soil, where it can germinate and take hold. The dead grass that remains provides a mulch for germinating seeds.

3 Cultivate the soil. Run a power rake over the grass, slicing through the thatch and into the soil (left). If the soil is compacted, core aerate to open it up (right). Rake the cores into the holes. You can also use a slit-seeder to cultivate and seed in one step (see step 6).

Renovating your lawn offers the opportunity to change over to new, improved grass varieties, which are more stress- and pest-tolerant.

4. Sow the seed at the rate you would use when starting a new lawn on bare soil. (You can sow up to 20 percent more seed than the normal rate.)

5. Go over the lawn one more time with the power rake (left) or with a leaf rake (right). This helps work the seed into the soil and improves germination. Finish with a final raking with a leaf rake to smooth uneven areas, then apply Scotts Starter Fertilizer. Water well until the grass germinates and is tall enough to mow.

6. Where compaction is not a problem, use a slit-seeder to combine Steps 3 through 6 into one. It drops seed as it slices through the soil. Sow the seed in two passes: half in one direction, the other half at a right angle to the first.

155

BRAND NEW LAWN

Anew lawn is like a brand new day—a clean slate, a fresh start. There are no weeds to taunt you, no bare patches to discourage you. A bright, healthy new lawn makes your entire yard and even the architecture of your home more appealing for the best possible impression.

Aside from the attraction of a beautiful lawn, if you have a newly built home, you can appreciate the urgency of establishing the lawn. In a heavy rain, its network of roots holds the soil in place better than any mulch. And if you have children or pets coming and going, you know the value of a lawn is in keeping the dirt in your yard and not on your clean kitchen floor.

A brand-new lawn figures heavily in a child's life. Lawns are, after all, places where childhood memories are made. That's why there are so many grass stains in the laundry. Grass makes an ideal playground and a soft mattress beneath a picnic blanket.

Choosing the right grass for your site, budget, and lifestyle is the secret to the success of your new dream lawn. Get it off to a good start, so your lawn will live up to your vision for it.

BRAND NEW LAWN DIGEST

Wait Out Weeds

If you sow seeds in spring or summer, you can expect weeds, as well as grass. But you can reduce their numbers. Here's how:

Prepare the soil for planting, water, then wait. In about 10 days a crop of weeds will appear. Kill the weeds without disturbing the soil—usually with an herbicide such as glyphosate. Or if you have the time to wait some more, kill them by lightly cultivating the seedlings. Water and wait for another 10 days, repeating a third or fourth time or until no new weeds appear.

TO DO

- Decide on a method.
- Get rid of existing grass and weeds.
- If you have time, send in a soil sample for testing two to four weeks before planting.
- Measure lawn.
- Buy materials: seed or sod, lime or sulfur, fertilizer, and topsoil.
- Grade the soil.
- Plant.

Q&A

Q When is a grass like James Dean?

A When it's cool. Cool-season grasses do best in northern regions. They prefer cool weather, growing best in spring and fall and slowing down during hot weather.

Warm-season grasses, on the other hand, prefer southern areas because they grow best during summer's warmest weather.

Q What's the point?

A Select a grass that's adapted to your region. And plant it just before or during its optimum growth period. That's late summer to early fall for cool-season grasses, late spring or early summer for warm-season grasses.

Did You Know?

- A lawn seed mixture that is 30 percent Kentucky bluegrass and 70 percent fine fescue will make a lawn that is 50 percent of each. Why? There are different size seeds and thus different amounts of seed per pound.

- A new lawn from seed has about 10 to 20 tiny grass seedlings per square inch. A well-maintained, mature lawn has about six plants per square inch.

- Sod weighs about 3 pounds per square foot. A typical strip of sod—2 feet wide and 6 to 8 feet long—weighs about 40 pounds.

Save Some Work

A soil test saves work two ways. First, you may discover that you don't need to till the soil or add amendments to it. That's rare, but it happens. More likely, you'll learn which specific amendments are needed—usually some lime or sulfur to change pH, a little fertilizer, and organic matter—and how much. That means you won't be wasting time, energy, or money on unnecessary materials. Second, soil tests save work because your lawn will be healthier and less problem prone.

Reading Between the Lines

By law, the label on a seed package must list all weed seed as a percentage of the bag's weight. But what's not clear is the fact that not all weeds are equal. Consider: One needlegrass seed weighs the same as 32 chickweed seeds. Let's say that in a typical bag of grass seed, these two weeds make up 0.27% of the total with the chickweed just 0.1% of the weight. Even with that small percentage, if all the seeds in the bag germinated, 560,000 chickweed seedlings would pop up in your new lawn, but only 18,000 needlegrasses.

Seed or Sod?

Why seed?	Why sod?
■ Lower cost. Savings are proportional to lawn size: The bigger the lawn, the greater the savings. Seed also gives you more choices in grass variety.	■ It's fast. Go from bare dirt to fancy lawn in a day. You can plant anytime, weather permitting.

Myths, Facts & Good Advice

Myth: Lawn seed is all the same. Save money and buy cheap.

Fact: Lawn seed is highly variable, and the most expensive seed is only a small fraction of the cost of a new lawn.

Advice: Plant the best seed you can find and make sure it's weed free.

Myth: Spring is the best time to sow seed.

Fact: Spring is OK for cool-season grasses, but fall is best. In spring, you'll get a good crop of weeds along with the grass. Sow seed of warm-season grasses in late spring.

Advice: Sow seed during the grasses' optimum growth period.

Myth: All those weeds came in the grass seed.

Fact: There are more dormant seeds waiting on or in soils than could possibly come in with lawn seed. Reduce weeds in prepared soil before sowing (see page 158).

Advice: Buy top-quality seed. Read the label to ensure it contains little weed, noxious weed, or other crop seed.

Myth: There's no need to improve the soil for sod.

Fact: For the best lawn, soil preparation should be the same whether you are starting the lawn from seed or from sod.

Advice: Prepare soil for sod as for seed. Add amendments as needed, eliminate weeds, grade to a level surface, and work soil into a fine tilth.

THE BASICS OF A NEW LAWN

Seeding vs. Sodding

Cost is the main difference between seeding a 1,000-square-foot Kentucky bluegrass lawn or sodding it. Seed runs about $10, sod about $200. Whichever you use, getting the site ready costs the same.

Although it's more expensive to start a lawn with sod, you will have a lawn when the job is done. Water daily until the sod is well rooted.

The steps involved in establishing a lawn include preparing and grading the soil, selecting a grass that will grow well in your region and that matches the way you'll use your yard, then installing it using the most appropriate method for the time of year and the type of grass you've chosen.

Seeding is the most popular method of planting simply because it is the easiest and least expensive. It also gives you a greater choice in varieties. However, not all grasses

can or should be grown from seed. And if the completion of your new home doesn't coincide with the best season for seeding, laying sod is the better option.

Sprigging and plugging are more economical than sodding when it comes to the amount of plant material you need to buy. But these methods take more labor to install the lawn and to control weeds until the grass has filled in.

Timing Is Everything

The ideal time for starting either warm- or cool-season lawns is at the beginning of the grasses' most active period of growth. For warm-season grasses, that time is summer. So spring and early summer are the best times for installing a warm-season lawn.

Cool-season lawns grow most actively in fall and spring and usually go semidormant during summer's heat and drought. The best times to install a cool-season lawn, then, are late summer, early fall, and spring.

Warm-season grasses Sod, seed, sprig, or plug warm-season grasses anytime from early spring on the Gulf Coast to June in the Transition Zone.

Warm-season grasses are usually grown vegetatively—that is, planted by sodding, plugging, or sprigging. Common bermudagrass can be seeded, but the finer-textured hybrids must be established vegetatively. Zoysiagrass seed is slow to germinate and so it is usually sodded or plugged. St. Augustinegrass also can be established by seed, but the improved,

GRASSES FOR SEEDING	GRASSES FOR SODDING
Bahiagrass	Bahiagrass
Bluegrass	Bluegrass
Buffalograss	Buffalograss
Centipedegrass	Centipedegrass
Common bermudagrass	Fescue
Fescue	Hybrid bermudagrass
Ryegrass	St. Augustinegrass
	Zoysiagrass

disease-resistant cultivars must be grown from plugs or sod. Centipedegrass, bahiagrass, and buffalograss can be established by seeding or sodding.

Cool-season grasses Cool-season grasses, which include bluegrass, ryegrass, and tall and fine fescues, are easy to start from seed. Bluegrass and tall fescue can also be sodded.

The best times to plant cool-season grasses are in late summer and early fall. Temperatures are warm enough then for seeds to germinate, yet moderate enough that the lawn is able to become established before winter arrives. Spring is the second best time to start a cool-season lawn. Avoid the temptation to sow seed too early in spring. The soil must be 55°F to 59°F at a 4-inch depth for the seed of most grasses to germinate. In some areas, this may not occur before the middle of May or later.

In spring, it's better to sod rather than seed. Although you can seed cool-season grasses easily enough in spring, you must control summer weeds such as crabgrass, goosegrass, and foxtail, which will overrun a new seeding when the weather turns hot. Siduron is the only preemergence herbicide that will stop crabgrass from growing while allowing the seeds of cool-season lawn grasses to germinate properly. Look for Scotts Starter Fertilizer, which includes this weed control. (Warm-season grasses don't have this problem because they continue to grow in hot weather.)

Late fall and winter are risky times to try to establish a lawn by seeding, especially in areas with freezing weather when soil erosion may be a problem. Wait for the soil to freeze, then seed. The seed germinates in spring when the soil warms, and the seedlings hold the soil during spring rains.

For more information on when to establish grasses in your area, contact your county extension service or a garden center. You can also call The Scotts Helpline (800/543-8873). Extension offices, located at universities in many states, will also have information on the Internet. Search the name of the university and the word *extension*. When you get to the site, link to information on the subject of lawn care.

Using seed to start a lawn is a less expensive option with an additional benefit: More varieties and types of grass are available as seed.

Sod, Sprigs, and Plugs

- Sod refers to the rectangular strips of grass cut from a sod farm field, transported fresh, then laid on prepared soil for an instant lawn.

- Plugs are 2- to 4-inch squares or circles that you cut from sod or buy precut, then plant in a grid, 6 to 12 inches apart. Zoysiagrass and St. Augustinegrass are most often grown this way. Plugs may take one or two seasons to spread and cover the soil, depending on how far apart you space them.

- Sold in bags, sprigs are grass plants with no soil attached. Scatter them across the surface of prepared soil, and keep them moist. Grasses sown this way spread readily to fill in the gaps. A sprigged lawn can fill in quickly, reaching maturity by the end of the first growing season. If the season is unusually dry or cool, this may take longer.

Sprigs

Plugs

Sod

BUYING SEED & SOD: RECOGNIZING QUALITY

Because high-quality seed is limited in quantity, it sells for a premium price. But when compared with the other expenses associated with establishing a new lawn—such as grading, topsoil, and amendments—the cost of seed is insignificant.

To ensure you get good-quality seed, buy from a reliable source and select the best cultivar available. Shop early, because at the end of the season most of the good seed will be gone. Buy seed that has been stored in a cool, dry location—and do the same at home until you are ready to plant.

Always read the label. Note particularly the date tested to be sure the seed is fresh. The germination percentage listed on the package tells you how much of the seed will actually grow into a plant; it should be at least 85 percent. Inert matter—nonseed material, such as chaff or dirt—should not exceed 3 percent.

The amount of weed seed is important, as is other-crop seed. A seed lot can be weed free yet contaminated if it contains a significant amount of other-crop seed. Many of the worst weeds in turf are perennial grasses such as smooth brome, orchardgrass, and timothy, which are listed as crops, not weeds. Noxious weeds are especially troublesome. Ideally, a package of seed will contain no weed, other-crop, or noxious-weed seed.

Mixtures and Blends

Most seed available to consumers is either a mixture (several grass species) or a blend (several varieties of one species). The reason seed is packaged as blends and mixtures is to ensure that the grass you buy is as adaptable to your particular conditions as possible. For example, one grass in the package may do better in sunny areas while another is good in shade. Or one grass may be resistant to a certain disease or insect, while another resists different pests. With a blend or mixture, you can buy one package of seed and successfully grow a new lawn, no matter how diverse the growing conditions in your yard.

Calculating How Much Seed

How much seed you'll need to buy depends on which grass you choose. You can start a lawn with as little as 1 pound of Kentucky bluegrass seed per 1,000 square feet or as much as 7 pounds of tall fescue seed.

The amount varies because the sizes of the seeds vary. Small-seeded grasses, such

Reading the Label

The label is the best way to learn about a seed's quality. Every label is required by law to have an analysis panel to tell consumers exactly what's in the bag. Here's how to read it:

- This is how much seed can germinate.
- These are the specific-named varieties.
- This assures that the named varieties and amount of other ingredients are as listed.
- Look for 0% or as close to 0% as possible.

SCOTTS™ PURE PREMIUM
SUN & SHADE MIX
GRASS SEED MIXTURE

Pure Seed	Variety/Kind	Germination	Origin
27.79%	Abbey Kentucky Bluegrass	87%	WA
25.35%	Badger Creeping Red Fescue	87%	CAN
24.47%	Evening Shade Perennial Ryegrass	90%	OR
20.43%	Affinity Perennial Ryegrass	90%	OR

Other Ingredients

0.45%	Other Crop Seed	Lot No. 60663
1.50%	Inert Matter	Tested 06/06 SELL BY: Feb. 28, 2007
0.01%	Weed Seed	In FL and LA SELL BY: Dec. 31, 2006

Noxious Weed Seeds: None Found
Net Weight 3 Lbs. (1.36 KG.)

In CO,IL,MT,NE,SD,WI and WY
SELL BY: May 31, 2007
In AK,AZ,CA,ID,MN,ND,NH,NV,NY,OH,OR,PA,
UT,VT,WA and DC SELL BY: Aug. 31, 2007

The Scotts Company
14111 Scottslawn Road
Marysville, Ohio 43041   AMS 238   111040s

as Kentucky bluegrass, have more seeds per pound than large-seeded grasses. The more seeds in a pound, the fewer pounds it takes to cover a yard. In addition, grasses that spread, such as Kentucky bluegrass and most of the warm-season grasses, can be started with less seed because they have stolons or rhizomes that quickly fill in the lawn. Bunchgrasses, such as perennial ryegrass or tall fescue, which do not spread, must be seeded at a higher rate.

The different size seeds could present a problem in mixes and blends. However, the seed supplier will have calculated the amount to sow to make sure the seed of each grass in the mix goes down at the right rate. You'll find that information on the package label, either as a spreader setting or as pounds of seed to sow for a certain size area. Be sure to follow those recommendations carefully.

Calculating how much seed or sod to buy requires knowing the square footage of your lawn-to-be. If the space is approximately square or rectangular, multiply its length by its width to get the square footage. If it is irregularly shaped or in separate pieces, divide it into uniform geometric areas, calculate the area of each, and add them together.

As an example of how to calculate the amount of seed to buy, let's say your lawn is 2,500 square feet, and you know from the bag that you need to sow 7 pounds of seed per 1,000 square feet. Multiply 7 by 2½ to find that you need 17½ pounds of seed ($2,500 \div 1,000 = 2.5 \times 7 = 17.5$).

Buying Sod, Sprigs, and Plugs

Sod Shopping for sod is like buying fruit at the market: Fresh is best. Order the exact amount you need and have it delivered directly to your home as close to installation time as possible. If you must hold the sod a few days, store it in a single layer in a shaded spot, and keep it moist.

Examine the sod. It should be green and healthy looking. Check for weeds and symptoms of diseases or insects. In addition, make sure that it was grown on

soil similar to your own. For example, if sod grown on muck (organic) soil is laid on clay, it will not root well. Likewise, sod grown on clay soil is unsuitable for a sandy site. You may be able to buy directly from a local sod farm that has the same kind of soil you do. If you're buying from a garden center, ask where its sod comes from.

From the producer's viewpoint, sod should be harvested so that a minimum amount of soil is removed from the sod farm. This not only conserves soil, it makes the sod lighter and easier to lay. In addition, thinner-cut sod roots faster. The proper cutting depth for mature sod is ½ to ¾ inch below the crown of the grass.

Calculating the amount of sod you need is easier than buying seed. Simply figure out how many square feet you want to cover, and that is how much sod you should order. Allow a little extra, about 5 percent, if you will be laying it around curves.

Plugs You can cut your own plugs from sod, but precut plugs are also sold in plastic trays and cloth bags, ready to be planted. How much to buy depends on how close you plan to space them. The closer you plant, the sooner they will cover the ground and the more expensive the project will be. Plant plugs on a staggered grid. If you space them 6 inches apart, figure on two plugs a square foot, or 2,000 for 1,000 square feet.

Sprigs Buy sprigs by the bag. They should be healthy, green, and as fresh as possible. The bag should be heavy, indicating the sprigs hold plenty of moisture. Depending on the condition of the sprigs, plan to use 5 to 10 bushels per 1,000 square feet.

Cheap Seed

Cheap product often contains low-quality grass seed with a low germination rate. So a good portion of the seed you put down won't germinate. Often the grass that does grow is an old variety that is neither disease nor drought resistant. Cheap seed mixes also contain more weed seed and inert matter, so you're really paying for stuff you don't want in your lawn.

EVALUATE THE SOIL

Soil is a key ingredient in making a beautiful lawn. The best seed or sod will not perform properly if the soil that supports it isn't as good as it can be.

Ideally, the soil will be fertile. It should contain all the elements the lawn needs for growth, and they should be in the proper balance and in a form the plants can use. To learn your soil's fertility, have it tested by a laboratory (see page 166).

The soil should also supply the lawn with the moisture and oxygen its root system needs to function. It should hold water yet drain well. A lawn that has standing water after a rain or irrigation is growing in soil that contains little oxygen. On the other hand, a fast-draining soil, because it cannot hold water in reserve, has plenty of oxygen but little moisture.

Physical characteristics—texture and structure—determine how much moisture and oxygen the soil contains. Texture refers to the size and arrangement of sand, silt, and clay particles in the soil. Structure is how the particles aggregate, or clump together, and is influenced by factors such as the amount of organic matter in the soil.

A soil that is predominantly clay tends to be fertile and is tightly structured. It is slow to absorb water but holds onto it once it enters the soil. Unless the soil is well aggregated into large crumbs, air and water won't move through it readily. Soil that is predominantly sandy is infertile, loosely structured, and does not hold water.

The best-textured soils for lawns are loam, clay loam, and sandy clay loam. Loams are well-structured soils made up of sand, clay, and organic matter in roughly equal amounts. However, the relative percentage of each particle making up the soil can vary somewhat. Loam soils hold moisture and nutrients while letting excess water drain through their pores.

Judging Soil

On a day when the ground is moist, neither too wet nor too dry, take a good look at

Tip
When building a new home, here's a way to protect the topsoil. Have the contractor stockpile it, scraping it off the lot and storing it out of the path of heavy equipment. Once construction is finished, let the contractor replace the topsoil before installing the lawn. This will cost a little extra at the front end but will save time, money, and aggravation later on. Note: Use glyphosate to kill weeds and grasses that germinate in the topsoil.

Ideally, topsoil will be at least 4 to 8 inches deep—the depth of the root zone.

If topsoil is thin, less than 2 inches, as here, consider having 1 to 2 inches of new topsoil brought in to augment it. Till the area after placing the topsoil.

your soil. Dig a few test holes around your yard, as you do when preparing a soil sample for fertility tests. Check several areas around the yard, because the topsoil could have been graded to different depths and because drainage can vary on a lot. Your test holes should be at least 12 inches deep.

Topsoil Measure the topsoil depth. You should find a minimum of 4 to 8 inches of good-quality topsoil in each hole. Topsoil is generally darker than subsoil and better structured. If the layer is thinner than 4 to 8 inches, you will need to have topsoil brought in to augment it.

Buried debris Look for buried debris such as rocks, bricks, leftover grade stakes, and other construction trash that contractors often bury rather than haul from the site. Problems arise when this debris is in the top 12 inches of soil. During dry weather, the lawn over these materials wilts and often looks diseased. Probe the soil with a long-bladed screwdriver to determine whether you have buried debris.

Structure A soil with good structure has a mix of large and small pores for water and air to move through. Watch how the soil breaks apart as it drops off your shovel or you gently work it in your hand. A well-structured soil is granular and readily breaks into small to medium, or pea-sized, crumbs. Soil that breaks into large clods rather than into crumbs holds more clay; powdery soil has no structure.

Texture The way to test texture is to feel the soil. Clay soils are heavy and sticky when wet. Because clay particles are very small and flat, they pack tightly together, which is why the soil breaks into clods. When clay is wet, it is slick, and when it dries, it becomes rock hard. Sandy soil, on the other hand, is gritty and crumbles readily whether wet or dry. Silty soils feel silky when wet.

To feel the soil, moisten a handful with water. Knead it to the consistency of moist putty, adding dry soil to soak up excess water. Then roll the soil into a ball in your hand. Pinch the ball between your index finger and thumb to form a ribbon. Let the ribbon hang over your finger without supporting it.

The longer and better formed the ribbon, the more clay the soil contains. Sandy soils will not hold together in a ribbon. If the soil is very sandy, it won't even make a ball. Loam soils form short, 1- to 2-inch-long ribbons, whereas clay soils form ribbons that are 2 inches or longer.

Drainage Fill a hole with water; let it drain, and then fill it again. Time how long it takes for the water to drain the second time. If the hole empties within a few minutes, the drainage is very good. If it drains in 3 to 4 hours, the drainage is good; in 5 to 12 hours, moderately good; in 12 to 24 hours, poor.

Remove all buried debris, including random rocks. The debris restricts the lawn's root system.

Clay soil is sticky and pliable when you worked in your hand. Although fertile, it is not the best growing medium.

If water drains from a 12-inch-deep hole in three to four hours, drainage is good.

SOIL TESTING

The pH scale measures acidity and alkalinity on a scale of 0 to 14. A pH of 7 is neutral. Soil with a pH below 7 is acid. Above pH 7, soil is alkaline. The ideal pH for growing a lawn is 6 to 7. In that range, the most nutrients are available to plants.

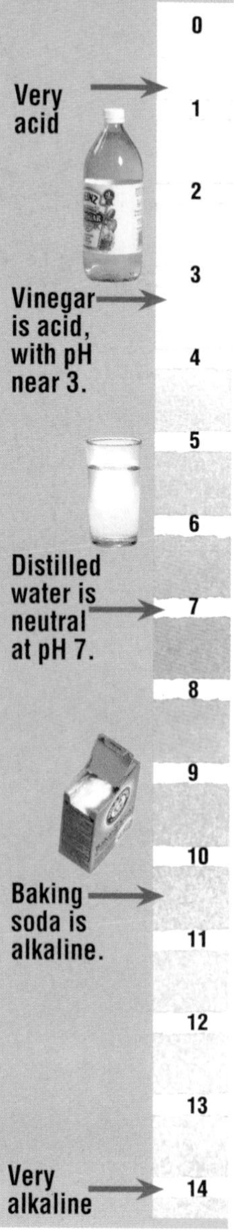

0

Very acid → **1**

2

3

Vinegar is acid, with pH near 3. → **4**

5

6

Distilled water is neutral at pH 7. → **7**

8

9

10

Baking soda is alkaline. → **11**

12

13

Very alkaline → **14**

Soil tests give you a very clear picture of your soil's nutrient status. More important, they tell you its pH level. If the soil is overly acid or alkaline, your goal is to bring the pH in line before the lawn is in place.

Because lime and sulfur—materials used to adjust pH—can burn grass, they should be worked into bare soil. And because it can take 200 pounds of the material per 1,000 square feet to change the pH, it's much easier to mix lime or sulfur into the soil before installing the lawn. So test first, make any adjustments, and then plant your lawn.

Soil tests are available at a relatively low cost. In many regions, the county extension service offers the tests. If this is not the case in your area, your extension agent should be able to direct you to a private laboratory. Allow up to four weeks to get the lab results.

Test Results

The standard items labs look at are pH, phosphorus, potassium, and organic matter. Nitrogen is not tested. Because it is highly mobile in soil, the amount of available nitrogen can change within hours. The results of a nitrogen test on soil samples that are several days old provide little useful information.

Soil test reports usually explain what the test results mean and provide specific recommendations on how much fertilizer and lime or sulfur to apply to bring the soil to optimal nutrient and pH levels.

pH The pH scale ranges from 0 to 14, with 7 the neutral point. Anything below 7 is acidic, which means it has a low pH; anything above it is alkaline, which means it has a high pH. Knowing the pH of your soil can tell you a lot about the availability of nutrients. Soils with a pH less than 6 are usually low in calcium, magnesium, and potassium; soils with a high pH are unable to supply sufficient amounts of other elements, including iron. The ideal

pH is in the range of 6 to 7. However, it is possible to grow a high-quality lawn when the pH is as low as 5 or as high as 8.

Lime is used to raise soil pH. You can reduce the pH in some high-alkaline soils by adding sulfur, although the task of lowering the pH is much more difficult than raising it. (And if the soil is high in calcium carbonate, it's impossible to lower the pH by using sulfur.)

Recommendations for raising or lowering pH may be given in pounds per acre. You can convert this figure to pounds per 1,000 square feet by dividing the recommended pounds per acre by 43.56. (Example: 2,180 pounds per acre ÷ 43.56 = 50 pounds per 1,000 square feet.)

Phosphorus and potassium The lab results will indicate how much of each nutrient is available for use by plants. On some reports, the amounts will simply be listed as low, medium, or high. On others, the actual amount in the soil may be provided in parts per million or pounds per acre. The chart below correlates parts per million and pounds per acre to very low, low, adequate, and high.

Fortunately, most reports also include recommendations on how much phosphorus and potassium to apply if these nutrients are lacking. Unless the soil

Potassium

Levels	Parts per million	Pounds per acre
Very low	0–40	0–80
Low	41–175	81–350
Adequate	176–250	351–500
High	above 250	above 500

Phosphorus

Levels	Parts per million	Pounds per acre
Very low	0–5	0–10
Low	6–10	11–20
Adequate	11–20	21–40
High	above 20	above 40

is very low in either element, the accepted practice is to spread Scotts Starter Fertilizer before planting.

Organic matter The percentage of organic matter offers more clues to soil fertility. Soils that are low in organic matter, such as sandy ones, are generally low in fertility. The ideal range of organic matter for lawns is 2 to 5 percent.

Taking Samples

Homeowner-friendly, do-it-yourself soil test kits are available, but a competent soil-testing lab will provide you with the most accurate results.

Soil tests must be performed on a sample that is representative of the entire lawn. Collect samples from several locations around your lot, roughly one sample per 1,000 square feet. On a 8,000- to 10,000-square-foot lawn, 8 to 10 randomly collected samples are sufficient to obtain reliable results. On a large lawn, more than one test may be needed; for example, test the front yard and backyard separately. If the lawn has distinctly different areas, such as a slope or a low-lying area, submit separate samples from each site.

Unless the laboratory specifies another depth, collect soil samples from 3 inches deep. Scrape away the thatch layer, dig up about a handful of soil with a clean trowel, shovel, or soil probe, and put the soil in a bucket. (Clean tools are important; any fertilizer residue, for example, may cause inaccurate results.)

Thoroughly mix the samples together, then measure out 1 to 2 cups of soil. Follow the lab's directions for submitting the sample. Indicate on the form that the test is for an area that you will be turning into lawn.

Reading the Report

Every laboratory has its own version of a soil test report. Some are easy to read; others aren't. These terms will help you understand your report.

Soluble salts, may be listed as EC: a measure of salts and sodium in the soil; the lower, the better

pH: 6 to 7 is ideal

CEC: capacity of the soil to hold nutrients; also called buffering capacity; the higher the number, the more fertile the soil

Organic matter: 2% to 5% is ideal

Available nutrients:

Recommendation: what you should do

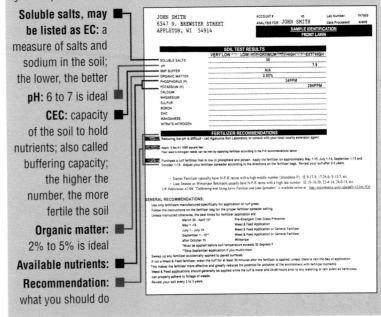

Testing the Soil

Soil tests are the most accurate gauge of a lawn's pH and need for phosphorus and potassium. Test the soil every three to five years or when your lawn is not up to snuff.

1 **Collect small amounts of soil from several locations.**

2 **Thoroughly mix all the samples together, then measure 1 to 2 cups of soil to send to the lab for testing.**

IMPROVING SOIL

Cultivate soil when it is moist, neither wet nor dry, to protect its structure. Avoid overworking the soil, which harms its structure.

Preparing soil for planting a lawn is within the ability of many homeowners, but it is hard work. You must till in amendments and establish the subgrade, then the finished grade. The following tips will help you do the job yourself or evaluate a contractor's work.

Working the Soil

Whether you seed or sod the lawn, preparing the soil is the same process. You want to end up with a fertile soil suitable for growing plants. It should slope away from the house, have few dips or high points, and be in good physical shape.

The first step is to establish the subgrade, which is covered on page 170. Then work the amendments into the topsoil. Do not work the soil when it is wet; nothing destroys soil structure or leads to a yard full of clods faster. To decide whether the soil is dry enough to work, pick up a handful. Squeeze it into a ball. Then drop it from about waist height. If it stays in one piece when it hits the ground, let the soil dry a few more days before tilling.

Stocking Up on Amendments

Before grading, order the amendments so they'll be on hand when you are ready to add them.

Changing pH How much lime or sulfur it takes to raise or lower the pH depends on how much the pH needs to be changed and on the type of soil. For example, to raise the pH of a sandy soil by a half unit (for example, from 6.0 to 6.5) takes 20 pounds of lime per 1,000 square feet, but 35 pounds are needed if the soil is loamy. Likewise, to lower the pH one unit takes 10 pounds per 1,000 square feet of sulfur for sandy soil, as opposed to 25 pounds for clay. (Most soil test labs will give you specific recommendations for your site.)

Lime and sulfur come in several forms, some more effective and easier to use than others. Ground limestone is a noncaustic powder that takes several weeks to change pH. The more finely it is ground, the faster it works. Dolomitic limestone supplies magnesium as well as calcium. Hydrated lime (also called quicklime) is much faster, but it is caustic and can burn when handled. Pelleted lime is the safest and

Buying New Soil

What can be done if the soil on a proposed homesite is unacceptable for plant growth? This problem often confronts people who build in mountainous regions, deserts, rocky areas, and other sites that may make attractive settings for a home but are not the best places to grow a lawn.

Basically, the solution is to bring suitable soil to the site. When large amounts of topsoil are needed, local landscape contractors are usually the best source. Their businesses depend on the quality of the soil they work with, and experienced firms generally have a good source available to them. Building contractors may also be a source of topsoil, but check the soil before it is delivered to be sure it is of good quality.

Do not use soil from road ditches or other areas where particles have been deposited by the wind.

This soil may look good, but the particles are small and drainage is generally poor. Likewise, silt from drainage ditches and lake excavations is not recommended.

Before buying soil from anyone, ask where it came from. If you are uncertain about the quality or source of the soil, pass on it. The detrimental effects of using inferior soil will last for a long time.

Gypsum

Although sometimes sold as a cure-all for clay soil, gypsum (calcium sulfate) works only when the soil is high in sodium—in areas near seacoasts, in the desert Southwest where effluent irrigation water is used, and in regions where sodium occurs naturally in the soil. Sodium destroys soil structure. Imagine water drops on fine talcum powder: They bead up rather than penetrate. That's how sodium affects soil, but gypsum helps reverse the process. How much gypsum to use varies with the sodium level, the percentage of clay in the soil, and other factors. You may need to work in as much as 100 to 350 pounds of gypsum per 1,000 square feet of soil. Follow soil test recommendations. Spread the gypsum evenly on top of the soil, and rototill it into the top 6 to 8 inches. Because gypsum resembles flour (in both color and texture), avoid spreading it in windy conditions.

easiest to apply. It combines both hydrated lime and ground limestone in pellets that are safe to handle yet act moderately fast.

Elemental sulfur is best for lowering soil pH. Granular sulfur is easiest to spread. If you can find sulfur only in a powdery form, which blows readily as you spread it, be sure to wear a dust mask when working.

Fertility Add fertilizer as recommended by the soil report. (This is in addition to the Scotts Starter Fertilizer you spread just before seeding.) The recommendations may suggest using a material such as superphosphate if the soil is very low in phosphorus. Not all garden centers carry this fertilizer; if you have trouble finding it, check a farm supply store.

Soil structure You'll find that soil structure takes time to build. The secret is mostly in organic matter, which aids both sandy and clay soils. The decomposing materials help soil particles to aggregate, opening pore spaces in clay soil and allowing sandy soil to retain moisture.

Compost is one of the best organic amendments for modifying soil. But the amount you need for an entire yard is probably more than you can make in a backyard compost pile. Look for a local source of commercially produced compost. For example, many local water

treatment plants sell composted sewage sludge, and some cities turn landscape waste into compost. Often you can buy these materials by the truckload.

Scotts Lawn Soil (available in bags at local garden centers) contains a mixture of composted materials that works well for small lawns.

Sphagnum peat moss is an inexpensive amendment. It too is available in bags or in bales. Apply a 2- to 4-inch layer of peat over the area to be prepared, then till it into the soil 4 to 6 inches deep. Not all peat is the same—quality varies a lot. Avoid peat with a high percentage of silt because it may cause serious problems with drainage. Look for peat with a minimum of 85 percent organic matter.

Do not till sand into clay soil, thinking it will improve drainage. The truth is, doing so is more likely to decrease drainage and to increase compaction. The small clay particles nestle into the spaces between the larger sand particles and pack down. Unless you add enough sand to make it the major component of the mixture (70 percent or more), it will do more harm than good.

Several other inorganic amendments, however, do help. These include porous ceramic clay materials, calcined diatomaceous earth, zeolite, and expanded slate. They can improve poor soils but are expensive and not readily available in all areas. Compare them with compost, sphagnum peat moss, bags of topsoil, and other materials before deciding whether to use them.

Topsoil If the topsoil layer is thinner than 4 inches, augment it with new topsoil. Either make up the full difference or spread 1 to 2 inches of topsoil over the yard. Rototill it into the existing soil so there's no sharp change between old and new; a change in texture between the two layers of topsoil can impair drainage.

Topsoil Calculator

Topsoil and other amendments are sold by the cubic yard. To calculate how many cubic yards to buy, you need to know the square footage of the lawn area and how thick you expect to spread the material.

Example: How much topsoil will it take to place 6 inches of soil over a 6,000-square-foot yard? First, imagine that you will spread the soil 1 foot thick. Each square foot, then, would be topped with 1 cubic foot of soil ($1 \times 1 \times 1$) for a total of 6,000 cubic feet.

There are 27 cubic feet in a cubic yard. Divide 6,000 cubic feet by 27, and you get 222 cubic yards of topsoil to cover the lawn 1 foot thick. Because you will actually spread 6 inches of topsoil, divide that amount by half: You need a total 111 cubic yards. It is always a good idea to have a little extra on hand to allow for spillage and settling. An order of 120 cubic yards is just right for this site.

SOIL PREP & SEEDING

The finished grade of your lawn is like an artist's canvas. If the canvas has wrinkles, so will the painting. If a lawn has low spots, water will collect in them and the grass will suffer. High places are apt to be scalped by the mower. So take the time and effort to create a smooth base before dropping a single seed or laying a roll of sod.

Grading begins before topsoil is brought in with the establishment of the subgrade, or rough grade. It is the foundation for the lawn and forms the broad contours of the finished lawn. Your home builder may do this step as a matter of course, but check to make sure it was done properly.

Establish the Subgrade

Soil should slope away from your home to keep water from accumulating at the foundation and creating moisture problems in the basement or crawlspace. A 1-foot fall in elevation for every 50 feet (a 2-percent slope) ensures that water flows away from your home.

To measure the slope, tie string to a stake driven into the soil next to your house. Stretch the string straight out from the house 50 feet, pull it taut, and tie it to another stake. Attach a string level and adjust the string's height until it is level. Measure the height of the leveled string at the house and at the other end. If the difference between the two is at least 1 foot, your lot has the slope it needs. Less than

Step-by-Step Soil Grading

1 Have the utility companies mark the location of all underground lines. Pick up construction debris. Locate, dig, and remove buried debris and rocks.

2 If there is hardpan (a hard compacted layer under the soil surface), break it up with a subsoiler, a plow, or a disk set 6 to 8 inches deep.

5 Install irrigation lines while you wait for the soil to settle.

6 Do the final grade on the soil. The purpose of this grade is to make the soil smooth with no dips or high points and to create a seedbed. Use a wide landscaper's rake to comb out rocks and clods and to fill in depressions. The seedbed should be firm but not packed and consist of fairly coarse particles, between the size of a pea and a golf ball. These particles prevent washing, reduce crusting, and provide crevices for the seed to lodge in.

that and you will need to excavate to create the required slope. Because good topsoil is so valuable, consider scraping it off and storing it out of the way beforehand if you must excavate extensively.

Before excavating, have all underground utilities flagged. Remove debris left over from construction. If the subsoil became compacted during construction, break it up.

Even if you don't have to excavate, remove debris. Fill in low spots and depressions in the yard, which can hold water. Knock down high spots so the entire surface is uniform.

Install Drain Tile

In wet climates or near downspouts, install drain tile in the subgrade to move excess water off-site. Dig trenches that are 1 foot wide and deep and 10 to 15 feet apart. The lines should slope so water entering the tile drains out. Direct the lines to a catch basin or storm-water drain, not your neighbor's property.

Fill the bottom of each trench with 2 inches of coarse, washed gravel. Lay 4-inch-diameter drain tile in the trench. Cover it with landscape fabric, which lets water in and keeps soil out. Add gravel around the sides and 2 inches over the tile. Then fill the rest of the trench with topsoil.

Replace Topsoil

Spread an inch or two of topsoil over the ground, and till it into the subgrade. Add the remaining topsoil to bring it up to

3 Measure the slope away from the foundation of your home. To ensure that your crawlspace or basement remains dry, the slope should be 1 foot for every 50 feet of distance. Rough-grade to that slope. Also knock down high points and fill in low spots to create a uniform surface. In wet areas, consider installing drain tile to ensure good drainage. Turn your rake upside down to smooth the soil afterward.

4 Replace set-aside topsoil; spread any necessary additional topsoil. Rototill to blend topsoil with the subsoil. Add the amendments recommended in the soil report, mixing them into the upper 4 to 6 inches of soil. Let the soil settle for a few weeks before planting to avoid leaving deep footprints. Rain and watering hasten soil settling.

7 When finished, the soil level should be about ½ inch lower than hard surfaces if you will be seeding, plugging, or sprigging the lawn. If you will sod the lawn, the soil should be about 1½ inches below hard surfaces.

4 to 6 inches deep. Let the topsoil settle for a few weeks to prevent depressions from forming in the new turf. Rain or irrigation after the topsoil is in place helps it settle. Any puddles that form will point you to low spots that need to be filled in before you plant the lawn.

After the topsoil has settled for two or three weeks, rototill it to a 4- to 6-inch depth, adding all amendments recommended in the soil report. Experienced contractors do a good job of firming soil as they place it. Where you use a contractor, you may be able to plant the lawn shortly afterward and not have to wait for the soil to settle.

However, if the soil needs time to settle, that's also an excellent time to install a permanent underground irrigation system. Seriously consider hiring a professional to do this job. Uneven coverage and water pressure problems often result when inexperienced people attempt to install a systems by themselves.

Finished Grade

The finished grade will be your seedbed. Smooth out wheel tracks and other depressions in the soil with a garden rake (one with steel tines) or an aluminum landscape rake, which has a broader head. Break up clods; remove rocks, debris, and large clods as you work. Rake out high or low spots. Recheck the slope to ensure that water will run off properly.

Step-by-Step Seeding

1 An optional first step is to lightly roll the soil before sowing seed. This helps firm the soil and may reveal any dips or high spots. Take care not to overfirm and compact the soil.

2 Set the spreader to the setting listed on the seed package for your brand of spreader, then fill the hopper with seed. Make sure the hopper is closed before pouring the seed into it.

3 You may think that you haven't put down enough seed when you're through, but you probably have. This photo shows an appropriate seeding distribution.

4 Mulch the seedbed to hold in moisture and prevent the seed from washing away if it rains. Use burlap, oat straw, or other material that will break down and doesn't carry weed seeds.

When finished, the soil should be about ½ inch below the driveway, sidewalk, and other adjacent hard surfaces if you are seeding. If you are sodding the lawn, the soil surface should be 1½ inches lower than the hard surface to make up for the soil attached to the sod. An optional final step is to lightly roll the area to firm the soil surface. If using a water–filled roller, fill it no more than halfway to prevent surface compaction. Even after rolling, you may need to rake down a few high spots and add soil to fill in depressions.

At this point, the methods for seeding and sodding part ways. If you plan to start your lawn by sod or other vegetative means (plugs or sprigs), skip to page 176.

Spread Fertilizer

Before seeding, apply Scotts Starter Fertilizer. Proper feeding is extremely important, even before seeds have germinated. High–quality starter fertilizers contain slow–release nitrogen and extra phosphorus. (New seedlings need phosphorus. Unless it is in the fertilizer, they will have a difficult time getting it until their root systems are more fully developed.) Spread the fertilizer over the soil surface, applying it at the rate specified on the label.

Sow Seed

It is important to sow the recommended amount of seed for each type of grass. Too much seed and the seedlings will have trouble becoming established because they will compete with one another for water, nutrients, and sunlight. Too little seed and the lawn will be slow to fill in.

Applied at the proper rate, seed is often not visible on the soil. Usually it will seem as though you haven't put enough down. If you spread seed to the point at which you can see it, you've probably used too much.

A drop spreader is the most accurate way to distribute seed over the prepared soil, particularly if the seeds are small. However, using a drop spreader may be too slow for seeding large areas. For these, a rotary spreader is a better choice. Be aware that when using a rotary spreader, wind can blow the seeds, making it more difficult to ensure that the seed is applied uniformly. On small areas, you can use a handheld rotary spreader.

Set the spreader to the setting listed on the seed package for your brand of spreader, and fill the hopper with seed. Then run the spreader over the yard the same way you would when applying fertilizer (see page 62).

If you are using a rotary spreader and sowing a mixture of seeds of varying sizes, split the total amount of seed in half. Sow one–half in one direction and the second half at a right angle to the first. Because rotary spreaders fling different–size particles out at different rates, this technique helps improve uniformity. With this method, be sure to use the half–rate spreader setting, if it is listed.

Lightly rake the soil surface with the back of a leaf rake. This helps mix the seed and fertilizer with the soil. Drag the rake over the surface only once so the seeds are incorporated without disrupting the uniformity of their distribution. Take care to cover the seed with no more than ¼ inch of soil. (If you have any leftover seed, you can store it for patching thin areas for up to a year.)

Mulch

Spread mulch over the seeding to hold in moisture and prevent soil and seeds from washing away. (This step may not be needed in small areas, which are easy to keep moist.) Use straw, burlap, peat, compost, or other materials. The ideal mulch carries few weed seeds and breaks down eventually on its own, so you don't have to remove it. If you are using straw, be sure to ask for straw, not hay. Oat straw is relatively free of weed seeds; hay is often full of them. Evenly spread the straw over the seedbed at approximately one and a half bales per 1,000 square feet; this is appropriately light coverage, leaving about half the soil showing through.

FINISHING THE JOB

Water often enough that the soil surface doesn't dry out until the seeds germinate. That may mean watering more than once a day.

Watering

When most of the grass has reached a uniform height of approximately 1 inch, the seedlings have developed a root system and are able to obtain water from the underlying soil. At that point, it's no longer necessary to keep the soil surface wet. Reduce irrigation frequency, as long as the underlying soil holds sufficient water. As the new lawn matures, water thoroughly once or twice a week (see page 70).

Fertilizing

Phosphorus is the most important nutrient in the Scotts Starter Fertilizer, but once the grass has emerged, nitrogen becomes more important. Scotts Starter Fertilizer should feed the lawn for six to eight weeks. When the grass has grown approximately 1 inch tall, it may begin to take on a yellow appearance, known as chlorosis, due to nitrogen deficiency. To prevent a deficiency, fertilize the new grass four to six weeks after sowing, using a high-quality lawn fertilizer. Then set up a regular fertilizer program for your lawn (see the chapter beginning on page 52).

Once seed, fertilizer, and mulch are in place, irrigate with enough water to moisten the soil surface without causing soil erosion or the seed to float. This generally requires about ¼ inch of water.

Then water lightly and frequently, never letting the soil surface dry out, until the seed has germinated and begun to form a root system that holds the soil in place. Lack of water is the main reason seedlings fail. If the seedlings dry out during this period, they will die. That can happen within just a few hours, particularly if the weather is hot, which is one reason midsummer planting often fails.

The time it takes for new seedlings to emerge depends on the grass species and environmental conditions. The cooler the soil, the longer it takes. Cool-season grasses emerge slowly in the cool soils of spring; they germinate faster in the warm soils of late summer and early fall.

Did You Know?

Nurse grasses germinate quickly and hold the soil in place while slower-germinating grasses become established. For example, Kentucky bluegrass is slow to germinate, particularly in spring. So it is often mixed with perennial ryegrass, which can begin to emerge in as little as three days. In some situations, one grass or the other may dominate, but in most yards, Kentucky bluegrass and perennial ryegrass make a beautiful, blended lawn.

Mowing

Mow the young grass as soon as it reaches normal mowing height. If you plan to keep the lawn at a 2-inch height, it should be mowed as soon as it reaches 3 inches tall. Remember, never take off more than one-third of the grass blade in a single mowing. Letting the lawn grow excessively long before the first mowing sets the grass back and could damage it.

The Mature Lawn

A lawn is considered to be mature when it has achieved full density and when the individual plants have formed all of the structures associated with an adult of that species. A rhizomatous grass is not mature until it has established a rhizome system. A stoloniferous grass requires dense stolon growth before it is considered mature.

The time required for a lawn to reach maturity varies with environmental conditions, the grass species, and the time of year. A newly seeded lawn may require a couple of months to settle in before it is mature. Perennial ryegrass germinates quickly and may achieve a dense stand in just a few weeks; Kentucky bluegrass becomes established much more slowly. The warmer the soil, the faster a new lawn will mature.

It's important for you to be able to know the degree of your lawn's maturity, especially when you begin thinking about using herbicides. Weed controls that can be safely applied to a mature lawn may severely damage or even kill seedlings. If your newly established lawn becomes heavily infested with broadleaf weeds, you may be tempted to treat it with a weed-and-feed. Don't. Wait until after the third or fourth mowing before applying a broadleaf weed control. This may take several weeks or perhaps months for some grasses. Herbicide tolerance also varies by species, so read the label carefully and follow the directions before using any product.

Begin mowing as soon as the seedlings reach mowing height. Take care if you use a riding mower though. Riding-mower wheels can damage new seedings.

Days to Germination

COOL-SEASON GRASSES		WARM-SEASON GRASSES	
Annual ryegrass	3–8	Bahiagrass	8–15
Fine fescues	7–14	Bermudagrass	7–15
Kentucky bluegrass	14–28	Buffalograss	7–14
Perennial ryegrass	3–14	Centipedegrass	7–15
Tall fescue	7–14		

Dormant Seeding

Dormant seeding refers to spreading seed in late fall or early to late winter after it is too late for germination to occur. The seed then germinates in spring when the soil warms. This process is sometimes used on football fields that sustain damage late in the season but is rarely used on home lawns. The mortality rate of seed sown in late fall and in winter is high. It is generally best to wait until the soil has warmed in spring before sowing seed.

SODDING, SPRIGGING & PLUGGING

Sodding lets you have a new lawn in a day.

You often have to wait a growing season for a seeded lawn to mature, but you can have a mature lawn in a single day with sod. A sodded lawn has the advantage of being uniform and weed free if good-quality sod is used. You can also plant over a much longer period of time. The window for seeding is limited to a few weeks during the optimum growing season, but sod can be laid anytime from early spring to late fall, as long as you are willing to provide sufficient moisture while it settles in. The main disadvantage of sod is its cost.

When you're laying sod, the soil should be ¾ to 1 inch lower than it would be for a seeded lawn.

Soil preparation is almost the same as for seeding. What differs is that the finished grade should be about ¾ to 1 inch lower than it would be for a seeded lawn, or about 1½ inches below hard surfaces. That is because the sod comes with its own soil, and the prepared bed needs to compensate for the increased thickness.

After preparing the soil and before laying the sod, apply Scotts Starter Fertilizer, which is high in phosphorus. Spread it over the soil at the rate specified on the label. Lightly rake it into the soil with a leaf rake.

Laying Sod

Sod should be moved to the site and laid as soon after harvest as possible. If left on a pallet or in stacks for more than 24 hours in warm weather, the rolls heat excessively, killing the grass. The cooler the weather, the longer the sod can remain in stacks before being laid, but it's best to store it in a single layer in the shade.

Lay sod in a staggered brickwork pattern, with the seams alternating. On slopes, place the sod perpendicular to the slope to prevent it from sliding when you water. On slopes of 10 percent or greater (a 10-foot difference per 100 feet of slope between the top and bottom), stake the sod in place.

Begin the first row of sod at a straight edge, such as a sidewalk, driveway, or straight line made with stakes and string. Place the first roll on the ground and unroll it. Set the second roll at the end of the first, tightly butting the seams together. Wedge successive rows tightly to adjacent rows.

As you add rows, putting a board over the previous row helps spread your weight uniformly as you work. Never stretch sod to make it cover more ground. Doing so creates gaps you will have to correct later.

Of course, lawns are not necessarily rectangular like pieces of sod. You will need to trim along curves or where the brick pattern leaves an irregular edge. Use a guide to cut straight lines and a garden hose for curves. Then cut the sod with a small hatchet or a hefty knife.

When all the sod is in place, lightly roll it or tamp it to remove air spaces between the soil surface and the sod. Air pockets can cause the sod to dry, then die, so take care to roll the seams.

Step-by-Step Sodding

1 Lay the first row out following a straight line, such as a sidewalk, a driveway, or a string pulled taut between stakes.

2 Tightly butt the ends of the sod rolls to each other.

3 Lay the sod in a staggered pattern so that the seams in one row of sod fall in the center of the sod pieces in the previous row, just like rows of brick.

4 Tamp the seams firmly with the back of a rake to help ensure that the edges of the sod make contact with the soil. Standing on a board laid over previous rows helps to distribute your weight and prevent you from gouging the sod as you work.

5 Cut the sod to fit curves exactly. The easiest tool to use is a heavy-duty knife or a small hatchet.

Like the Pros

Groundskeepers installing sports fields use big roll sod in order to have fewer seams and less drying out of the sod. Landscapers and lawn care contractors are using this technique more often, so if your lawn is large enough, be sure to ask about big roll sod.

Sprigging

Sprigging involves establishing grasses by spreading cut-up pieces of grass stolons—the sprigs—on the soil. Nodes, the swollen sections of the stolon, contain buds. When they are in contact with soil and the sprigs have sufficient moisture, these buds produce new plants.

The main reason for sprigging rather than sodding is to save money. All the grasses that are sprigged can be established by sod. (If seed is available for the grass, seeding is the easiest and cheapest method.)

Only species that form stolons can be established by sprigging. Most warm-season grasses can be established in this way, but most cool-season grasses lack stolons. This method is used most often with improved bermudagrasses. Several types are hybrid crosses between common and African bermudagrass. Because hybrids produce seedlings that differ from the parents these lawns must be established by vegetative means.

Stolons are highly perishable. They may have to be refrigerated during transport and storage. Use them as quickly as possible after they arrive. Prepare the soil for sprigging as you would for seeding or sodding, and apply Scotts Starter Fertilizer that is high in phosphorus before planting.

Spread the sprigs uniformly over the site at a rate of 5 to 10 bushels per 1,000 square feet. Then press or slice them into the soil. This is a crucial step; it ensures that the sprigs root and begin to form new plants. On small areas, you can simply press them down with a shovel. For large lawns, rent a sprigger machine to slice them into the soil. Run the machine over the lawn from one direction, then go over it again at a right angle to the first pass. You can also use a roller to press the sprigs.

Until the sprigs have rooted and begun to take moisture from the underlying soil, keep them moist. Do not allow the soil surface to dry until new growth has begun. Once the sprigs are established, water normally.

Lay sod perpendicular to a slope to prevent it from sliding down the hill.

Water the newly laid sod long enough to wet the upper 4 to 6 inches of soil. To ensure you're wetting the underlying soil and not just the sod's surface, lift the edge of the sod and check underneath it. The soil needs to be wet to encourage roots to grow into it in search of moisture, but avoid overwatering sod. Rooting will be delayed if the soil is continuously saturated.

Avoid walking on the lawn until the soil has stabilized and the sod has rooted to the underlying soil. This will take 10 to 14 days. To check whether the sod is rooting, gently tug on the grass. If it doesn't lift up, it is rooting.

One month after sodding, apply a standard lawn food and begin treating the grass like a mature lawn. Water at least ½ inch twice a week and follow an annual fertilizer program (see the chapter beginning on page 52).

If the slope is very steep, stake the sod roll in place. Use two to four stakes per roll.

An alternate sprigging method uses stolons to establish the lawn, but here the stolons are placed in narrow trenches 6 to 8 inches apart. This conserves material and uses only four to five bushels of stolons per 1,000 square feet. The disadvantage is that more time is needed for the lawn to become established.

Plugging

To plug, you plant 2- to 4-inch pieces of sod in a grid across the yard. You can obtain plugs by cutting strips of sod in squares or circles, or you can purchase them precut. A square yard of sod yields 324 2-inch plugs.

Plugging saves money; you can establish a 1,000-square-foot lawn with just 63 square feet of sod. However, it is a much slower way to establish a lawn than sodding. Weeds present a considerable challenge until the grass fills in. It takes one to two seasons for complete coverage, depending on the spacing of the plugs and on environmental conditions. You'll be looking at a work in progress for some time.

Any spreading grass can be established by plugging. But the ones most often grown this way are zoysiagrass, buffalograss, and St. Augustinegrass. Zoysiagrass is difficult to grow from seed, and its sod is expensive. For zoysia and the others, vegetative means of establishment allow you to grow disease-resistant cultivars, for which no seed is available. St. Augustinegrass has delicate stolons that are easily damaged in harvest.

Prepare the soil in the same way as with the other establishment methods. Spread Scotts Starter Fertilizer over the soil prior to planting. Before obtaining the plugs, dig the holes for them. A tool is available for this job; it takes plugs from the soil so that the sod plugs can be easily put in place. You can also use a trowel. The holes should be no deeper than the depth of the plug. Space them 6 to 16 inches apart on a staggered grid pattern.

Plugs can dry quickly after planting, so keep the area moist for the first 10 to 14 days, or until the plugs have rooted.

Evenly broadcast 5 to 10 bushels of stolons over 1,000 square feet of soil. Press the sprigs into the soil with the back of a shovel or use equipment that slices them in.

Space plugs 6 to 16 inches apart on a staggered or triangular grid pattern.

Fertilize with a standard lawn fertilizer. Then water routinely as you would for a mature lawn.

Weeds are usually a problem in the open areas between the plugs. Apply a preemergence herbicide to prevent germination of annual weeds or a postemergence weed control for broadleaf weeds. The choice of herbicides will depend on the grass species. Read the label carefully before applying any herbicide.

Strip-sodding is the process of laying sod in long rows with 6 to 10 inches between each row. As in plugging, the bare areas are filled in by the spreading stolons and/or rhizomes. Strip-sodding is faster and easier than plugging, but it uses more plant material and is more expensive than plugging. Zoysiagrass is the species most often established by strip-sodding, although any spreading species could be established in this way. Use the same irrigation, weed control, and fertilization methods for strip-sodding as for plugging.

The basis for a beautiful lawn is simple. Grow a grass that's well adapted to the environmental conditions and the amount and type of use it will receive in your yard.

Grasses differ in their ability to adapt to the climate of a region, to minor variations in environmental conditions within a region, and to the amount of use they receive. Some grasses grow best where it's cool; others do better in warm climates. Most grasses must have full sun to survive, but some tolerate shade. Many grasses rapidly recover from regular use, such as from the dog wearing a path along a fence or from the daily beating of kids playing. Other grasses can't take such wear.

Climate is the most important factor bearing on which grass you can grow. There are warm- and cool-season grasses, and they are limited to their areas of adaptation: cool-season grasses in the North, warm-season grasses in the South.

So climate determines the broad category of grass you can grow. Within each category are a number of species, such as Kentucky bluegrass and tall fescue in the cool-season group and bermudagrass and zoysiagrass in the warm-season category. Each is suited to different parts of the cool- and warm-season regions. Also, each species has numerous cultivars, or varieties, which are similar to the species but may have a distinctive color, tolerance to certain diseases, adaptations to stressful conditions such as shade or drought, insect resistance, or any other desirable trait. From these, you can select the particular species or variety of the species that best thrives in all the conditions your yard offers.

Climate Breakdown

The map on the opposite page shows the five major climatic regions for turfgrass in North America. It will help you further narrow your grass choices.

Cool–Humid This diverse region includes areas with mild, wet winters and warm, dry summers and ones with frigid winters and hot summers. Rainfall totals 30 inches or more a year. All of the cool-season grasses grow well in this region, but in dry weather, they may go dormant for short periods unless watered. Zoysiagrass also grows in the southern portion of the cool-humid zone and along the Atlantic coast; it has a short growing season in these areas and is brown much of the year. Buffalograss grows in interior sections of the region.

Cool–Arid Cold to mild, snowy to dry winters and warm to hot, dry summers define this region. Rainfall totals less than 20 inches a year. Cool-season grasses, especially Kentucky bluegrass and fine fescues, grow here but must be irrigated to stay green. In warm parts of the region, buffalograss does well without irrigation.

Warm–Humid Winters are mild, rainfall is high, and summers are hot and humid. The area along the Gulf Coast is almost tropical, with rainfall totaling 60 inches or more a year. Warm-season grasses dominate in this region. Bermudagrass grows throughout this region. Zoysiagrass is better adapted to the northern part of it; St. Augustinegrass, bahiagrass, and centipedegrass do better along the Gulf Coast. In the mountainous sections, cool-season grasses will grow.

Warm–Arid Hot summer temperatures, mild winters, and little to no rain at any time of year are the norm here. Warm-season grasses grow here, with bermudagrass the most common. Buffalograss grows in northern parts of the region. Because the soil is very alkaline and often saline, some of the minor grasses may be more appropriate for parts of this region.

Transition Zone Overlapping parts of all four regions, the Transition Zone has hot summers, cold winters, and wet and dry periods throughout the year. Here you can grow either cool- or warm-season grasses, but neither does especially well. Both are on the edge of their adaptation range. It is too cold in winter for most warm-season grasses to thrive and too hot in summer for most cool-season grasses.

Only grasses that tolerate extremes do well in the Transition Zone. These include tall fescue, a cool-season grass better suited to hot summers than most other cool-season grasses which survives winter in most of the region. Of the warm-season grasses, cold-tolerant varieties of bermudagrass do well in the southern part of the zone; zoysiagrass grows farther north but is brown much of the year. Kentucky bluegrass and perennial ryegrass, or a mix of these two with tall fescue, are successful in the cooler parts of the Transition Zone.

In the Transition Zone, shade, elevation, soil conditions such as pH, salinity, moisture, and other factors are important criteria to have in mind as you select a grass for your lawn. Decide, too, whether it matters to you if your lawn is green year-round or goes dormant in winter.

Narrowing Your Choices

The pages that follow profile the main turfgrasses. They point out the regions in which each grass grows best, the

environmental conditions it tolerates, and the levels of use it can support. The profiles will help you narrow your search to the grass or grass mixture that is best suited to your yard.

The profiles do not recommend varieties or provide detailed information about them. Breeding efforts are in a constant state of flux, with new cultivars being discovered and released each year and older ones taken off the market. So finding a particular cultivar we might name here could be frustrating.

Before purchasing seed, check with local experts, such as a county extension agent or staff at local garden centers. They have information on which grasses are available in your area, and can offer advice geared to your region. You can also get advice from The Scotts Helpline (800/543-8873).

Transition Zone

ADAPTATION MAP
Key to the Regions
☐ Cool–Humid
☐ Cool–Arid
☐ Warm–Arid
☐ Warm–Humid
☐ Transition Zone

About Names

All plants have two names: a common name and a scientific name. Common names derive from everyday use and vary from one region to another. Scientific names are written in Latin and are the same around the world. By knowing the scientific name, everyone, no matter the region or country, can find the grass being discussed, using the combination of names. To avoid confusion, this book uses the most widely recognized common name for each grass and pairs it with the scientific name.

KENTUCKY BLUEGRASS

Kentucky bluegrass (*Poa pratensis*) is among the most popular cool-season grasses. It has excellent color, texture, and density and can easily be established from seed, forming one of the highest-quality lawns. Use it wherever you desire a dense, durable, beautiful turf.

One of the biggest advantages of this grass is its system of rhizomes, aggressive underground stems that spread and quickly repair damaged areas without your having to reseed. Because they live underground, protected from damage, these stems help Kentucky bluegrass tolerate many types of stress. You could burn a Kentucky bluegrass lawn, eliminating all living tissue on the surface, yet the lawn would quickly return. That's because buds on the rhizomes would remain alive, allowing new plants to emerge from below the soil surface.

The rhizomes also allow Kentucky bluegrass to survive months of drought. The lawn may look dead, only to emerge quickly from the protected rhizomes when sufficient water is again available.

Kentucky bluegrass is the standard by which most other turfgrasses are compared. It forms a beautiful lawn. Fine texture and good density are a hallmark of Kentucky bluegrass.

Buyer Beware

Occasionally, advertisements show up in magazines and newspapers about a miracle grass that needs no fertilizer or mowing. That grass is alpine bluegrass (*Poa alpina*). Unfortunately, the reports are not true, at least not when it's growing in typical North American home lawns. In fact, no grass lives up to that billing.

Deep shade is one stress that Kentucky bluegrass generally does not tolerate. The lawn readily thins out in the limited sunlight available under trees and on the north side of buildings. For these areas, you should choose mixtures formulated for shade. These contain shade-tolerant species, such as fine fescues, along with the bluegrass. In such a case, the Kentucky bluegrass will dominate in full sun, and the other grasses will take over in the shade.

Kentucky bluegrass survives extended drought by going dormant during dry periods. Maintaining a high-quality, always-green lawn requires supplemental irrigation. In dry regions or where irrigation is not available, choose another species.

When establishing a lawn, select either a blend containing three or four Kentucky bluegrass cultivars or a mixture containing Kentucky bluegrass along with fine fescues or other species. If a single cultivar is used and it develops a disease or an insect problem, the entire lawn could be lost. Diversity ensures the lawn's survival.

Breeding Efforts

Older cultivars are best suited to low-maintenance regimes, in which they are not irrigated or fertilized and high quality is not expected. In situations where they receive higher maintenance, they develop leaf spot diseases.

Improved cultivars are more tolerant of leaf spot and other diseases, have a more prostrate growth habit, and grow more slowly.

Summary

- **Regional adaptation:** cool-season grass: good cold tolerance, so grow it in cooler portions of the Transition Zone, as well as in Cool–Humid and Cool–Arid regions

- **Good for:** home lawns, parks, school yards, golf courses, cemeteries, and athletic fields

- **Shade tolerance:** poor to moderate

- **Wear resistance:** good

- **Maintenance level:** average to high

- **Fertilizer:** three to five feedings a year

- **Water:** needs irrigation for ideal lawn but survives drought by going into summer dormancy

- **Mowing height:** 2 to 4 inches

- **Planting method:** seed or sod

- **Pests:** bluegrass billbugs, chinch bugs, dollar spot, leaf spot, rust, sod webworms, white grubs

ID Clues

- Keel- or boat-shaped leaf tip
- V-shaped blade
- Membranous ligule
- Folded in cross section
- Translucent lines parallel to the midrib, one on each side
- Rhizomes

Perennial ryegrass (*Lolium perenne*) is a bunchgrass known for good wear tolerance and rapid seed germination. When conditions are ideal, its seedlings peek through the ground within three days. Other grasses may take a week or two before the first green shoots appear. For this reason, ryegrass has traditionally been used as a nurse grass. In other words, ryegrass seed is usually mixed with that of slower-emerging grasses. It germinates and holds the soil in place while the primary grass establishes itself.

Ryegrasses are also known for having tough, difficult-to-mow leaf blades with tips that shred badly with mowing. The leaves contain a lot of silica, so even with a well-sharpened mower blade, the tips rarely stay intact. The whole lawn may take on a whitish cast.

Although perennial ryegrass forms a good, wear-tolerant lawn, it is a bunchgrass and doesn't readily spread to fill in damaged areas. Turf-type perennial ryegrass and Kentucky bluegrass are compatible, so the two are often combined in cool-season seed mixtures. The turf-type perennial ryegrass provides rapid germination and wear tolerance; the Kentucky bluegrass provides the spreading rhizome system to repair damage. Together, the two form a high-quality turf that is ideal for use on sports fields and other high-traffic areas, such as playgrounds and home lawns.

Perennial ryegrass is a cool-season grass, but it has limited use in northern states, such as Minnesota and Wisconsin, because it dies during severe winters. If you live in a region with very cold winters, don't worry if it is in a seed mixture you are considering buying. Ryegrass in the mixture will get your lawn going; if it doesn't survive the cold weather, the other grasses will take over.

Breeding Efforts

Common perennial ryegrasses, such as 'Linn', shred much worse than newer cultivars. Coarse-textured and difficult to mow, they are best suited for use in pastures. Luckily, better turf-type cultivars have been developed for home and commercial use.

Improved cultivars mow better and have a color, texture, and growth rate similar to that of Kentucky bluegrass. Many have also been bred to contain endophytes, fungi that give the grasses better insect resistance and stress tolerance.

Grass that shines is usually perennial ryegrass. You can even pick it out when it's mixed with other grasses in a lawn.

You may find both common and turf-type ryegrass on the shelf in garden stores. The common ryegrass may look like a bargain when you compare costs—but remember, there are no bargains in turf seed. Turf-type cultivars are much better suited to lawns.

Annual Ryegrass

Annual ryegrass (*Lolium multiflorum*) is not recommended for use in lawns, even as a nurse grass. This may surprise you, in light of the fact that much of the lawn seed on the shelves of garden stores in the northern United States and in Canada contains annual ryegrass.

As the name implies, annual ryegrass lives for one 12-month period; then it dies, and the lawn must be replanted. Homeowners often find this out the hard way. They buy annual ryegrass seed because it is inexpensive. It germinates quickly and the lawn looks good for a few months, only to be gone the next season.

Summary

- **Regional adaptation:** cool-season grass: poor heat and cold tolerance; does well in cooler parts of the Transition Zone, as well as the warmer parts of the Cool–Humid and Cool–Arid regions

- **Good for:** use as nurse grass, home lawns, sports fields, and high-traffic areas such as playgrounds

- **Shade tolerance:** relatively good

- **Wear resistance:** good

- **Maintenance level:** average

- **Fertilizer:** three to five feedings per year

- **Water:** needs irrigation for an ideal lawn but survives drought

- **Mowing height:** 2 to 4 inches

- **Planting method:** seed

- **Pests:** billbugs, gray leaf spot, leaf spot

ID Clues

- Shiny back side of leaf
- Pointed tip
- Prominent veins on upper leaf
- Broad collar
- Small to medium-size, clawlike auricles
- Membranous ligule
- Improved cultivars may lack auricles and ligule
- Tufted bunchgrass
- Folded in cross section

TALL FESCUE

Turf-type tall fescue forms a fine-textured lawn. A good choice for the Transition Zone, its deep root system helps it to survive dry periods. It is occasionally mixed with Kentucky bluegrass (less than 20 percent bluegrass), to form a beautiful lawn that stands up to heavy use.

Although tall fescue (*Festuca arundinacea*) is a cool–season grass, it tolerates hot, dry conditions better than other cool–season species. As a result, it is widely used throughout the Transition Zone, where neither cool– nor warm–season grasses are particularly well adapted.

Because tall fescue tolerates foot traffic well, it is often the grass of choice for athletic fields and other areas where heavy play is anticipated. It is also relatively shade tolerant. In shaded areas in warm regions where fine fescues succumb to heat and drought, tall fescue is frequently the grass of choice.

Like ryegrass, tall fescue is a bunchgrass. Although some cultivars may have short rhizomes, tall fescue is not a spreading species. Even though it can tolerate heavy use, it doesn't readily recover from damage. If your kids use the backyard for a football field, you may need to periodically overseed a tall fescue lawn to maintain a

Words Make a Difference

Because many turf-type tall fescue cultivars have a much finer texture than the older cultivars, they are sometimes referred to as fine-leaved fescues. This can lead to confusion because of the term's similarity to the fine fescue group of grasses. The finer-bladed, turf-type tall fescues are still quite coarse compared with the fine fescues. Read seed labels carefully when buying mixtures. A mixture containing fine fescues and Kentucky bluegrass is excellent for shade; the grasses are compatible. But if the mixture actually contains fine-leaved tall fescue, the lawn will not be what you expect.

dense cover. Do it in late summer or early fall, using half the seeding rate you would use for a new lawn.

Also like perennial ryegrass, tall fescue is less tolerant of cold weather than are Kentucky bluegrass and fine fescues. In the coldest regions of the northern United States and Canada,

tall fescue can die during the winter and require reseeding in spring.

Because of their texture and bunch-type growth, older tall fescue varieties are not compatible with fine-textured grasses. They have a tendency to segregate into coarse-textured clumps. Patches of older varieties will stand out, looking weedy; they are difficult to eliminate. For that reason, tall fescue is generally not included in mixes containing finer-textured grasses. It is generally best to establish tall fescue as a single-species blend of three or four cultivars adapted to your region.

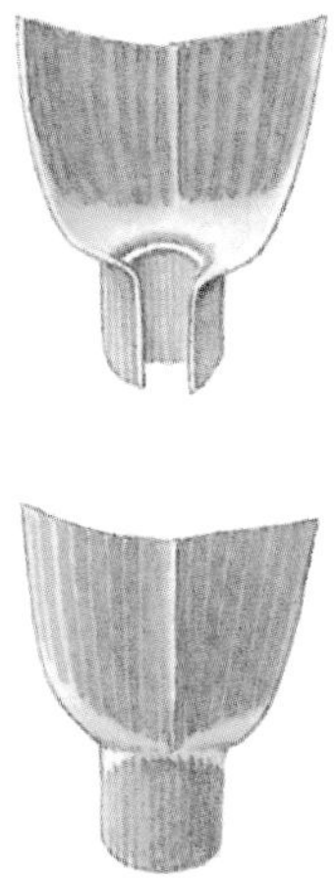

Breeding Efforts

Until about 10 years ago, only coarse-textured 'Kentucky 31' tall fescue was available. Turf-type tall fescues and other improved cultivars are markedly finer in texture, but even so they cannot compare with fine-textured grasses such as Kentucky bluegrass, perennial ryegrass, and fine fescues.

Varieties with improved disease and insect resistance are also available.

Summary

- **Regional adaptation:** cool-season grass: does well in warmer parts of Cool–Arid and Cool–Humid regions, as well as most of the Transition Zone

- **Good for:** home lawns, athletic fields, and other high-use areas, and for shady lawns where it's too warm to grow fine fescue

- **Shade tolerance:** good

- **Wear resistance:** good

- **Maintenance level:** average

- **Fertilizer:** two to four feedings a year

- **Water:** much better drought tolerance than Kentucky bluegrass but requires some irrigation for best results

- **Mowing height:** 2½ to 4 inches

- **Planting method:** seed or sod

- **Pests:** brown patch, leaf spot; few insects bother it

ID Clues

- Coarse texture
- Prominent veins on upper leaf surface; no midrib
- Pointed leaf tip
- Broad, shiny, light-green collar
- Short ligules and rounded auricles on older cultivars
- Rolled in cross section
- Bunchgrass with short rhizomes

187

FINE FESCUES

Fine fescues have the narrowest of leaf blades. In shade they become the dominant grass, forming a lush, softly textured lawn.

Several species make up the group of grasses known as fine fescues. Among them are red fescue (*Festuca rubra*), chewings fescue (*F. r. commutata*), hard fescue (*F. longifolia*), and sheep fescue (*F. ovina*). These species are among the finest-textured turfgrasses, having almost needlelike leaf blades.

All fine fescues are native to northern Europe and are well adapted to the cool, moist conditions found there. In fact, in Scotland they are the primary grass used on lawns and on golf courses, where they produce a high-quality playing surface that needs little care other than regular mowing.

The North American market values fine fescues for their shade tolerance. They persist in shady areas where most other grasses don't.

Mixtures and Blends

A blend is a combination of several cultivars of the same species; a mixture is a combination of different species, such as Kentucky bluegrass and ryegrass.

Seed companies usually sell blends and mixtures rather than single grasses. A typical cool-season mixture for shade includes one or more fine fescues, Kentucky bluegrass, and maybe some perennial ryegrass. Such mixtures let you seed a lawn and get a good stand of grass no matter how the growing conditions vary across your yard. Where the growing conditions favor one species over the others, that species will prevail.

In the shade mixture, for example, the fine fescues flourish in the shady areas; the Kentucky bluegrass is dominant in sunnier, warmer, drier parts of the yard, and the perennial ryegrass bridges the two. It can fill in for the fine fescue in hot weather.

Grasses in a mixture are chosen to look good together and to grow in a complementary fashion. If conditions are just right for all the grasses in the mixture to grow, you'll have a beautiful lawn. In addition, the lawn will be better able to withstand extreme conditions, such as periods of drought or insect attack.

Fine fescues are best suited to the northeastern United States and to eastern Canada, areas where soil moisture levels stay within a relatively narrow range. Fine fescues need moisture but do not tolerate excessively wet conditions.

Most fine fescues do not tolerate heat and drought and so are not well adapted to the dry, hot western states or to heat–prone areas in the Transition Zone. However, they will grow in the higher elevations of the Transition Zone. Within cool–season regions, hard, sheep, and chewings fescues are better for dry areas; red fescue does better in cooler, wetter regions.

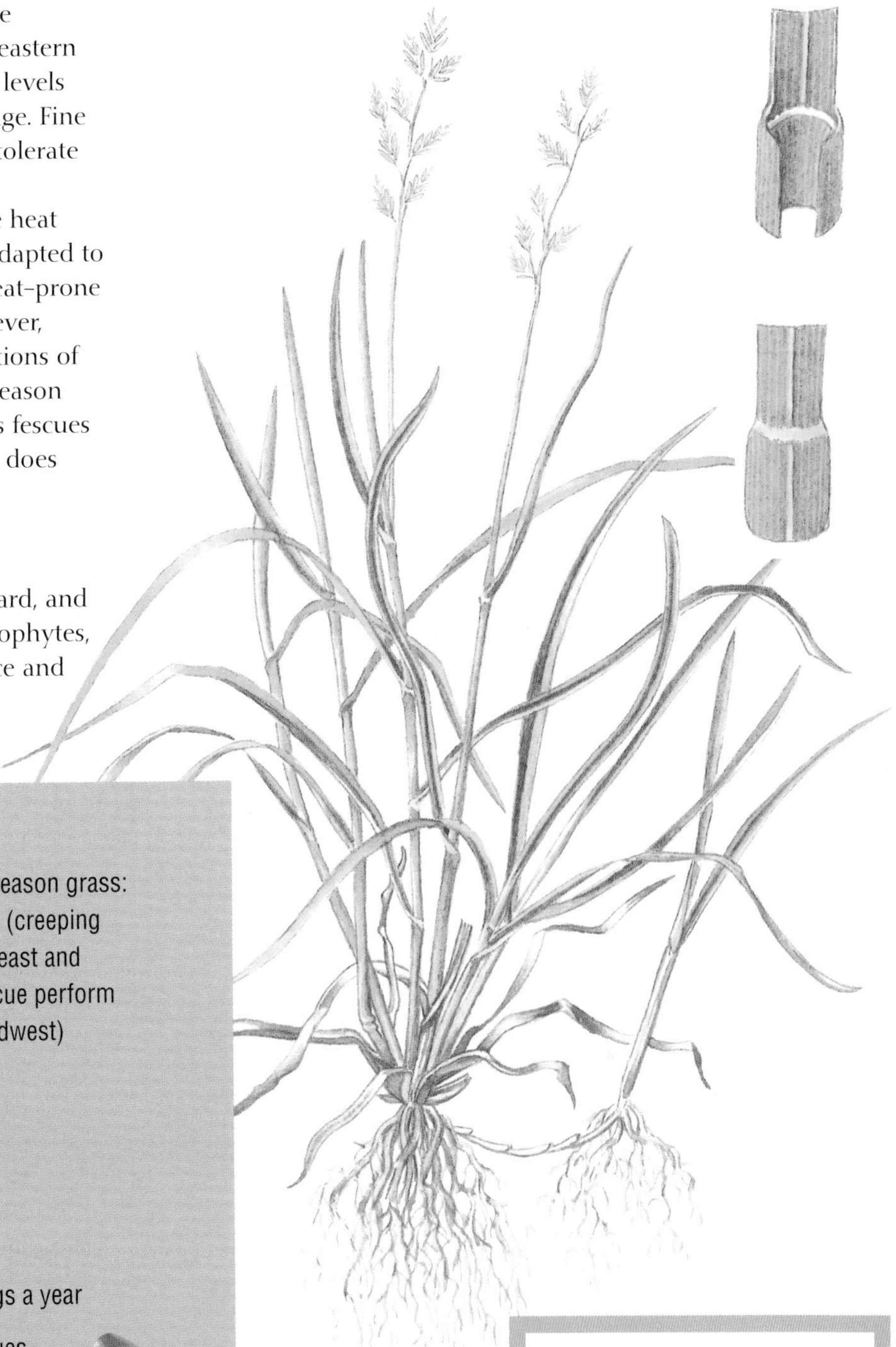

Breeding Efforts
Improved cultivars of chewings, hard, and red fescue have high levels of endophytes, fungi that improve insect resistance and extend the range of the grasses.

Summary

- **Regional adaptation:** cool-season grass: does well in Cool–Humid region (creeping red fescue is better in the Northeast and Canada; hard and chewings fescue perform well in the drier states of the Midwest)

- **Good for:** shaded lawns

- **Shade tolerance:** excellent

- **Wear resistance:** good

- **Maintenance level:** low

- **Fertilizer:** two to three feedings a year

- **Water:** chewings and red fescues require moist conditions; hard and sheep fescues tolerate drought

- **Mowing height:** 2 to 4 inches

- **Planting method:** seed

- **Pests:** dollar spot, leaf spot, red thread

ID Clues

- Very fine leaf texture
- Hard and sheep fescues: gray-green leaf blades
- Red fescue: short rhizomes
- Hard, chewings, and sheep fescues: bunchgrasses

BERMUDAGRASS

Originating in Africa, bermudagrass (*Cynodon* spp.) makes a fine lawn for homes and other areas where a dense, uniform turf is desired. The grass has both rhizomes and stolons, hence the density and ability to form a high-quality lawn, if you provide good care. Some types can tolerate very low mowing heights and are used on golf course greens, tees, and fairways.

The most popular bermudagrasses are common bermudagrass (*C. dactylon*) and hybrids between common and African bermudagrass (*C. transvaalensis*). Common bermudagrass is a coarse-textured grass; the hybrids are much finer textured. Hybrid bermudagrasses include cultivars such as 'Midiron', 'Tiflawn', and 'Tifway'.

One advantage of common bermudagrass is that it can be established by seed. However, its seedheads may detract from the lawn's appearance. Hybrid bermudagrass doesn't produce viable seed and must be established vegetatively.

Bermudagrass makes a dense, close-cropped turf suitable for warm-season lawns like this one in California, as well as for lawns in states in the Transition Zone.

Neither common bermudagrass nor the hybrids tolerate cold temperatures, although the hybrids are somewhat hardier. The range of bermudagrass adaptation extends into the Transition Zone as far north as Kansas City. Bermudagrass will not survive as far north as zoysiagrass and buffalograss. In the South, it is more often found in western Texas than on the Gulf Coast or in Florida.

Common bermudagrass has relatively good drought tolerance compared with the hybrids, which tend to thin during extended drought periods. However, irrigation is usually necessary to keep bermudagrass growing in midsummer; like Kentucky bluegrass, it has the ability to survive extended periods of drought by going into dormancy. Bermudagrass withstands wear and soil compaction pretty well and has a high nitrogen requirement. Most types do not tolerate shade.

Many of the hybrids are well adapted to low mowing heights and have been the best warm-season choices for golf courses and other lawns where a closely mowed turf is needed. Some varieties have even

Hybrid bermudagrasses, on the right, are finer textured—both leaves and stolons—than common bermudagrasses (left).

been used on putting greens. Common bermudagrass should be mowed taller than the hybrids.

Breeding Efforts

Improved varieties of common bermudagrass, including 'Cheyenne', 'NuMex Sahara', 'Yuma', and 'Sonesta' have finer texture and, unlike hybrid bermudagrasses, they can be seeded. Improved varieties require the same level of maintenance as common bermudagrass.

Don't confuse improved bermudagrass varieties with hybrid bermudagrass. The hybrids are finer-textured than either common bermudagrass or its improved varieties and are considered to be superior-quality turfgrasses.

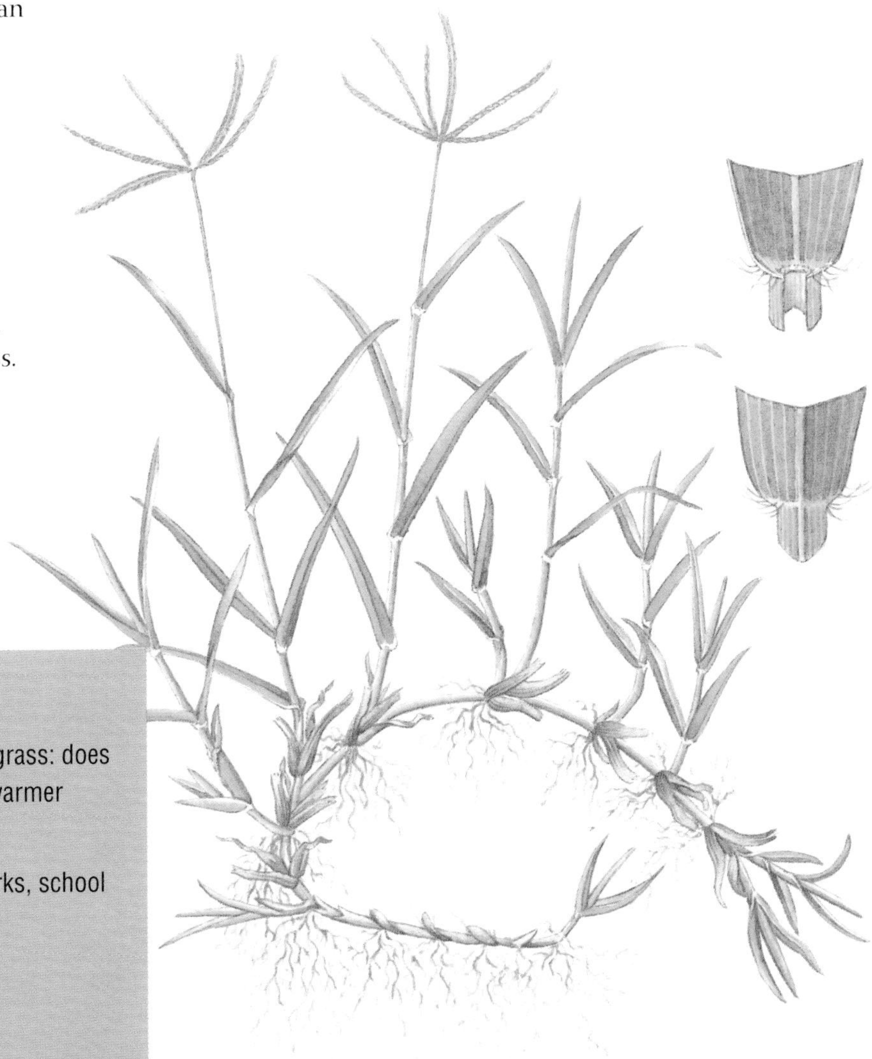

Summary

- **Regional adaptation:** warm-season grass: does well in Warm–Humid, Warm–Arid, and warmer parts of the Transition Zone

- **Good for:** home lawns, cemeteries, parks, school yards, and sports fields

- **Shade tolerance:** poor

- **Wear resistance:** good

- **Maintenance level:** average to high

- **Fertilizer:** four to six feedings a year

- **Water:** tolerates drought but needs water weekly to remain green and growing

- **Mowing height:** ½ inch to 2 inches, depending on type (some of the newer hybrids can be mowed as low as ⅛ inch, which is suitable for putting greens)

- **Planting method:** seed, sod, sprigs, or plugs (hybrids must be established vegetatively)

- **Pests:** armyworms, bermudagrass dead spot, dollar spot, mole crickets, sod webworms

ID Clues

- Ligule a fringe of hairs
- Folded in cross section
- Has both rhizomes and stolons
- Space between nodes (joints) varies between plants
- Dense, deep root system with tough stolons
- Distinctive three- to five-fingered seedhead

ST. AUGUSTINEGRASS

St. Augustinegrass (*Stenotaphrum secundatum*) is a coarse-textured species forming extensive stolons, or aboveground stems, that reach out several feet. In some ways, especially in its texture, St. Augustinegrass looks like tall fescue.

It is widely used in the coastal plains of the Carolinas, Georgia, and Florida and along the Gulf Coast through Alabama, Mississippi, Louisiana, and Texas. St. Augustinegrass grows as far north as Dallas, but cold temperatures usually restrict its use to the warm southern United States and to the Tropics.

Although St. Augustinegrass is best adapted to humid regions, it will grow in Warm–Arid climates, such as in California. There, it requires regular irrigation for good performance; in fact, plenty of moisture is essential for survival.

Except for one variety—'Floratam'— St. Augustinegrass has excellent shade tolerance and is well adapted to lawns that have both full sun and shade.

Of all turfgrasses, St. Augustinegrass has one of the broadest and coarsest leaf blades.

Establish St. Augustinegrass by sod or plugs. Seed and sprigs are not generally available for this grass.

You can expect a number of insects to attack St. Augustinegrass. The grass is also susceptible to fungal diseases, including brown patch and gray leaf spot.

One disease especially common in Texas and Louisiana, St. Augustinegrass decline (SAD), is unusual in that it is caused by a virus, not by a fungus. There are no chemical controls for it, and the best defense is to establish SAD–resistant cultivars, which include 'DelMar', 'Floratam', 'Raleigh', and 'Seville'. 'Floratam' and 'Seville' are best adapted to warmer regions; 'Raleigh' and 'DelMar' tolerate cooler conditions in the northern part of the St. Augustinegrass range.

Breeding Efforts

Improvements have focused on developing SAD resistance and a semidwarf growth habit. The smaller cultivars have good density and finer texture and can be mowed lower than other St. Augustinegrass varieties.

Warning

St. Augustinegrass can be damaged or killed by 2,4-D, an ingredient in many weed-and-feed products formulated for cool-season grasses, bermudagrass, and bahiagrass. Before using a broadleaf weed control on St. Augustinegrass, read the label carefully to ensure that the product is recommended for use on this grass.

St. Augustinegrass stolons are easily damaged in harvesting. It's common to see two shoots at a node (joint).

Summary

- **Regional adaptation:** cool-season grass: does well in Warm–Humid region and southern part of the Transition Zone

- **Good for:** home lawns, golf course roughs

- **Shade tolerance:** excellent

- **Wear resistance:** moderate

- **Maintenance level:** average

- **Fertilizer:** four to five feedings a year

- **Water:** needs weekly watering for optimum growth but survives drought moderately well

- **Mowing height:** 2 to 4 inches

- **Planting method:** sod or plugs

- **Pests:** armyworms, brown patch, cutworms, gray leaf spot, mole crickets, SAD virus, sod webworms, southern chinch bugs, white grubs

ID Clues

- Narrow, constricted collar on a leaf with a broad blade and sheath
- Blade grows at a 90-degree angle to the sheath
- Stolons are several feet long
- Slightly boat-shaped leaf tip

ZOYSIAGRASS

'El Toro' is an improved zoysiagrass. It has better cold tolerance and color than the species in cool weather, forms less thatch, and resists rust.

You know when you are walking on a zoysiagrass lawn. The stiff blades and puffy thatch layer feel like a thick, prickly carpet.

Zoysiagrass (*Zoysia* spp.) comes from Asia, and of the 10 species, only two are widely used as turfgrass in North America: Korean (or Japanese) lawngrass (*Z. japonica*) and manilagrass (*Z. matrella*). Manilagrass is not well adapted to cold temperatures and is grown only in the southernmost regions. Korean lawngrass—most people call it simply zoysiagrass or zoysia—is the most widely used and is the one discussed here.

Zoysia is grown primarily in the Transition Zone, from Kansas to Missouri through the central states to the Carolinas. Although it survives as far north as the Canadian border, the growing season is so short in the North that zoysia is brownish-yellow for most of the year. It also grows throughout the South. In the Deep South, bermudagrass, St. Augustinegrass, and bahiagrass are better adapted to the climate.

In addition to forming an outstanding lawn, zoysia is suited for use on golf course fairways and tees. Golfers like it because the stiff leaf blades make the ball sit up higher, where it is easier to hit.

Zoysiagrass produces seed, which is very slow to germinate and may remain dormant in the soil for an extended period of time. For this reason, zoysia lawns are generally established by vegetative means, usually by sodding or plugging. The grass is relatively slow growing, and it may take more than one season to become fully established if you install it by plugging.

Be aware that the broadleaf weed control 2,4-D can damage zoysiagrass if applied while the lawn is emerging from dormancy and greening up. Avoid applying any products containing 2,4-D, including weed-and-feeds at that time.

Breeding Efforts
Improved cultivars have better winter color, reduced water needs, and rapid sod establishment.

Summary

- **Regional adaptation:** primarily the Transition Zone; a warm-season grass that survives in cold and warm areas

- **Good for:** home lawns, parks, school yards, athletic fields, golf course fairways and tees

- **Shade tolerance:** good

- **Wear resistance:** moderate

- **Maintenance level:** average

- **Fertilizer:** three to five feedings a year

- **Water:** weekly watering is ideal but tolerates some drought

- **Mowing height:** ¾ inch to 2 inches

- **Planting method:** sod, plugs

- **Pests:** armyworms, grubs, mole crickets, sod webworms, zoysia patch

ID Clues

- Ligule a fringe of hairs
- Rolled in cross section
- Stiff leaf blades, which may have fine hairs protruding from inner and outer surfaces
- Both stolons and rhizomes present
- Uniform space between nodes (joints) on stolon
- Nodes on stolon may be covered with a tan "husk"
- Seedhead a single spike

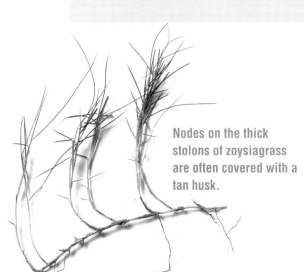

Nodes on the thick stolons of zoysiagrass are often covered with a tan husk.

Bahiagrass *(Paspalum notatum)*

Once considered best suited to low-maintenance areas such as roadsides, bahiagrass is now used in lawns thanks to a selection called 'Argentine', which grows into a compact, deep green sod. It is ideal for unirrigated Florida lawns. The sandy soils in Florida dry quickly, but bahiagrass has an extensive root system that allows it to survive even in drought.

Although it has thick rhizomes, bahiagrass is not an aggressive spreader. It can be established inexpensively from seed, or it can be sodded. Sodding avoids the many weeds that appear before a seeded lawn fills in. Whichever establishment method you use, water weekly until your lawn has a well-developed root system. Even if it goes dormant and turns brown from drought, it should green up again soon after watering or rain.

Bahiagrass requires less fertilizer than other grasses (except for centipedegrass) and, as a result, grows well in infertile soil. What little fertilizer it does need on occasion should contain iron, especially if the soil pH is greater than 7.

It is poorly adapted to cold temperatures and does not do well in shade. St. Augustinegrass is a better choice for shady sites.

Once in place, bahiagrass is better behaved than other warm-season grasses, such as bermudagrass or St. Augustinegrass, and will not invade surrounding shrub beds and flowerbeds as quickly. Unfortunately, owners of bahiagrass lawns must deal with the numerous tall seedheads that pop up. Regular mowing will keep their number in check.

Summary

- **Regional adaptation:** Florida primarily, except in the southeastern part of the state; some use in Texas
- **Good for:** low-maintenance home lawns and roadsides
- **Shade tolerance:** moderate
- **Wear resistance:** good
- **Maintenance level:** low
- **Fertilizer:** two to four feedings during the growing season; on soils with pH greater than 7, the fertilizer should contain iron
- **Water:** drought tolerant
- **Mowing height:** 2 to 4 inches
- **Planting method:** seed or sod
- **Pests:** brown patch, dollar spot, mole crickets

BUFFALOGRASS

Buffalograss has a distinctive blue-gray color. Left unmowed, it has a soft, puffy appearance.

A warm-season species, buffalograss (*Buchloe dactyloides*) is known for its outstanding heat and drought tolerance, as well as its cold hardiness.

It is the only major turfgrass species that is native to the United States. Buffalograss is somewhat of a regional grass, growing best in the central plains states— Kansas, Colorado, Nebraska, Oklahoma, northern Texas—and other arid states. It will survive in the northern plains up into central Canada.

Buffalograss, which spreads by stolons, is gray-green. It does not form a high-quality, deep green turf, so where moisture or irrigation is readily available, another grass may be better to use. On lawns that cannot be irrigated, it is an alternative to moisture-loving warm- and cool-season species.

This grass has good wear tolerance but does not grow well in shade. It can provide an acceptable turf without much mowing. It grows slowly and not very tall; generally it only reaches 8 to 10 inches tall during the entire growing season. For lawns, the preferred mowing height is 2 to 3 inches.

Buffalograss is best adapted to dry areas where it has little competition from weeds. Although it will grow in humid climates, more aggressive grasses can crowd it out. In wetter regions, avoid fertilizing, which encourages weed competition. In dry climates, buffalograss needs little fertilizer but will benefit from one or two feedings a year, one in spring and one in summer. Establish buffalograss lawns by seeding, sodding, sprigging, or plugging.

Breeding Efforts

Turf-type buffalograsses are being developed for use in low-maintenance lawns. Among them are 'Comanche', 'Plains', 'Sharps Improved', 'Texoka', and 'Top Gun'. These varieties have an aggressive growth habit and form a denser turf.

Because male flowers are a major detraction to the appearance of a buffalograss lawn, breeding efforts have also focused on finding female cultivars. (Buffalograss has male and female plants. When no male flowers interrupt the surface of the turf, the lawn appears more uniform.) The female clones must be established vegetatively.

Summary

- **Regional adaptation:** warm-season grass: Warm–Arid and Cool–Arid, below 6,500 feet elevation

- **Good for:** lawns, unirrigated roadsides, parks, cemeteries, school yards, even low-maintenance golf course fairways in the drier western states

- **Shade tolerance:** poor

- **Wear resistance:** good

- **Maintenance level:** low

- **Fertilizer:** zero to two feedings a year

- **Water:** very drought tolerant (water every 21 to 45 days)

- **Mowing height:** 2 to 3 inches, or leave unmowed

- **Planting method:** seed, sprigs, or plugs

- **Pests:** chinch bugs, leaf spot

Centipedegrass *(Eremochloa ophiuroides)*

Centipedegrass is remarkably low maintenance. Spreading by stolons, the grass forms a dense sod with a mowing height of 1 to 3 inches. It has such horizontal growth that homeowners find they don't have to mow as frequently. And because the grass spreads on the soil surface, it is easy to edge and keep in bounds.

Centipedegrass has better cold tolerance than St. Augustinegrass and bahiagrass, and its range of adaptation extends throughout the Warm–Humid zone. 'Oaklawn' and 'TifBlair' have more improved cold tolerance than the species.

Unlike many of the other warm-season grasses, centipedegrass is less tolerant of drought. It quickly goes dormant in drought conditions and requires frequent watering to remain green in dry summers. It has moderately good shade tolerance and will persist under trees if some sunlight reaches it during the day.

Centipedegrass can be seeded, but seed is expensive and slow to sprout. For that reason, it is usually sodded or established from sprigs. Be sure to supply plenty of water to a young lawn.

One of the worst things you can do to this grass is to overfertilize. It needs only 2 pounds of nitrogen per 1,000 square feet a year, applied 1 pound at a time in spring and summer. Centipedegrass often needs extra iron.

Summary

- **Regional adaptation:** warm-season grass: Warm–Humid zone

- **Good for:** low-maintenance lawns

- **Shade tolerance:** fair

- **Wear resistance:** low

- **Maintenance level:** low

- **Fertilizer:** two feedings a year, supplement with iron as needed

- **Water:** tolerates moderate drought but requires water to stay green and vigorous

- **Mowing height:** 1 to 3 inches

- **Planting method:** seed, sod, or sprigs

- **Pests:** centipede decline, caused by overfeeding and overwatering

ID Clues

- Gray-green leaf blades with fine hairs on both sides (hold the blade up to the light to see the hairs)
- Leaves curl and twist
- Ligule a fringe of hairs
- Rolled in cross section
- Stolons only

OTHER TURFGRASSES

Many grasses fill small niche markets for particular climates or specific uses. Here are a few grasses that may prove suitable for your situation.

Warm-Season Grasses

Carpetgrass Common carpetgrass (*Axonopus affinis*) thrives in poor, wet soil and is used mainly in Florida and coastal areas of the Warm–Humid region. It is well adapted to roadsides and other low-maintenance sites. Tropical carpetgrass (*A. compressus*) grows in the same areas as common carpetgrass, but it does not tolerate cold. Both species form a thin turf.

Seashore paspalum Closely related to bahiagrass, seashore paspalum (*Paspalum vaginatum*) is a finer-textured species. In fact, it looks a little like bermudagrass, only shinier. Its niche is salty soil. The grass is so salt tolerant that you could water it with seawater if you had to. This makes it particularly well adapted to warm, coastal regions such as Florida and Hawaii, where salt spray can damage turf, and areas where soil and water contain excessive amounts of sodium. Seashore paspalum does not grow well in shade.

Kikuyugrass Kikuyugrass (*Pennisetum clandestinum*) is a weed grass that got out of hand in Southern California. It's not one you'd plant, but if it has taken over your lawn, you can manage it to form an acceptable lawn. Mow it ½ to 1 inch tall, and feed it once or twice a year. Kikuyu needs plenty of rainfall, so it is ideal where other grasses may suffer from excess water. Vertical-mow frequently to control thatch.

Dichondra A broadleaf species rather than a grass, dichondra (*Dichondra micrantha*) can be mowed and maintained like a turfgrass in warm regions, such as Southern California and parts of Arizona. It does well in part shade and on hot, dry, low-maintenance sites. Few herbicides are labeled for use on dichondra, so weeds can be a problem.

Cool-Season Grasses

Bulbous bluegrass Bulbous bluegrass (*Poa bulbosa*) has a swollen bulblike stem base in which it stores water. This allows it to endure dry conditions and persist where unirrigated Kentucky bluegrass will not. It is less adapted to cold temperatures than Canada bluegrass, so its use is limited to dry areas such as in California, Kansas, Nebraska, and eastern Colorado.

Canada bluegrass Canada bluegrass (*Poa compressa*) is suited to very dry and cold climates, such as those found east of the Rocky Mountains in central Canada and in the drier regions of northern states such as Montana and North Dakota.

Where no irrigation is available, Canada bluegrass may make the difference between bare ground and a reasonably good cover. Its leaf blades are similar to those of Kentucky bluegrass but tend to be shinier. Its stems are distinctly flattened. The biggest problem with Canada bluegrass is that its stems elongate in warm weather, resulting in an open and thin turf.

Rough bluegrass Rough bluegrass (*Poa trivialis*) fits two very different niches. Most commonly, it is used to overseed golf courses in the South for the winter. In cool-season regions, it is suited to continuously moist, shaded areas, such as along riverbanks and lakefronts.

Closely related to Kentucky bluegrass, rough bluegrass has many distinctive features. Its color is lighter green than Kentucky bluegrass with a silvery cast that comes from the outer sheaths at the base of the plant. Patches of it show up clearly in a Kentucky bluegrass lawn. They are particularly noticeable in dry weather because rough bluegrass turns brown much sooner than Kentucky bluegrass.

In the drier regions of the upper Midwest, rough bluegrass is dormant for much of the season while the surrounding grass remains green. Rough bluegrass is less traffic tolerant than Kentucky bluegrass but is better adapted to shade. It does not survive drought, so it does not do well in dry shaded areas.

Creeping bentgrass Many golfers long to have a lawn of the beautiful, close-mown grass that is used on putting greens. In most areas, that grass is creeping bentgrass (*Agrostis palustris*). Fine textured and highly stoloniferous, creeping bentgrass is particularly well adapted to low mowing heights and can maintain a dense, uniform stand even if mowed as low as $1/10$ inch.

Although it is used in home lawns in the Pacific Northwest, creeping bentgrass requires expert skills to maintain. It is also expensive to grow compared with other grasses. You must use expensive equipment to mow creeping bentgrass because it does not perform well at standard mowing heights. If mowed tall, it develops masses of puffy stolons. And the lower mowing height puts a lot of stress on the turf, requiring specialized care such as fungicide applications that other grasses generally don't need.

Patches of creeping bentgrass stand out and disrupt the uniformity of a lawn. Its dense, stoloniferous growth is not compatible with the upright growth of other cool-season grasses, and its color is lighter green. There are no selective controls for it, which means that to eliminate it, you have to kill all the grass in an affected area and reestablish the lawn.

Weeping alkaligrass This species is adapted to soils containing high levels of sodium. Such soils are found in coastal areas, many western states, and areas where salt is used to melt snow and ice on roads.

Weeping alkaligrass (*Puccinellia distans*) is a bunchgrass and does not form a high-quality turf, but it is preferable to bare soil. It's unlikely you'll find it on the shelf of the local garden center. Your county extension service may know of a source.

Wheatgrasses There are places in Montana, North Dakota, South Dakota, Wyoming, and central Canada where it is too dry to grow most cool-season grasses without irrigation and too cold to effectively manage drought-tolerant, warm-season grasses such as buffalograss. For these areas, the wheatgrasses—fairway crested wheatgrass (*Agropyron cristatum*) and western wheatgrass (*Pascopyrum smithii*)—form reasonably good lawns.

Creeping bentgrass forms an elegant close-cropped lawn that's perfect for lawn enthusiasts who love to pamper their grass.

Dichondra is a groundcover for shady areas in warm climates. It tolerates close mowing like a turfgrass.

hat better way to
appreciate the full
potential of a healthy
lawn than to get out there
and play on it? Games
on the lawn can be rowdy
and action packed or just a peaceful way to
spend an afternoon working on the perfect
putt. Not many lawns can be transformed
into a football field, but that doesn't mean
you can't play.

Almost any game can be adapted to fit
any size lawn. And it doesn't have to be a
complicated or expensive process—just put
up a net or set a few stakes and start having
fun. Of course, for the more serious athlete
or avid aficionado, there is always the
pursuit of the perfect backyard field—and
that can be just as much fun itself.

LAWN SPORTS

PREPARE THE FIELD

Marking tools include cones, paint, tape, and flags. If you're really into the games, consider buying a measuring-marking wheel so that you can do two jobs at once.

Choosing the best area for your home playing field is the first item on the agenda. Make sure the area chosen is level, large enough for play, and free of obstructions. Clear the play area and the area around it, removing yard equipment, furniture, storage containers, or anything else that can be tripped over or run into. Check the lawn carefully for objects hidden in the grass—sticks, rocks, or small toys—that could turn an ankle.

Overhead obstructions, such as tree branches, wires, or roof overhangs, not only can thwart a perfectly good hit in a game but can also be a potential hazard to the players. Any game that requires either a racket or sends a ball flying through the air will need wide-open space (both on the ground and overhead) for safety's sake.

Care for the Lawn

Even though your regular lawn care program keeps the grass in good shape

Prune or remove obstructions as much as possible or find a different site for the games.

for the occasional weekend barbecue or touch football game, establishing a more permanent game area calls for some special attention before and after setting up the field.

To begin with, make sure the lawn is as healthy as it can be. The grass will need to be at its absolute best to survive repeated play. Make sure the lawn has enough water and nutrients and that the soil isn't compacted before setting up the play area. Continue to take care of the lawn between games. Monitor the condition of the grass to keep the damage to a minimum and to support recovery from the stress of heavy use.

Marking the Field

Although you don't have to officially mark off a field—the field is just for fun, after all—marking helps keep the players within the bounds of the playing area. A few tools will help you get your playing field measured, marked, and ready for play.

You'll need a large measuring tape and ground-marking materials. Landscapers paint, field-marking paint, or chalk (available at hardware stores, athletic stores, or online) can be used to outline the boundaries of the field and delineate areas inside the boundary lines.

If you don't want to go to the trouble of marking the field, place flags or cones at the corners of the area to help the players see the edges of the playing area. Or simply mark the area with a piece of scrap cloth tied to stakes or cones to indicate the general definition of the field. How you mark the area depends on how slick you want your playing field to look and how necessary it is to keep players within a safe playing area.

Whatever you use to delineate your field of play, be sure that the markers are set up correctly so they themselves are not a hazard to participants. Use a hammer or mallet to drive in net stakes or pole markers if necessary.

Marking a Playing Field

Not every game needs to have a well-marked play area. But your friends and children will get a kick out of having an official-looking, well-defined playing field with crisp lines.

To mark a straight-lined field, locate one corner and drive a stake there. From this stake, measure the length of the field and drive a second stake at this corner. Continue on around the field until you have staked out all four corners of the field.

Tie mason's string between each stake, then outline the field with paint or chalk, following along the string as you spray.

To mark circular areas, drive a stake at the center point of the circle. Cut string to the length of the circle's radius and tie it to the stake. Stretch the string taut, hold a spray can at the end of the string and walk around the circle while spraying.

Suppliers

Consult these online resources for field-marking supplies:

www.kuzsports.com—temporary and permanent marking chalk and paint
www.markersinc.com—backyard golf flags
www.soccersupplies.com—field-marking paint and equipment and corner flags

BADMINTON

contact with a player's body or clothing, or is hit again before it crosses the net. If the serving team commits a fault, no points are scored, but the receiving team gets the bird and becomes the serving team. Games are played to either 11 or 15 points.

Setup

An official badminton court measures 20 feet wide for doubles play and 17 feet wide for singles play. For either doubles or singles, the court is 44 feet long. If your yard is too small for a regulation court, you can shrink the court to fit the space available. You can also resize it to accommodate younger players, who may not be able to get the bird over the net from the far reaches of a regulation court.

Mark the boundaries of the court with string first, then with marking paint or chalk. Or just use cones or flags to mark off the corners of the court. The net should

A regulation-size badminton court will fit in most suburban backyards but can be scaled to fit any space.

Badminton was introduced to North America in the 1890s and has been a backyard favorite since. It became an Olympic sport in 1992. The game is similar to tennis in that a racket and a net are used, but badminton requires a bird (also known as a shuttlecock or a birdie) to be hit back and forth, and play is in the air only.

Badminton is played with either two or four people, yet informal games have seen many more people on the court—just for fun. Recreational badminton sets can often be purchased at sporting goods stores and come as a complete kit for a backyard doubles or singles game. This makes for a relatively inexpensive family activity that can be enjoyed throughout the entire outdoor season.

Badminton can be a demanding game with plenty of strategy involved to keep your opponents on edge. Simply, the game is played by hitting the bird back and forth across the net between the serving team and the receiving team. Points are scored when the receiving team commits a fault—the bird is hit out of bounds, hits the ground, is hit into the net, comes in

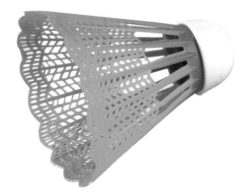

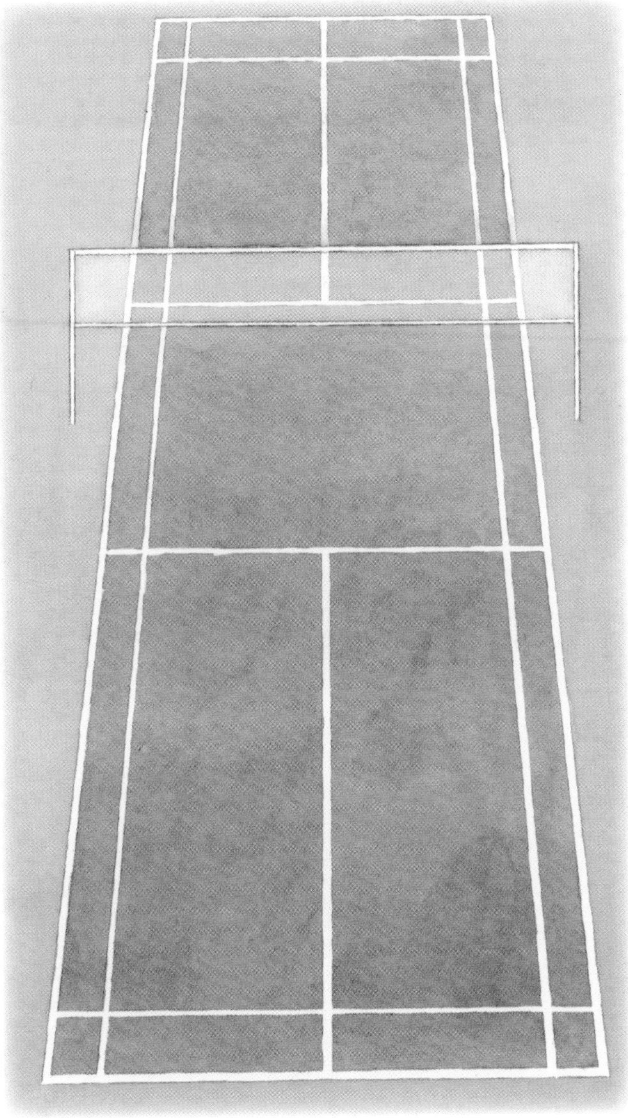

Badminton

For more information on badminton, check out:

www.badminton.ca
www.badmintoncentral.com
www.usabadminton.org
www.worldbadminton.com
Badminton (Backyard Games),
by Steve Boga
Badminton (magazine published by Badminton England)

Volleyball

If you have space enough to set up for badminton, you could probably stage a credible game of volleyball too. The differences are slight, mainly that a volleyball court is longer (60 feet) and wider (30 feet) and calls for a sturdier, higher (7- to 8-foot) net. Regulation indoor volleyball calls for six players on each team. As with all backyard sports, though, you can adapt the size of the court to fit your yard and play with as many or as few folks as you can corral into a game. Just be sure your net is tough enough to withstand all that stuffing, spiking, and serving.

be placed in the middle of the court and stretched to about 5 feet high in the middle. The height of the net can be adjusted, if need be, to help the players get the bird over the net.

Care

The lawn can take a beating from repeated badminton games, but it should bounce back pretty quickly from a game or two over the weekend. Try not to play on wet grass, as this will increase the amount of damage to the grass. For court areas that see frequent play, be on the lookout for compacted soil and pay attention to the condition of the grass.

If the grass is suffering, the soil underneath may have become compacted and is not allowing water or nutrients to get to the grass roots. If you can't bring the grass back with a good watering and fertilizing regimen, you may need to suspend play for a while and aerate the lawn to allow the grass to recover. Water as regularly as the lawn needs, and keep to a fertilizing schedule. This regimen should keep the grass hardy and ready for play.

CROQUET

Croquet is an easy game for players of all ages and abilities.

Croquet lends itself beautifully to backyard play. Wickets are set up around a course, and players use mallets to hit balls through the wickets in a certain order. The player who does this first is the winner. The game isn't without peril, as many backyard players know. Skill and calculation are required, and competition can be fierce among true aficionados.

Croquet became popular in North America in the 1860s, due in part to the fact that women enjoyed playing as much as men. It was a hit in the social circles of the rich, where croquet courts popped up all over on expansive lawns. To this day, croquet is enjoyed by people of all ages, and croquet sets are found in many a garage and shed. If you don't yet own a set, you can pick one up at a sporting goods store, or you may even find one at a local garage sale.

Setup

A regulation croquet court measures 105 feet long by 84 feet wide. If your backyard isn't that big, you can scale down the court. Use a basic court ratio of 5:4 (or five units long by four units wide), so that the wickets can be set up at equal distances around the playing field. For example, courts that are 50 feet long by 40 feet wide, 30 by 24 feet, or 25 by 20 feet have the proper ratio.

Mark the four corners of the court with flags or golf tees; line the boundaries with athletic-field paint or chalk if you'd like. Hammer in a stake at the exact center point of each end of the court. Place two wickets in front of each stake. Then set up the rest of the wickets around the court at specific intervals and positions so that play follows the wickets through once, then reverses and follows through the opposite way to finish the game. (See the diagram of a nine-wicket setup, opposite.)

If there are no objections from the other players, a far more casual game of croquet can be played, placing the wickets wherever you please, or adopting custom rules and penalties—in other words, just having fun playing the game.

Care

Although there may be more activity around the wickets than in the far reaches of the court, croquet is generally a very gentle game in terms of the grass.

The only thing that will affect the game is the length of the grass. The shorter the lawn, the faster and farther the ball can travel. The longer the grass, the harder the ball will have to be hit to travel through the lawn. Cutting a special croquet court into your lawn might not be desirable, but it's not a bad idea to mow the lawn and rake the clippings from the court area just before you plan to play.

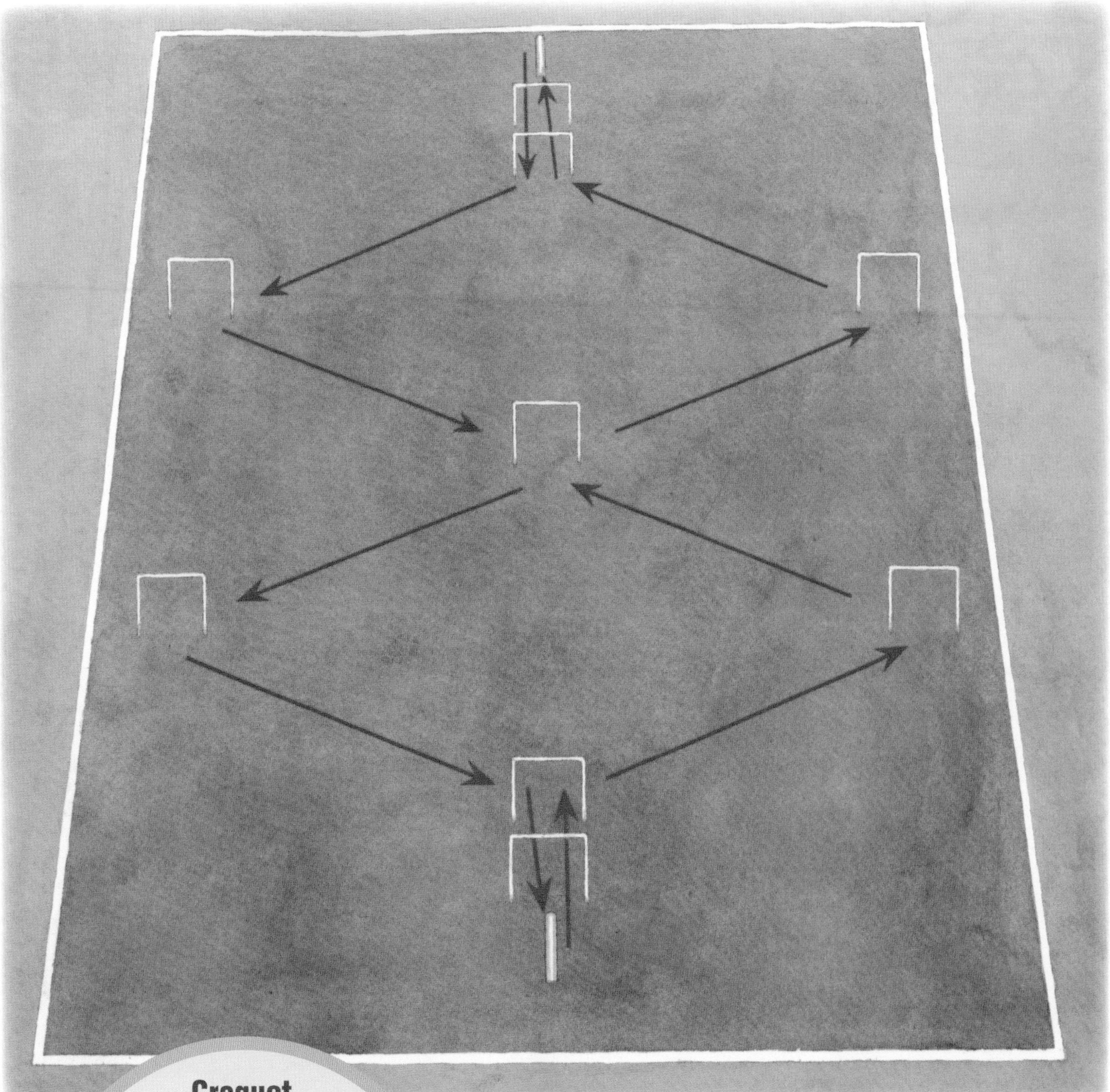

Croquet
For more information about
croquet, check out:

www.croquet.ca
www.croquetamerica.com
Croquet (Backyard Games), by Steve Boga
Croquet (Know the Game)
by Croquet Association

HORSESHOES

The area around the stake in a horseshoe court receives the heaviest wear and requires the most care.

Horseshoes evokes memories of lazy, sunny afternoons and the sound of metal shoes clanging against a stake—that is, if you're lucky enough for your shoe to come near the stake. Horseshoes is a simple game that takes good aim and skill to score points.

Basically, a player pitches a horseshoe toward the stake, and earns points for coming close, leaning, or actually hooking the horseshoe on the stake. The team that gets to 40 points first (in a point-based game) or has the most points after pitching 40 shoes (in a shoe-limit game) wins.

Setup

A horseshoe court measures 46 feet long and 6 feet wide. At both ends of the court are pitchers' boxes, which should measure 6 feet square. These consist of the stake, the pit, and the pitching platform. The stakes are located in the center of each pitcher box, 40 feet apart. In official horseshoe courts, pits are dug around the stakes and filled with sand, sawdust, or clay. Unless you plan on installing a

Horseshoes
For more information about horseshoes, check out:

www.horseshoepitching.com
Horseshoes (Backyard Games),
by Steve Boga

permanent horseshoe court in your yard, you can simply mark a pit in the grass around each stake with some athletic paint (chalk is easily rubbed off the grass by the horseshoes and the players). The pit should measure 6 feet long by 3 feet wide.

The pitching platforms are located on each side of the pits, extending from the edges of the pits to the outer lines of the court. Players toss from the top of each pitching platform. Mark these "shot" lines (also called foul lines) at 37 feet from the target stake (for adult men) or 27 feet from the target stake (for female, elderly, handicapped and junior players).

Care

The grass can suffer damage from the heavy horseshoes and therefore should be cared for after especially heavy play. Maintain both ends of the court with plenty of water and nutrients.

Unless the court is used constantly, soil compaction should not be much of a problem. If it does become an issue in the pit areas, aerate them to allow moisture, air, and nutrients to get into the soil. Seed the areas around each pit if the grass is thinning to keep weeds out. To maintain the grass and keep it in shape for a game anytime, water as needed and keep to a fertilizing schedule.

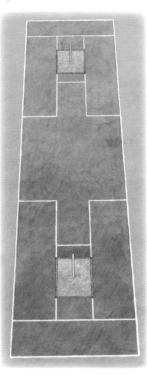

BOCCE

Bocce, a game with roots that can be traced to ancient Egypt, is a close cousin of bowling. Competition games are played on courts of packed dirt or gravel, but bocce is just as easily enjoyed on a backyard grass court. It is a simple game of skill, strategy, and luck and is a social activity enjoyed by generations of friends and family.

The essence of the game is that players roll a ball (a boccia) toward a target, which is a smaller ball called a pallino. The players are not necessarily out to hit the pallino, merely trying to come as close to it as possible. Of course, if another player's ball is closer to the target, the thrower may hit it or the pallino out of the way to gain a better position. If side boards define the bocce court, the ball can be rolled against them to get a better angle to the pallino, similar to the way billiards is played. If the ball needs to travel a greater distance it may be lobbed in the air to get it closer to the pallino: This is called volo shooting.

Setup

A bocce court is generally 10 to 13 feet wide (12 feet is standard) and 60 to 100 feet long (76 feet is standard), so a good stretch of narrow lawn can accommodate a bocce court nicely. If there isn't enough room for a regulation court, a shorter play area is fine. As long as the playing field is marked with the pitch lines and the volo lines, it is considered a proper bocce court.

In a regulation bocce court, the pitch lines are marked 16 feet from each end of the court to create the inbound area of play. The volo lines are then marked 8 feet past the pitch lines, or 24 feet from the back line. If side boards are used, they are placed along the sides of the court.

Home Play

These dimensions can be adjusted to whatever size bocce court will fit in your backyard. The one requirement for any bocce court is that it should be completely open—no trees, shrubs, or other obstructions.

Care

Playing bocce puts little stress on a lawn because play takes place all over the court. Inbound areas may see more wear than the middle of the court, but a good maintenance program should keep the grass in shape. If your court has side boards, take them out when the court is not in use. Side boards can be up to 1½ feet high and could shade the grass, potentially causing problems. A well-kept lawn should withstand regular play, but if the lawn is showing signs of stress, up your maintenance routine or suspend games until it recovers.

Neatly mowed grass will make it easy to roll the balls on a bocce court. Avoid cutting it too short.

Bocce

For more information about bocce, check out:

www.bocce.ca
www.bocce.com
www.bocce.org
www.boccestandardsassociation.org
Bocce: A Sport for Everyone,
by Rico C. Daniele
The Joy of Bocce,
by Mario Pagnoni

WIFFLE BALL

ball is hit, so you don't need a big-league space to play. Another great thing about the game is that it can be played with as few as two players (a pitcher and a batter) or as many as 10 players. Perfect for a neighborhood pickup game.

Setup
A Wiffle ball field is triangular in shape with the point of the triangle at home base. The field is broken up into four areas from home plate to the back of the field: single, double, triple, and home run. The sides of the field are foul lines.

The recommended size of the field is 60 feet long by 20 feet wide in the home-run section. Each section of the field is 15 feet long, so that the home-base markers are 60 feet from home plate. Mark the dimensions with sand, sports paint, or flags.

Home Play
There is no rule that says the field has to be exactly these dimensions or officially marked. Many a Wiffle ball field has been informally marked with a lilac bush or an elm tree as base markers. However, to take any guesswork out of foul lines and base markers, outline the field in athletic paint, chalk, or plastic cones, and use whatever dimensions fit the space you have.

Care
Wiffle ball isn't as tough on a lawn as baseball. Since the batters don't have to run to bases, there won't be telltale baselines through the grass.

The places that will get the roughest treatment are the pitcher's mound and home plate. Treat these areas gently with plenty of water and nutrients and watch for soil compaction. These small areas can easily be aerated to reduce compaction. If a more permanent Wiffle ball field is set up, you may want to consider using sand to mark the pitcher's mound and home plate, instead of letting the grass be damaged to the point where weeds and diseases easily infiltrate the lawn.

If the Wiffle ball field markings could detract from their surroundings, it's ok to leave them off. Wiffle ball is fairly easy on your lawn.

Wiffle ball is a game quite literally invented for the backyard. It's for baseball lovers who like to hear the crack of the bat but not the crash of a window. It's played with a plastic bat and an aerodynamically distinct lightweight plastic ball that makes a "wiffing" sound as it flies through the air.

Scoring Wiffle ball is the same as in baseball, but the uniqueness of the official Wiffle ball game is that there is no running around the field from base to base. A player "reaches base" determined by how far the

Wiffle ball
For more
information about
Wiffle ball, check out:
www.wiffle.com

Baseball and Softball

Nothing evokes what we love about spring
and summer better than a game of baseball
or softball with all the fixin's—worn leather
gloves and bats and balls and plenty of folks
to field a couple of teams. But that tricky part
about hardballs flying fast through the air near
windows and innocent bystanders makes playing
on your home lawn—no matter how large a yard

you have—inadvisable. Save the big nine-inning
bonanza for a local park or Little League field.
You can, though, use your yard to work on your
skills with terrific training aids such as portable
hitting and pitching machines or playback
screens for throwing and fielding. You can even
install a full-scale batting cage—but then all your
neighbors will know you're a baseball fanatic.

FOOTBALL

Depending on how rigorous and frequent the games, football can be pretty hard on a lawn. Ensure a good lawn care routine if your kids regularly play this sport.

Fall is all about football. Something about the crisp air and bright sunshine brings out the gridiron greatness in all of us. Professional football is as slick as a Hollywood production, but the homegrown variety is as much of a fall favorite.

Regulation teams consist of 11 players. Pickup backyard football can feature teams of any size; teams of five or six, providing enough players to run, pass, kick, and pretend it's the NFL, complete with victory spikes upon scoring in the end zone.

Setup

A regulation football playing field (for both professional and college teams) is 100 yards long and 53⅓ yards wide. The field is divided into 10-yard increments, with smaller 1-yard increments ticked off with hash marks. Goal lines denote the beginning of the end zones, which are 10 yards deep. Lines at the end (end zones) and along the sides of the field (sidelines) mark the areas of out-of-bounds play.

Home Play

Establishing a backyard football field is a snap. Scale the proportions to fit your playing area, and outline just the basics—the sidelines, end zones, end lines, and goal lines—with athletic-field paint, chalk, or plastic cones. Mark the middle of the field (your "50-yard line") and, if desired, ten "10-yard" lines along the sideline. You can just as easily use shrubs or other landmarks to define your end zones. No goal posts are required; any ball reasonably within the end zone is in bounds.

Care

Football can be hard on grass. Lots of people flattening it as they play can weaken a lawn. If you only play a few rigorous games, setting up a regular maintenance routine is usually enough to let the lawn bounce back. Keep an eye on the condition of the grass, though; it may need some time off from play so that regular maintenance can get it back into game shape.

If you've played extensively, your lawn will need special attention. Give grass that is turning brown enough water and fertilizer to bring it back to life. And where heavy play has compacted the soil, aerate to allow moisture, nutrients, and air to reach the roots.

Some backyard fields may show signs of extreme wear, with bare spots popping up in the grass. Patch these areas with seed or sod so that weeds won't have a chance to gain a foothold. Stay off the field until the new grass is well rooted and can be mowed with the rest of the lawn.

GOLF GREEN

A backyard putting green could be the ultimate luxury where kids and parents alike master their strokes. Lawn care on the green can be tricky.

What could be more indulgent—or fun—than a backyard golf green? You can practice putting, take strokes off your game, and achieve a state of blissful relaxation—all in the privacy of your backyard.

Building a backyard putting green is an undertaking that few homeowners tackle themselves. It requires planning to ensure the area is properly drained, and has adequate sunlight, and that the soil underneath the green is precise so the grass survives. Plenty of companies specialize in the design and construction of putting greens. With that in mind, there are still some things to know about a backyard green that will affect the choices you make during planning and construction.

Start with the grass. Most putting greens are planted with either bermudagrass or bentgrass, both of which tolerate short mowing. Which one you choose depends on the part of the country in which you live. Neither grass can tolerate shade well, so choose a very sunny part of the yard for the green.

A putting green requires specific growing conditions. It must have good drainage, and the soil needs to be sandy to maintain the green's structural integrity. Simply plunking sandy soil on top of the existing soil will affect drainage through the green. When drainage is poor, it's easy to overwater the green. This in turn may damage the grass and lead to disease.

To make sure drainage is right, avoid building the green in a low-lying part of the yard. Also consider having the green built so it is above the grade of the

Choosing the Right Contractor

Get estimates from several contractors for building your putting green. Ask for local references, and arrange to take a look at some of the work they've done. Ask the references about the quality of the process of installing a green, as well as the quality of the product—the green itself. Most important, be a part of the planning and be actively involved in overseeing the construction of your green to be sure it's exactly what you want.

surrounding lawn. This allows excess water, whether from watering or from rain, to roll off the green into the lawn.

Care

The time required to maintain a putting green discourages most backyard golf enthusiasts. First is the mowing. A properly maintained putting green should be cut ¼ to 1 inch tall. Any taller, and the grass will develop a layer of thatch that can wreck the green. Keeping the grass so short means you must mow at least three times a week to avoid cutting off more than one-third of the grass blade at a time. Scalping the grass will leave it weak and unplayable.

Also use a reel mower. Keep its blades impeccably sharp to avoid shredding the leaves. Shredded leaves are an invitation to diseases and pests and can affect the quality of your putts. Change mowing patterns every time you mow to prevent the grass from growing in one direction only.

Because short-cut turf is more prone to diseases and weeds, which readily move in from the rest of the lawn, regular maintenance of the rest of the lawn is essential in keeping the putting green healthy.

Water with care and monitor the grass to make sure it's getting enough moisture but not so much that the excess won't run off. A week of rain can put your putting green at risk.

Fertilizing a putting green is also different from feeding the rest of the lawn. The trick is to get the grass to grow, but not to become so thick and lush that you can't keep up with mowing. As it is, you may be mowing as much as you're putting, but that's what it takes to indulge this particular passion.

Golf
For more information about home golf greens, check out:

www.putting-greens.com
The Golf Instruction Manual by Steve Newell

SOCCER

of the field marked with cones, flags, or even paper cups. The side boundaries are called touchlines, and the end boundaries are goal lines. The actual goal zones are centered at the edge of each goal line.

Halfway between the goal zones, a line bisects the field, and a center circle is drawn around the exact center of the field. This is the area where play begins. Penalty boxes are centered around the goals, and corner kicks are marked by 1-yard quarter circles inside the four corners of the field.

Home Play

You can mark as little or as much as you like to delineate your field of play. For casual games, the goal, the four corners of the field, the touchlines, goal lines, and the midfield line are probably enough. Serious casual games might feature marks at the goal area and the field corners. Portable goal nets are convenient because they keep attempted goals from getting away from the game, but they're not necessary.

Care

As with football, the traffic of a soccer game can do some damage to a lawn. Most of the play is on the ground, so the possibility of injuring the grass is reason enough to make sure the grass is in prime shape before setting up the field. Good lawn maintenance gives the grass a fighting chance before all those feet even start scurrying furiously around your yard.

After the field is set up and your games begin, the area needs care to keep the grass healthy. Regular watering and a fertilizing schedule will help the lawn maintain the vitality it needs to withstand the use.

Repairing damaged areas, especially around the goals, may require some seeding or sod placement to fill in bare spots. The soil in the field may become compacted from lots of play, so consider aerating the lawn to get the water, air, and nutrients down to the roots of the grass.

Soccer requires only an open space and a ball. Because it's a high-traffic game, it can do some damage to the grass if played frequently with lots of players.

Soccer is hot. It's played in every corner of the globe, in huge stadiums and on tiny dirt lots, by world-famous professionals and barefoot boys and girls. It really is the world's favorite game, and best of all, you can play it nearly anywhere. All that's needed is a flat, unobstructed stretch of lawn and a soccer ball.

The object of the game is for one team to score more points than their opponents in a set time. In an official game each team has 11 players, but as with any backyard adaptation, as few as two players can have fun playing this classic game.

Setup

A regulation soccer field is 60 feet wide by 100 yards long. Backyard fields are scaled to fit the available space, with the four corners

Soccer
For more information
about soccer, check out:

www.usyouthsoccer.org
Soccer: How to Play the Game,
by Dan Herbst
Soccer (How-To Sports),
by Paul Joseph

RESOURCES

The Scotts Company

Whenever you have lawn problems or questions about lawn care, you can call a Scotts lawn specialist at 800–543–TURF (8873) or email your questions via the "Contact Us" link at www.scotts.com. The Scotts Web site offers numerous other services, tools, and tips. Among them:

Identify Your Grass: If you don't know the type of grass in your lawn, this handy online tool will help.

Weed Finder and Bug Finder: Identify your problem weeds and pests, then learn the product solutions to eliminate them.

Annual Program Builder: Just enter your ZIP code and grass type, and this interactive tool will prescribe a year–round schedule of the right products for your lawn.

Email Reminder Service: Sign up to receive a message when it's time to fertilize or apply weed or insect controls. In addition, this service will warn you if a lawn problem is developing in your region. Scotts lawn specialists track calls by ZIP code and, if they start logging calls from your area asking the same questions, they'll send out an alert telling you how to prevent or control the problem.

Brand names for the products mentioned

WEED PREVENTERS

pendimethalin	Halts Crabgrass Preventer, Scotts® Lawn Pro Super Turf Builder with Halts Crabgrass Preventer, Scotts Turf Builder with Halts Crabgrass Preventer
ferrous sulfate monohydrate	Moss Control Granules, Scotts Turf Builder with Moss Control
siduron	Scotts Starter Brand Fertilizer Plus Crabgrass Preventer

WEED CONTROLS

atrazine	Scotts Bonus S Weed Control, Scotts Lawn Pro Weed & Feed for St. Augustinegrass, Ortho Weed-B-Gon Spot Weed Killer for St. Augustine Lawns
glyphosate	Roundup Weed & Grass Killer, Roundup Extended Control Weed & Grass Killer Plus Weed Preventer
MCPA, triclopyr, and dicamba	Ortho Weed-B-Gon Max
MCPP plus dicamba	Ortho Weed-B-Gon Max, Ortho Weed-B-Gon Weed Killer for Southern Lawns
quinclorac, MCPP, 2,4-D, and dicamba	Ortho Weed-B-Gon Max Plus Crabgrass Control (kills broadleaf weeds and crabgrass)
triclopyr	Ortho Weed-B-Gon Chickweed, Clover & Oxalis Killer for Lawns
2,4-D and MCPP	Scotts Turf Builder with Plus 2 Weed Control, Scotts Turf Builder WinterGuard with Plus 2 Weed Control, Scotts Super Turf Builder with Plus 2 Weed Control

INSECT CONTROLS

acephate	Orthene Fire Ant Killer
bifenthrin	Scotts Bonus S Max Southern Weed & Feed with Fire Ant Killer, Scotts Turf Builder Plus SummerGuard, Scotts Lawn Pro Insect Control Plus Fertilizer, Ortho Bug-B-Gon Max Insect Killer for Lawns, Ortho Bug-B-Gon Max Lawn & Garden Insect Killer Concentrate, Ortho Fire Ant Killer Mound Treatment, Ortho Max Fire Ant Killer Broadcast Granules
imidacloprid	Scotts GrubEx Season-Long Grub Killer

DISEASE CONTROLS

thiophanate-methyl	Scotts Lawn Fungus Control

Extension Services

Extension service offices are found in most counties throughout the United States, however, in some states, several counties may be combined into one district. To find a nearby office, check "extension" in the phone book blue pages under county government or call your state's land–grant university. (These are usually the ones named State University.)

You can also find offices through an internet search. Type in "extension" or "cooperative extension" plus your state name in the search engine box, and the home page for the service should pop up. Usually this page provides the contact information for the county offices.

INDEX

Numbers in **boldface** indicate pages with photographs or illustrations.

Metric Conversions

U.S. Units to Metric Equivalents			Metric Equivalents to U.S. Units		
To Convert From	**Multiply by**	**To Get**	**To Convert From**	**Multiply by**	**To Get**
Inches	25.4	Millimeters	Millimeters	0.0394	Inches
Inches	2.54	Centimeters	Centimeters	0.3937	Inches
Feet	30.48	Centimeters	Centimeters	0.0328	Feet
Feet	0.3048	Meters	Meters	3.2808	Feet
Yards	0.9144	Meters	Meters	1.0936	Yards

To convert from degrees Fahrenheit (F) to degrees Celsius (C), first subtract 32, then multiply by ⁵⁄₉.

To convert from degrees Celsius to degrees Fahrenheit, multiply by ⁹⁄₅, then add 32.

Scotts Lawns

Editor: Marilyn Rogers
Contributing Designer: Lyne Neymeyer
Contributing Writers: Nick Christians, David R. Mellor, Ashton Ritchie
Copy Chief: Terri Fredrickson
Publishing Operations Manager: Karen Schirm
Senior Editor, Asset & Information Management: Phillip Morgan
Edit and Design Production Coordinator: Mary Lee Gavin
Editorial and Design Assistant: Kathleen Stevens
Book Production Managers: Pam Kvitne,
    Marjorie J. Schenkelberg, Rick von Holdt, Mark Weaver
Contributing Copy Editor: Carolyn Garrick Stern
Contributing Proofreaders: Fran Gardner, Susan Lang, Ginny Perrin
Contributing Photographer: Image Studios
Contributing Map Illustrator: Jana Fothergill
Contributing Indexer: Kathleen Poole
Other Contributors: Janet Anderson, Susan Ferguson

Additional Editorial Contributions from Art Rep Services

Director: Chip Nadeau
Designer: Ik Design
Illustrator: Michael Surles

Additional Editorial Contributions from Lark Productions

Project Manager: Karen Watts
Principal Writer: David R. Mellor

Meredith® Books

Executive Director, Editorial: Gregory H. Kayko
Executive Director, Design: Matt Strelecki
Managing Editor: Amy Tincher-Durik
Executive Editor: Benjamin W. Allen
Senior Editor/Group Manager: Michael McKinley
Senior Associate Design Director: Tom Wegner
Marketing Product Manager: Brent Wiersma

Publisher and Editor in Chief: James D. Blume
Editorial Director: Linda Raglan Cunningham
Executive Director, New Business Development: Todd M. Davis
Executive Director, Sales: Ken Zagor
Director, Operations: George A. Susral
Director, Production: Douglas M. Johnston
Director, Marketing: Amy Nichols
Business Director: Jim Leonard

Vice President and General Manager: Douglas J. Guendel

Meredith Publishing Group

President: Jack Griffin
Senior Vice President: Karla Jeffries

Meredith Corporation

Chairman of the Board: William T. Kerr
President and Chief Executive Officer: Stephen M. Lacy

In Memoriam: E. T. Meredith III (1933–2003)

Note to the Readers: Due to differing conditions, tools, and individual skills, Meredith Corporation assumes no responsibility for any damages, injuries suffered, or losses incurred as a result of following the information published in this book. Before beginning any project, review the instructions carefully, and if any doubts or questions remain, consult local experts or authorities. Always read and observe all of the safety precautions provided by manufacturers of any tools, equipment, or supplies that you use, and follow all accepted safety procedures.

Photographers

Photographers credited may retain copyright © to the listed photographs. L=Left, R=Right, C=Center, B=Bottom, T=Top

Dean Abramson/AgPix: 214; **Bill Adams:** 98B, 102C, 125B, 128T, 128C, 133B, 143B; **Shawn Askew:** 97BC, 107B; **Fred Baxendale:** 122T; **Joseph Berger:** 117-4; **Patricia Bruno/Positive Images:** 105C, 111T; **Ron Calhoun:** 99C; **Nick Christians:** 96T, 96CL, 96CR, 98T, 99T, 101T, 105B, 106B, 107C, 108C, 108B, 117-3, 129T, 130T, 135B, 142T, 142C, 143T; **Julie Cordeiro:** back cover right; **Chuck and Barbara Crandall:** 195L; **Karl Danneberger:** 131T; **Alan and Linda Detrick:** 4–5; **Jason Donnelly:** 28, 87T; **Derek Fell:** 110T, 182, 184, 192, 199T; **Roger Foley:** 197; **Christopher Frame/Scag Power Equipment:** 50T; **Susan Glascock:** 104B; **Image Studios:** 18, 52–53, 60T, 60C, 65C, 65B, 83T, 87B, 152, 155T, 158, 162, 166T, 166B, 167T, 200–201, 202T, 203BR, 204BL, 205, 206B, 207B, 208BL, 208BR, 209B, 210, 212T, 212B, 213B; **Bill Johnson:** 97T, 97B, 98TC, 100B, 101B, 102T; **Jim Kalisch:** 85BL, 113T, 116C, 118, 119T, 122C; **John Kaminski:** 85TR, 128BC, 128B, 131B, 132C, 133BC, 134T, 135T; **Dwight Kuhn:** 123BC, 123B; **Frank Lane Picture Agency:** 113B; **Frank Lane Picture Agency/Holt Studios:** 133T; **Richard Latin:** 132T, 133TC; **Charles Lewallen:** 97C; **David Liebman:** 98C; **Charles Mann:** 196L; **Mike McCaskey:** 102B; **Phil Nixon:** 85BR, 116TC, 119TC; **Richard Old/XIDservices.com:** 101C; **PACE Turfgrass Research Institute:** 117-1, 117-2; **Jerry Pavia:** 3; **Bryan Pinchen:** 120T; **Luigi Rignanese:** 109T; **Leonard Rue Jr.:** 123C; **The Scotts Company:** 19, 36, 40, 42, 43, 46, 47, 48TL, 48BL, 54, 61, 64B, 69B, 70, 71-4, 72, 73C, 73B, 75T, 75B, 83BR, 84TR, 84B, 119BC, 119B, 121L, 125T, 126C, 130C, 130B, 132B, 134BC, 137T, 149, 150T, 151, 154, 155TC, 155BCL, 155BCR, 155B, 159, 164, 165L, 165R, 167C, 167B, 168, 170, 171, 172, 174, 175, 176B, 177, 178, 179, 186, 190C, 190R, 193, 196T, 196R; **David Shetlar:** 116BC, 116B, 120B, 121TR, 121BR, 122B, 134TC, 134B; **Joseph G. Strauch Jr.:** 99B, 103C, 104T, 108T, 109B, 129B; **Michael Thompson:** 100T, 188

Cover Photographer: Jerry Pavia

All of us at Meredith® Books are dedicated to providing you with the information and ideas you need to enhance your home and garden. We welcome your comments and suggestions about this book. Write to us at:
Meredith Corporation
Meredith Gardening Books
1716 Locust St.
Des Moines, IA 50309–3023

If you would like more information on other Scotts products, call 800/225-2883 or visit us at: www.scotts.com

BEAUTIFY YOUR YARD with Scotts® and Miracle-Gro

Pick up these exciting titles from the brands you trust for gardening expertise—wherever gardening books are sold.